Bus Handbook

September 1996

British Bus Publishing

The East Midlands Bus Handbook

The East Midlands Bus Handbook is part of the Bus Handbook series that details the fleets of stage carriage and express coach operators. Where space allows other significant operators in the areas covered are also included. These handbooks are published by *British Bus Publishing* and cover Scotland, Wales and England north of London. The current list is shown at the end of the book. Together with similar books for southern England published by Capital Transport, they provide comprehensive coverage of all the principal operators' fleets in the British Isles.

The operators included in this edition cover those who provide stage and express services in the counties of Derbyshire, Leicestershire, Lincolnshire and Nottinghamshire. Also included are a number of those operators who provide significant coaching activities.

Quality photographs for inclusion in this, and other areas of Great Britain, are welcome and a fee is payable. The publishers unfortunately cannot accept responsibility for any loss and request you clearly show your initials on each picture or slide. Details of changes to fleet information are also welcome.

More information on the Bus Handbook series is available from:

British Bus Publishing Ltd,
The Vyne,
16 St Margaret's Drive
Wellington
Telford,
Shropshire TF1 3PH

Series Editor: Bill Potter
Principal Editor for *The East Midlands Bus Handbook* is Steve Sanderson

Acknowledgements:
We are grateful to Richard Belton, David Donati, Paul Hill, Mark Jameson, Colin Lloyd, Tony Wilson, the PSV Circle and the operating companies for their assistance in the compilation of this book.
The front cover photo is by Tony Wilson
The rear cover and frontispiece photographs are by Steve sanderson and Tony Wilson

Contents correct to August 1996

ISBN 1 897990 16 2
Published by *British Bus Publishing*
The Vyne, 16 St Margarets Drive, Wellington,
Telford, Shropshire, TF1 3PH
© British Bus Publishing, September, 1996

CONTENTS

A B C	4	Hylton & Dawson	59
A & S	5	Isle Coaches	60
Albert Wilde Coaches	6	Johnson's	61
Andrews	6	Johnson Bros	62
Applebys	8	Kettlewell's	65
Avisdors	12	Kime's	66
Bestwicks	13	Kinch	67
Blands of Cottesmore	14	Lamcote	70
Bowers	15	Leicester Citybus	71
Brylaine	16	Lincoln City Transport	103
Butler Brothers	18	Macpherson	75
Camms	19	Marshall	76
Carnell	20	Maun Crusader	77
Cavalier	21	Midland Fox	78
City Rider	22	Moxon	86
Confidence	26	Nottingham City Transport	87
Cropley	27	Nottinghamshire Community	95
Daisy	28	P C Coaches	96
Dee Ward	28	Pam's Coaches	98
The Delaine	30	Pathfinder	98
Dunn-line	32	Paul James	100
Eagre	35	Paul S Winson	101
East Midland	36	Reliance	102
Elsey	43	Roadcar	103
Emmerson	44	Skills	112
Enterprise & Silver Dawn	45	Scutt	115
Everett	46	Skinner	115
Express Motors	46	Sweyne	115
Felix	46	Sleafordian	116
Fowler's Travel	48	TRS	117
Glovers	49	Travel Wright	118
Graycroft	50	Trent	119
Hail and Ride	51	Trent Motors	126
Haines	52	Unity	126
Hodson	52	Virgin Bus	126
Holloways	54	Wide Horizon	128
Hulley's	55	Wing	129
Hornsby	56	Woods	130
Hunt's	58	Vehicle index	131

A B C

M V Patel, 5 Woodside Close, Leicester, LE4 7UJ

Depot : McHugh Close, Beveridge Lane, Ellistown, Leicester

STO529R	Leyland Atlantean PDR1A/1	Northern Counties	H47/30D	1970	Ex British Shoe, Leicester, 1996
TJI6713	Volvo B58-56	Duple Dominant	C49F	1974	Ex Accord Coaches, Portslade, 1994
SIB1358	Volvo B58-56	Plaxton Viewmaster IV	C57F	1974	Ex P & B Coaches, Barking, 1992
UIA7089	Volvo B58-61	Duple Dominant	C57F	1977	Ex Curtis, Gorefield, 1994
SIB3709	Leyland Leopard PSU3E/4R	Duple Dominant II	C53F	1978	Ex Riley, Royton, 1992
RSK584W	Volvo B58-61	Duple Dominant IV	C53F	1981	Ex Stagecoach, 1993
PJI5631	Volvo B10M-61	Berkhof Esprite 350	C49FT	1983	Ex Parr, West Derby, 1993
A546HEF	Volvo B10M-61	Duple Caribbean	C53F	1983	Ex Bold, Melling, 1996
TXI8757	Volvo B10M-61	Jonckheere Jubilee P90	CH49/9FT	1983	Ex Goodwin, Stockport, 1994
A261OWL	Mercedes-Benz L608D	Reeve Burgess	C21F	1984	Ex Ash, Wooburn Moor, 1995
C127PPE	Leyland Tiger TRCTL11/3RH	Berkhof Everest 370	C53F	1985	Ex Riversdale, Brighouse, 1996
TJI6298	MCW Metrorider MF150/15	MCW	B25F	1987	Ex Stevensons, 1994
SJI1978	Mercedes-Benz 609D	Coachcraft	C24F	1988	Ex Waylands, Beccles, 1994
F350WCS	Mercedes-Benz 609D	Scott	C24F	1988	Ex B & M Coaches, Ferryhill, 1994
F78TDE	Mercedes-Benz 609D	PMT	B24F	1988	Ex Silcox, Pembroke Dock, 1994
F180CGN	Sanos S315-21	Sanos Charisma	C49F	1988	Ex Anglo-Polish, Nottingham, 1993
G961SND	Mazda E2200	Made-to-Measure	M13	1989	Ex Hornsby, Ashby, 1993
M14ABC	Mercedes-Benz 709D	Alexander Sprint	B29F	1995	
M19ABC	Mercedes-Benz 709D	Alexander Sprint	B29F	1995	

Previous Registrations:

M19ABC	M496JRY	SJI1978	E129YJC
PJI5631	BDV866Y, KSV832, RBD46Y	TJI6298	E805UDT
RSK584W	MCS991W, 145CLT, RSK584W, MDZ7209	TJI6713	SEC554M
SIB1358	TGE5R, 24PAE, ANP608R	TXI8757	MRP837Y, GSV937, LHO942Y
SIB3709	WTV964S	UIA7089	ACK754R

Livery: White and red

Seen in the centre of Leicester is ABC minibus, A261OWL, a Mercedes-Benz L608D converted by Reeve Burgess. It is the oldest minibus in the A B C fleet. The board in the windscreen indicates that the bus is performing a tendered service on behalf of Leicestershire County Council.
Tony Wilson

A & S

A A, A A & N A Sarang, 34 Hartington Road, Leicester, LE2 0GL

Depot : Vulcan Road, Charnwood Ind Est, Leicester

C663MCN	Mercedes-Benz L307D	Reeve Burgess	M12	1985	Ex Kingsway, Blyth 1994
329FBH	Mercedes-Benz 709D	Coachcraft	C24F	1987	
329FTU	Mercedes-Benz 811D	Coachcraft	C26F	1989	
A14ABU	Mercedes-Benz 609D	?	C24F	1988	Ex McFall & McFadden, Clydebank, 1994
A16ABU	Mercedes-Benz 609D	Coachcraft	C26F	1989	
A19ABU	Mercedes-Benz 508D	Coachcraft	C16F	1990	
A20ABU	Mercedes-Benz 811D	Dormobile Routemaker	B33F	1990	Ex Barnes, Bedlington, 1994
A17ABU	Mercedes-Benz 609D	Whittaker Europa	C23F	1991	
M18ABU	Mercedes-Benz 709D	Alexander Sprint	B29F	1995	

Previous Registrations:

329FBH	D329WVL	A16ABU	G384MAG	A19ABU	G89NRH
329FTU	F319TJV	A17ABU	H996TAK	A20ABU	G492TYS
A14ABU	F820XEG				

Livery: White and green

The index number on minibus A16ABU relates to the name of the proprietors. A & S stands for Abu and Sons. Despite carrying an 'A' plate, this Mercedes-Benz 609D, which carries bodywork by Coachcraft, was built in 1989. *Tony Wilson*

The East Midland Bus Handbook

ALBERT WILDE COACHES

P J Wilde & D A Ward, 121 Parkside, Heage, Derbyshire, DE56 2AF

BTB692T	Ford R1114	Duple Dominant	C53F	1979	Ex Smith, Wigan, 1984
ENF514Y	Ford R1114	Duple Dominant IV	C44FT	1983	Ex Stone, Rochdale, 1988
A522LCX	Ford R1114	Duple	C53F	1983	Ex Nationwide, Lanark, 1989
ADC176A	Bova EL26/581	Bova Europa	C51F	1982	Ex Nichols, Carlton, 1991
A206LPP	Bova EL26/581	Bova Europa	C53F	1983	Ex Graham, Gilsland, 1995
A737HFP	Bova EL26/581	Bova Europa	C53F	1984	Ex Channel, Rochford, 1992

Previous Registrations:
ADC176A   VWX348X

Named vehicles; ADC176A, Heage Windmill; ENF514Y, Windmill Cruiser

Livery: White and red

ANDREWS

Andrews of Tideswell Ltd, Anchor Garage, Tideswell, Buxton, Derbyshire, SK17 8RB

EUA366	Ford R1114	Plaxton Supreme IV	C53F	1979	Ex Smith, Alcester, 1980
PIW8618	Ford R1114	Plaxton Supreme IV	C53F	1980	Ex Temple, Up Hatherley, 1994
RIW8127	Ford R1114	Plaxton Supreme IV	C53F	1980	Ex Gray, Hoyland Common, 1995
PIW8619	Ford R1114	Plaxton Supreme V	C49F	1982	Ex Mitchell, Birmingham, 1994
PUA917	Ford R1114	Plaxton Supreme IV	C53F	1982	
476BTO	Volvo B10M-61	Plaxton Paramount 3200	C53F	1983	Ex Richmond, Barley, 1995
NIB6064	Volvo B10M-61	Van Hool Alizée	C49FT	1984	Ex Crossland, Sheffield, 1995
345BLA	Volvo B10M-61	Plaxton Paramount 3500	C49FT	1984	
C550TJF	Ford Transit 190	Rootes	B16F	1986	Ex The Bee Line, 1991
C311LWG	Mercedes-Benz L307D	Reeve Burgess	M12	1986	
PJI5529	Volvo B10M-61	Van Hool Alizée	C53F	1986	Ex Shearings, 1993
PJI3746	Volvo B10M-61	Van Hool Alizée	C53F	1986	Ex Shearings, 1993
E477GBV	Mercedes-Benz 609D	Reeve Burgess	DP24F	1987	Ex East Pennine, Halifax, 1989
RIW8126	Mercedes-Benz 609D	Reeve Burgess Beaver	C19F	1988	
RBA480	Scania K113CRB	Plaxton Paramount 3500 III	C49FT	1989	
BAZ8577	Volvo B10M-60	Van Hool Alizée	C49FT	1990	Ex Shearings, 1995
BAZ8578	Volvo B10M-60	Van Hool Alizée	C49FT	1990	Ex Shearings, 1995

Named vehicles: 345BLA, *Peakland Queen XII* ; EUA366, *Peakland Queen IX* ; PUA917, *Peakland Queen X* ;
PJI5529, *Peakland Queen XVII* ; E667KCX, *Peakland Queen XV* ; RBA480, *Peakland Queen XVI* ;
PJI3746, *Peakland Queen XVIII* ; BAZ8577, *Peakland Queen XX* ; BAZ8578, *Peakland Queen XXI* ;
PIW8619, *Peakland Queen XXII* ; 476BTO, *Peakland Queen XXIII* ; PIW8618, *Peakland Queen XIX*.

Previous Registrations:

345BLA	B853KRY	PIW8619	VJT616X
476BTO	RMU964Y	PJI3746	C338DND, XTW359, C440GVM
BAZ8577	G877VNA	PJI5529	C337DND, 205CCH, C441GVM
BAZ8578	G878VNA	PUA917	BUR140X
EUA366	DWK413T	RBA480	G33HKY
NIB6064	A795TGG	RIW8126	E814WAK
PIW8618	HVR105V	RIW8127	CDN649V

Livery: Cream and red

Albert Wilde Coaches operate a daily service from Ripley to Belper through the operator's home village of Heage. The fleet contains a trio of Bova Europa coaches one of which now carries the older mark ABW178X, the letters of which reflect the owner's name. *Steve Sanderson*

An early attempt to create what is now known as the midibus was made by Midland Red to meet operational needs. This operator had several full-sized Plaxton Derwent-bodied Fords shortened, the modified vehicles having a seating capacity of only 27. Now in the Andrew's fleet is one of the conversions, YHA362J. *Tony Wilson*

APPLEBYS

R W Appleby Ltd, Conisholme, Louth, Lincolnshire, LN11 7LT
Halcyon Leisure Ltd, Conisholme, Louth, Lincolnshire, LN11 7LT

Depots : Bardney ; Bessingby Industrial Estate, Bridlington ; Brighowgate, Grimsby ; Julian Street, Grimsby ; Horncastle ; Wincolmlee, Hull ; Newark Road, Lincoln ; North Somercoates and Queen Margaret Road, Scarborough.

Reg	Chassis	Body	Seating	Year	History
869NHT	Bristol Lodekka FS6G	Eastern Coach Works	CO33/27R	1961	Ex North, Sherburn, 1989
WJY760	Leyland Atlantean PDR1/1	Metro Cammell	O43/34F	1962	Ex Plymouth, 1991
HCS795N	Leyland Leopard PSU3/3R	Alexander AY	B53F	1975	Ex Chiltern Queens, 1994
JTD387P	Daimler Fleetline CRL6-33	Northern Counties	O49/31D	1975	Ex NPT, Bilsthorpe, 1993
MFR17P	Leyland Leopard PSU3C/2R	Alexander AY	DP49F	1976	Ex Clydeside, 1996
MNU479P	Leyland Leopard PSU3C/4R	Plaxton Supreme III Express	C53F	1976	Ex Trent (Barton), 1996
KMW176P	Daimler Fleetline CRG6LX	Eastern Coach Works	O43/31F	1976	Ex Emblems Jazz Band, Knottingley, 1992
KMW177P	Daimler Fleetline CRG6LX	Eastern Coach Works	H43/31F	1976	Ex Thamesdown, 1991
KMW178P	Daimler Fleetline CRG6LX	Eastern Coach Works	H43/31F	1976	Ex Thamesdown, 1991
KON326P	Leyland Fleetline FE30ALR	MCW	O43/33F	1976	Ex SS Suncruisers, Scarborough, 1994
RRC484R	Leyland Leopard PSU3C/4R	Plaxton Supreme III Express	C53F	1976	Ex Thornton Dale Coaches, 1993
PAU205R	Daimler Fleetline CRG6LX	Northern Counties	H47/30D	1976	Ex Darlington, 1994
NKU570R	Leyland Fleetline FE30ALR	East Lancashire	H45/29D	1977	Ex Smith, Alcester, 1993
SUR278R	Leyland Leopard PSU3C/4R	Plaxton Supreme III	C53F	1977	Ex Holloway, Scunthorpe, 1984
VAT176S	Bedford YLQ	Plaxton Supreme III	C45F	1977	Ex Boddy, Bridlington, 1983
SDA517S	Leyland Fleetline FE30AGR	MCW	H43/33F	1977	Ex Midland Fox, 1995
SDA563S	Leyland Fleetline FE30AGR	MCW	H43/33F	1978	Ex Amberley Travel, Pudsey, 1993
YRH808T	Bedford YMT	Plaxton Supreme III	C53F	1978	Ex Boddy, Bridlington, 1983
EGB68T	Leyland Leopard PSU3C/5R	Alexander AYS	B53F	1978	Ex KCB Network, 1996
OFV287T	Bedford YMT	Duple Dominant II	C53F	1978	Ex Tours IOM, Douglas, 1988
MGR915T	Leyland Leopard PSU3E/4R	Duple Dominant	B55F	1979	Ex United, 1996
GSU835T	Leyland Leopard PSU3E/5R	Alexander AYS	B53F	1979	Ex KCB Network, 1996
GSU844T	Leyland Leopard PSU3E/5R	Alexander AYS	B53F	1979	Ex KCB Network, 1996
GSU857T	Leyland Leopard PSU3E/5R	Alexander AYS	B53F	1979	Ex KCB Network, 1996
GSU858T	Leyland Leopard PSU3E/5R	Alexander AYS	B53F	1979	Ex KCB Network, 1996
GSU860T	Leyland Leopard PSU3E/5R	Alexander AYS	B53F	1979	Ex KCB Network, 1996
ANJ304T	Leyland Leopard PSU3E/4RT	Plaxton Supreme IV Express	C49F	1979	Ex Timeline, 1994
ANJ313T	Leyland Leopard PSU3E/4RT	Plaxton Supreme IV Express	C49F	1979	Ex Timeline, 1994
YUH115T	Bedford YMT	Plaxton Supreme IV	C53F	1979	Ex Hawthorn, Barry, 1982
ETL508T	Bedford YMT	Plaxton Supreme IV Express	C53F	1979	
FFE477T	Bedford YLQ	Plaxton Supreme IV Express	C45F	1979	
FFW263T	Bedford YLQ	Plaxton Supreme IV Express	C45F	1979	
FRH615T	Bedford YMT	Plaxton Supreme IV	C53F	1979	Ex Boddy, Bridlington, 1983
FTL817T	Bedford YMT	Plaxton Supreme IV Express	C53F	1979	
GFE343T	Bedford YMT	Plaxton Supreme IV Express	C53F	1979	

Appleby's fleet has for many years contained a large number of Plaxton Supreme-bodied Bedfords most of which are the Express variant. This featured a wider entrance door that made the vehicle eligible for then *new bus* grant. Seen in Lincoln is MTL750V.
Tony Wilson

The mainstay of Appleby's double deck fleet is the Fleetline. SDA563S is an MCW-bodied 76-seat model of the Leyland variant and was new to West Midlands PTE in 1977. It came to Applebys via Amberley Travel of Pudsey. *David Longbottom*

WOC740T	Leyland Leopard PSU3E/4R	Plaxton Supreme IV Express	C53F	1979	Ex Stephenson, Easingwold, 1993
WDA948T	Leyland Fleetline FE30AGR	MCW	H43/33F	1979	Ex Amberley Travel, Pudsey, 1993
FTO544V	Leyland Leopard PSU3E/4R	Plaxton Supreme IV Express	C53F	1979	Ex Trent (Barton), 1996
DAK220V	Leyland Leopard PSU5C/4R	Duple Dominant II	C53F	1979	Ex Barnard, Kirton-in-Lindsey, 1993
MGE8V	Bedford YMT	Plaxton Supreme IV	C53F	1980	Ex Haldane, Glasgow, 1982
MRH398V	Bedford YMT	Plaxton Supreme IV	C53F	1980	Ex Boddy, Bridlington, 1983
MTL750V	Bedford YMT	Plaxton Supreme IV	C51F	1980	
MVL750V	Bedford YLQ	Plaxton Supreme IV Express	C41F	1980	
NVL692V	Bedford YMT	Plaxton Supreme IV	C53F	1980	
NFW110V	Bedford YMT	Plaxton Supreme IV	C53F	1980	
JGV317V	Bedford YMT	Duple Dominant	B55F	1980	Ex Rider York, 1993
HSD86V	Leyland Fleetline FE30AGR	Alexander AD	H44/31F	1980	Ex Clydeside, 1996
LMS161W	Leyland Fleetline FE30AGR	Alexander AD	H44/31F	1980	Ex Clydeside, 1996
ORJ366W	Leyland Atlantean AN68A/1R	Northern Counties	O43/32F	1981	Ex GMN, 1996
UVL89W	Bedford YNT	Plaxton Supreme IV Express	C53F	1981	
UVL653W	Bedford YNT	Plaxton Supreme IV Express	C53F	1981	
VNH160W	Leyland Leopard PSU3F/4RT	Duple Dominant IV Express	C49F	1981	Ex Oban & District, 1995
VNH162W	Leyland Leopard PSU3F/4RT	Duple Dominant IV Express	C49F	1981	Ex Oban & District, 1995
PWT279W	Leyland Leopard PSU3F/4R	Willowbrook 003	C49F	1981	Ex West Yorkshire, 1988
LJI8027	Volvo B10M-61	Duple Dominant III	C57F	1981	Ex The Isleworth, 1995
DSV721	Volvo B10M-61	Duple Dominant IV	C57F	1982	Ex Lothian Transit, Newtongrange, 1993
795BFU	Volvo B10M-61	Duple Goldliner IV	C57F	1982	Ex McDade, Uddingston, 1995
BJV787	Volvo B10M-61	Plaxton Supreme V	C53F	1982	Ex Stagecoach Midland Red, 1996
OHE273X	Volvo B10M-61	Duple Dominant IV	C53F	1982	Ex Sykes, Appleton Roebuck, 1996
VUD32X	Leyland Leopard PSU3G/4R	Eastern Coach Works B51	DP51F	1982	Ex KCB Network, 1996
EAT170Y	Leyland Leopard PSU3F/5R	Plaxton Supreme IV	C53F	1982	Ex Boddy, Bridlington, 1983
105NHY	Bedford YNT	Plaxton Supreme V	C53F	1982	
FJV931	Volvo B10M-61	Duple Dominant IV	C53F	1983	Ex Gregory, Blaencwm, 1995
841TPU	Volvo B10M-61	Plaxton Paramount 3200 II	C53F	1985	
NEE496	Volvo B10M-61	Plaxton Paramount 3200 II	C53F	1985	
957XYB	Volvo B10M-61	Plaxton Paramount 3200 II	C53F	1986	
6257RO	Volvo B10M-61	Plaxton Paramount 3200 II	C53F	1986	
WSV317	Volvo B10M-61	Plaxton Paramount 3200 II	C53F	1986	
D22SAO	Renault-Dodge S56	Reeve Burgess	B23F	1986	Ex AJC Coaches, Leeds, 1994

Scania coaches now form the backbone of the Applebys touring fleet. These modern vehicles can be seen far from their Lincolnshire base, throughout Britain and other parts of Europe. YNA887 was photographed in Kent when on tour. The vehicle carries a Berkhof Excellence 1000L body finished to their high standard, known as the Royal Class specification. *Steve Sanderson*

	Reg	Chassis	Body	Layout	Year	Notes
	D32SAO	Renault-Dodge S56	Reeve Burgess	B25F	1986	Ex Preston Bus, 1994
	D768YCW	Renault-Dodge S56	Northern Counties	B24F	1987	Ex Preston Bus, 1994
	D769YCW	Renault-Dodge S56	Northern Counties	B24F	1987	Ex Preston Bus, 1994
	YJV178	Volvo B10M-61	Plaxton Paramount 3200 III	C55F	1987	
	XAT586	Volvo B10M-61	Plaxton Paramount 3200 III	C53F	1987	
	E459WJK	Renault-Dodge S56	Alexander AM	DP25F	1987	Ex Brighton, 1995
	RVL445	Volvo B10M-61	Plaxton Paramount 3200 III	C53F	1987	
	5517RH	Volvo B10M-61	Plaxton Paramount 3200 III	C53F	1988	
	E824MDO	Iveco Daily 49.10	Robin Hood City Nippy	B21F	1988	Ex Bloomsbury HA, 1994
	E48MCK	Renault-Dodge S56	Northern Counties	B25F	1988	Ex Preston Bus, 1996
	E75LFR	Renault-Dodge S56	Northern Counties	B25F	1988	Ex Preston Bus, 1996
	E985GFW	Volkswagen Caravelle	Volkswagen	M8	1988	
	UTL798	Scania K112CRB	Van Hool Alizée	C53F	1988	
	F970GJK	Iveco Daily 49.10	Robin Hood City Nippy	B21F	1989	Ex Translink, Folkestone, 1994
	251CNX	Scania K93CRB	Van Hool Alizée	C53F	1989	
	XJV146	Scania K93CRB	Plaxton Paramount 3200 III	C53F	1989	
	YNA887	Scania K93CRB	Berkhof Excellence 1000L	C53F	1990	
	ORJ442	Scania K93CRB	Berkhof Excellence 1000L	C53F	1990	
	990ULG	Toyota Coaster HB31R	Caetano Optimo	C18F	1989	Ex Davidson, Edinburgh, 1994
	HVL611	Scania K93CRB	Van Hool Alizée	C53F	1990	
	UJV489	Scania K93CRB	Van Hool Alizée	C53F	1990	
H	G495VFU	Mazda E2200	Coachwork Walker	M8	1990	
	WAC828	Aüwaerter Neoplan N122/3	Aüwaerter Skyliner	CH57/20T	1988	Ex Randle, Padiham, 1993
H	485DKH	Scania K113CRB	Berkhof Excellence 2000HL	C49FT	1990	
H	G545PRH	Scania K113TRB	Berkhof Excellence 2000HD	CH57/17CT	1990	
H	G698PRH	Scania K113CRB	Berkhof Excellence 2000HL	C49FT	1990	
	KRO718	Toyota Coaster HB31R	Caetano Optimo	C18F	1990	Ex Travellers, Hounslow, 1993
	5447FH	Scania K113CRB	Berkhof Excellence 2000HL	C49FT	1991	
H	H894AAT	Scania K113CRB	Berkhof Excellence 2000HL	C49FT	1991	
	UVE288	Scania K93CRB	Berkhof Excellence 1000L	C49FT	1991	
H	J23HRH	Scania K113CRB	Berkhof Excellence 2000HL	C49FT	1992	
	VFW721	Scania K113CRB	Berkhof Excellence 2000	C49FT	1992	
	WEE584	Scania K113CRB	Berkhof Excellence 2000HL	C49FT	1992	
	388XYC	Scania K113CRB	Berkhof Excellence 1000	C53F	1992	
	LJV273	Scania K113CRB	Berkhof Excellence 1000	C50FT	1993	
	361EKH	Scania K113CRB	Berkhof Excellence 1000	C49FT	1993	

Applebys operate an increasing number of services with minibuses. A number of Northern Counties-bodied Dodge S56 examples have been obtained from the Preston Bus fleet. D768YCW is to be found on services in Bridlington and Scarborough. *David Longbottom*

	520FUM	Scania K113CRB	Berkhof Excellence 1000	C49FT	1993
H	K860RRH	Scania K113CRB	Berkhof Excellence 2000HL	C49FT	1993
	L230RDO	Scania K113CRB	Irizar Century 12.35	C49FT	1994
	L502YFE	Scania K113CRB	Irizar Century 12.35	C49FT	1994
	L542JJV	Scania K113CRB	Irizar Century 12.35	C49FT	1994
	M433GFE	Scania K113TRB	Irizar Century 12.37	C49FT	1995
	M135NBE	Scania K113TRB	Irizar Century 12.37	C49FT	1995
H	M985LAG	Scania K113TRB	Irizar Century 12.37	C49FT	1995
	M594GFE	Volkswagen Caravelle	Volkswagen	M8	1995
	N875AKY	Mercedes-Benz 811D	Mellor	B33F	1995
	N539OFE	Scania K113CRB	Irizar Century 12.35	C49FT	1996
	N135OFW	Scania K113CRB	Irizar Century 12.35	C49FT	1996
	N764RBE	Scania K113TRB	Irizar Century 12.37	C49FT	1996
	N356REE	Scania K113TRB	Irizar Century 12.37	C49FT	1996

Previous Registrations:

105NHY	DFW782X	990ULG	G864VAY	UJV489	G649WFE
251CNX	F327OVL	ARW163X	YKV811X, 3669DG	UTL798	E562FFW
361EKH	K669SFE	DSV721	FGD826X	UVE288	H960FFW
388XYC	J677LVL	E75LFR	E77LFR	VFW721	J559MTL
485DKH	G402PRH	FJV931	ENF553Y	WAC828	F618CWJ
520FUM	K671SFE	HVL611	G592WFW	WEE584	J884MFE
5447FH	H82FVL	KRO718	H167DJU	WJY760	From new
5517RH	E899HFW	LJI8027	BKF348X	WSV317	From new
6257RO	C320NFW	LJV273	K668SFE	XAT586	D413SFW
795BFU	FGD825X	NEE496	B273ETL	XJV146	F141DCT
841TPU	From new	OFV287T	OFV287T, B111MAN, MAN1578	YJV178	D240WTL
869NHT	From new	ORJ442	G288VTL	YNA887	G630VVL
957XYB	From new	RVL445	From new		

Livery: Ivory, green and red (Appleby) ; pink, green & yellow (Halcyon - which are also marked H above)

AVISDORS

W C Heath, Twingates, Stapleton Lane, Barwell, Leicestershire, LE9 8HE

PCA797M	Bedford CFL	Deansgate	C17F	1974	Ex Williams, Bala, 1994
PNK94R	Bedford YMT	Duple Dominant	C53F	1976	Ex Sanders, Holt, 1994
WAD642S	Ford R1114	Plaxton Supreme III	C53F	1978	Ex Crutwell, Ramsey, 1994
XRW510S	Leyland Leopard PSU5C/4R	Plaxton Supreme III	C50F	1980	Ex British Shoe, Leicester, 1996
C395RRY	Ford Transit 190	Dormobile	B16F	1985	
D817KWT	Freight Rover Sherpa	Dormobile	B16F	1987	Ex West Riding, 1991
D41TKA	Freight Rover Sherpa	Dormobile	B16F	1987	Ex Shaw, Werrington, 1992
D163KDN	Volkswagen LT55	Optare CityPacer	B25F	1987	Ex MacLennon, Laxy Lochs, 1995
E405BHK	Volkswagen LT55	Optare CityPacer	B25F	1987	Ex Derby Blue Bus, 1995
E738VWJ	Freight Rover Sherpa	Whittaker	C16F	1988	
F307EKP	Freight Rover Sherpa	Dormobile	B16FL	1989	

Livery: Various ; most vehicles are in former owner's colours

Avisdors predominantly operates minibuses from a base in Barwell near Hinckley in south west Leicestershire. This view is of D817KWT a Freight Rover Sherpa from the West Riding fleet which displays the blue and red North Western-style livery carried by some Avisdors minibuses.
Steve Sanderson

BESTWICKS

P Bestwick, Ford Lodge, Winkpenny Lane, Tibshelf, Derbyshire, DE5 5LN

Depot : Back Lane, Tibshelf.

GNN220N	Leyland Leopard PSU3B/4R	Plaxton Elite III Express	C53F	1974	Ex Trent (Barton), 1994
GNN222N	Leyland Leopard PSU3B/4R	Plaxton Elite III Express	C53F	1974	Ex Trent (Barton), 1994
HHE217N	Bristol LHS6L	Plaxton Supreme III	C33F	1975	Ex Kirkham, Doncaster, 1995
KBD22V	Bristol LHS6L	Eastern Coach Works	DP30F	1979	Ex DeeWard, Mkt Harborough, 1993
JTH54W	Volvo B58-61	Plaxton Viewmaster IV	C53F	1981	Ex Brian Isaac, Morriston, 1993
UDU891W	Volvo B58-61	Jonckheere Bermuda	C49FT	1981	Ex Cumming Upholland, 1992
FVL353X	Leyland Tiger TRCTL11/3R	Plaxton Supreme IV	C57F	1981	Ex Hornsby, Ashby, 1996
BLN591Y	Ford R1115	Duple Dominant IV	C53F	1982	Ex Chalfont, Greenford, 1988

Previous Registrations:

FVL353X	YUM551X, 1642RH	UDU891W	WNV817W, TGE93
JTH54W	SLH2W, 431DWN		

Livery: White and red

Bestwicks of Tibshelf operate service 5 which runs from Holmewood to Tupton through Clay Cross. Seen at Holmewood is KBD22V. This Eastern Coach Works-bodied Bristol LHS was new to the Northampton municipal fleet and unusually is fitted with 30 high-backed seats. *Tony Wilson*

BLANDS OF COTTESMORE

I R & A R Bland, 27 Main Street, Cottesmore, Oakham, Leicestershire, LE15 7DH

SND85X	Leyland Leopard PSU3B/4R	Duple Dominant IV(1982)	C51F	1975	Ex Greater Manchester, 1986
OTD827R	Leyland Leopard PSU3E/4R	Plaxton Supreme III Express	C51F	1977	Ex Busways, 1994
BUA705X	Leyland Leopard PSU3F/5R	Plaxton Supreme V	C53F	1981	Ex Clarkson, South Elmsall, 1992
CNH170X	Leyland Leopard PSU3G/4R	Eastern Coach Works B51	C49F	1982	Ex Whitelaw, Stonehouse, 1995
RJU129Y	Bedford YNT	Plaxton Paramount 3200 E	C53F	1983	
FP5992	Dennis Javelin SDA1907	Duple 320	C53F	1989	
F22TBC	Mercedes-Benz 811D	Reeve Burgess Beaver	C25F	1989	
G709LKW	Scania K93CRB	Plaxton Paramount 3200 III	C55F	1990	
J518LRY	DAF SB2305DHS585	Caetano Algarve	C53F	1992	

Previous Registrations:
BUA705X   RLJ89X, MIW2422   RJU129Y   BAY644Y, FP5992
FP5992   F21TBC   SND85X   KDB...P

Livery: White, orange and brown.

Blands of Cottesmore operate a service from an R.A.F station near the operator's depot, to Peterborough. Seen setting down passengers in Cottesmore village on return from Peterborough, RJU129Y, a Plaxton Paramount-bodied Bedford YNT that was purchased new by Blands.
Steve Sanderson

BOWERS

E W Bowers (Coaches) Ltd, Aspincroft Garage, Town End,
Chapel-en-le-Frith, Derbyshire, SK12 6NU

WKY676K	AEC Reliance 6U3ZR	Plaxton Elite II	C51F	1973	Ex Lonsdale, Heysham, 1989
PFN787R	AEC Reliance 6U3ZR	Duple Dominant	C51F	1974	Ex East Kent, 1985
PNK152R	AEC Reliance 6U3ZR	Plaxton Supreme III	C53F	1976	Ex Saxton, Heanor, 1991
RVE651S	AEC Reliance 6U3ZR	Plaxton Supreme III Express	C49F	1977	Ex Premier Travel, 1989
ETU531X	Mercedes-Benz L207D	Mercedes-Benz	M12	1982	
LIL2512	DAF SB2300DHS585	Plaxton Paramount 3200	C53F	1985	Ex AMR, Bedfont, 1995
D930ARE	Mercedes-Benz L608D	PMT	C17F	1986	
805AFC	Volvo B10M-61	Jonckheere Jubilee	C49FT	1987	Ex Club Cantabrica, St Albans, 1994
E186UWF	Renault-Dodge S56	Reeve Burgess	B25F	1987	Ex Moffat & Williamson, Gauldry, 1994
LIL7568	Mercedes-Benz 609D	Reeve Burgess Beaver	C25F	1988	
E650KYW	MCW Metrorider MF158/2	MCW	DP33F	1988	Ex East London, 1996
LIL3068	MCW Metrorider MF150/36	MCW	C23F	1988	Ex Geoff Willetts, Pillowell, 1995
PRD34	Scania K113CRB	Van Hool Alizée	C53F	1988	Ex Scania demonstrator, 1991
YWH978	Scania K113CRB	Van Hool Alizée	C51FT	1989	Ex Fowler, Holbeach Drove, 1993
LIL2612	Leyland Swift ST2R	Reeve Burgess Harrier	C37F	1989	Ex AMR, Bedfont, 1995
B6WER	Volvo B10M-60	Van Hool Alizée	C49FT	1990	Ex Shearings, 1996
LIL7910	Mercedes-Benz 814D	Reeve Burgess Beaver	C33F	1991	
LIL7912	Mercedes-Benz 811D	Reeve Burgess Beaver	C25F	1991	
B8WER	Scania K113CRB	Van Hool Alizée	C51F	1994	Ex Holmeswood Coaches, Rufford, 1996

Previous Registrations:

805AFC	D847UBH, 612CCH, D32RKX, LIL2512	B232RRU	LIL7912	J282YWJ
B6WER	G879VNA, XTW359, G792YND, LIL3068	E148NAD	PRD34	F113JPP
B8WER	L839KHD, L4HWD, L749NEO, LIL7568	E468AWF	WKY676K	HJP999K, PRD34
LIL2612	G341VHU	LIL7910	J281YWJ	YWH978	F373CHE, 805AFC

Livery: Red ; PRD34 & 805AFC carry North British Tours livery

The Peak District village of Hartington is the location of this view of Bowers LIL7910. This Reeve Burgess Beaver-bodied Mercedes-Benz 800 series is the more powerful 814D model rather than the more common 811D. Along with many of the Bowers fleet, this midicoach carries a date-less LIL registration.
Tony Wilson

The East Midland Bus Handbook   **15**

BRYLAINE

B W & E R Gregg, Peck Avenue, Boston, Lincolnshire, PE21 8DT

Depots: Main Road, Benington ; Peck Avenue, Boston ; Old Boston Road, Coningsby and High Mill, Old Bolingbroke.

w	CNG525K	Bristol LH6P	Eastern Coach Works		B45F	1972	Ex Hogg, Boston, 1990
w	DLJ112L	Daimler Fleetline CRL6	Alexander AL		H43/31F	1973	Ex Burman, Dordon, 1992
w	DLJ118L	Daimler Fleetline CRL6	Alexander AL		H43/31F	1973	Ex Burman, Dordon, 1992
w	NBF744P	Ford R1114	Duple Dominant		C53F	1976	Ex Sanders, Holt, 1994
	URN154R	Bristol VRT/SL3/6LXB	East Lancashire		H43/32F	1977	Ex Hogg, Boston, 1990
	URN155R	Bristol VRT/SL3/6LXB	East Lancashire		H43/32F	1977	Ex Hogg, Boston, 1990
	URN158R	Bristol VRT/SL3/6LXB	East Lancashire		H43/32F	1977	Ex Hogg, Boston, 1990
	OJD434R	Leyland Fleetline FE30ALR	Park Royal		H44/24D	1977	Ex Cardiff Bluebird, 1995
	OJD444R	Leyland Fleetline FE30ALR	Park Royal		H44/32F	1977	Ex Cardiff Bluebird, 1995
	OJD455R	Leyland Fleetline FE30ALR	Park Royal		H44/24D	1977	Ex Cardiff Bluebird, 1995
	THX305S	Leyland Fleetline FE30ALR	MCW		H44/24D	1977	Ex Cardiff Bluebird, 1995
	PJV36S	Ford R1114	Plaxton Supreme III		C53F	1977	Ex Atkins, Skegness, 1991
	USO184S	Ford R1114	Alexander AYS		B53F	1977	Ex Strathtay Scottish, 1987
	BRO486T	Ford R1114	Plaxton Supreme III Express		C53F	1978	Ex Evag Cannon, Bolton, 1994
w	OGU131	Leyland Leopard PSU5C/4R	Duple Dominant II		C50F	1978	Ex Sam's, Skegness, 1991
	GBH511T	Bedford YMT	Duple Dominant II		C57F	1978	Ex Hogg, Boston, 1990
	OJS27T	Ford R1014	Duple Dominant II		C45F	1978	Ex Bowers, Chapel-en-le-Frith, 1994
	YNY586T	Bedford YRT	Willowbrook		B52F	1978	Ex Hogg, Boston, 1990
w	YJL655T	Bedford YMT	Duple Dominant II		C53F	1978	Ex Hogg, Boston, 1990
	KIB6844	Bedford YLQ	Duple Dominant II		C45F	1979	Ex Sam's, Skegness, 1991
	GTM123T	Bedford VAS5	Plaxton Supreme IV		C29F	1979	Ex Chartercoach, Dovercourt, 1993
	JDB939V	Ford R1114	Plaxton Supreme IV		C53F	1979	Ex Salopia, Whitchurch, 1984
	CJL639V	Bedford YMT	Plaxton Supreme IV Express		C53F	1979	Ex Hogg, Boston, 1990
	DJL581V	Bedford YMT	Duple Dominant II		C53F	1980	Ex Hogg, Boston, 1990
	JRF161V	Bedford VAS5	Plaxton Supreme IV		C29F	1980	Ex Clark, Barnsley, 1994

URN158R is an East Lancashire-bodied Bristol VRT which was new to Burnley and Pendle and is seen here leaving Boston for Spilsby. This trio, from the same batch, have recently been joined in the Brylaine fleet by four Leyland Fleetline DMS types. All carry the Brylaine white and blue livery.
Steve Sanderson

Bedford and Ford coaches dominate the Brylaine fleet. GTM123T is one of the smaller Bedfords, a VAS5 type with Plaxton Supreme coachwork. It is seen at the Meadowhall shopping complex near Sheffield, a favourite venue for coach excursions. The fleet name is a combination of the first names of the proprietors, Brian and Elaine Gregg. *Phillip Stephenson*

	HVU81V	Ford R1114	Plaxton Supreme IV	C53F	1980	Ex Evag Cannon, Bolton, 1994
	WIA7680	Ford R1114	Plaxton Supreme IV	C53F	1980	Ex Evag Cannon, Bolton, 1994
	PFW839V	Ford R1014	Duple Dominant II	C45F	1980	Ex Sleafordian, Sleaford, 1995
	JAF208W	Ford R1114	Plaxton Supreme IV Express	C53F	1980	Ex Hambly, Pelynt, 1995
	VUR118W	Ford R1114	Duple Dominant	B55F	1980	Ex Rover Bus Service, Chesham, 1994
	GDO27W	Ford R1114	Duple Dominant II	C53F	1980	Ex Hogg, Boston, 1990
	LNU577W	Bedford YMT	Plaxton Supreme IV Express	C53F	1980	Ex Beeline, Warminster, 1992
	MUT777W	Bedford YMT	Plaxton Supreme IV	C53F	1980	Ex Hogg, Boston, 1990
	YDM354W	Ford R1114	Duple Dominant II	C53F	1980	Ex TRS, Leicester, 1989
	JCT73W	Ford R1114	Duple Dominant II	C53F	1980	Ex Hogg, Boston, 1990
	ENP666W	Bedford VAS5	Plaxton Supreme IV	C29F	1981	Ex Swansdown, Inkpen, 1993
	LJX401W	Ford R1114	Plaxton Supreme IV	C53F	1981	Ex Sanders, Holt 1994
	ODJ587W	Ford R1114	Duple Dominant IV	C53F	1981	Ex Capitol Coaches, Cwmbran, 1994
w	ODJ593W	Ford R1114	Duple Dominant IV	C53F	1981	Ex Capitol Coaches, Cwmbran, 1994
w	ODJ599W	Ford R1114	Duple Dominant IV	C53F	1981	Ex Capitol Coaches, Cwmbran, 1994
	LTG278X	Ford R1114	Plaxton Supreme IV	C53F	1981	Ex Sanders, Holt, 1994
	XNK199X	Ford R1014	Plaxton Bustler	B47F	1981	Ex Provence, St Albans, 1994
	MVK881X	Ford R1114	Duple Dominant IV	C53F	1982	Ex Express Motors, Bontnewydd, 1996
	BBY430Y	Ford R1114	Duple Dominant IV	C53F	1982	Ex Long, Freshwater, 1996
	FDV142Y	Ford R1114	Duple Dominant IV	C53F	1983	Ex Thomas, Portchester, 1996
	YRB652Y	Ford R1115	Plaxton Paramount 3200	C49F	1983	Ex Plastow, Wheatley, 1995
	ACX783Y	Ford R1114	Duple Dominant IV	C53F	1983	Ex Evag Cannon, Bolton, 1994
	A680JCM	Ford Transit	Ford	M12	1983	Ex private owner, 1992
w	OIB3509	Quest VM	Plaxton Paramount 3200	C53F	1984	Ex Weeks, Uxbridge, 1994
w	A820LEL	Quest VM	Plaxton Paramount 3200	C53F	1984	Ex Rees Travel, Llanelly Hill, 1993
	C603NPU	Ford Transit 190	Carlyle	B20F	1985	Ex Midland Fox, 1995
	C62LHL	Ford Transit 190	Carlyle	DP20F	1986	Ex Rover, Bromsgrove, 1995
	C572TUT	Ford Transit 190	Carlyle	B16F	1986	Ex Midland Fox, 1995
	E903DRG	Ford R1114	Plaxton Elite III	C53F	1988	Ex Bob Smith Travel, Langley Park, 1994
	KSU363	Bedford YNT	Plaxton Paramount 3200 III	C53F	1988	Ex Sproat, Bouth, 1994

Previous Registrations:

KIB6844	BNL137V	OIB3509	A808LEL
KSU363	F327YTG	VUR118W	PNM663W, 662JJO
OGU131	AFH197T	WIA7680	BCY248V

Livery: White and blue

The East Midland Bus Handbook 17

BUTLER BROTHERS

R & R Butler, 60 Vernon Road, Kirkby-in-Ashfield, Nottinghamshire, NG17 8ED

OSJ1X	Leyland Tiger TRCTL11/2R	Duple Dominant IV Express	C53F	1982	Ex Brown, Dreghorn (A1), 1994
BGS287X	Leyland Leopard PSU5E/4R	Duple Dominant IV	C57F	1982	Ex Capital, Gatwick, 1987
B217WEU	Leyland Tiger TRCTL11/3RH	Duple Laser	C51F	1984	Ex Elsey, Gosberton, 1990
B220WEU	Leyland Tiger TRCTL11/3RH	Duple Laser	C51F	1984	Ex Edwards Bros, Tiers Cross, 1991
BUT2B	DAF MB200DKFL600	Van Hool Alizée	C53FT	1984	
68BUT	DAF MB200DKTL600	Van Hool Alizée	C53F	1984	
83BUT	Leyland Tiger TRCTL11/3RZ	Duple 340	C57F	1986	
E393HNR	Dennis Javelin 12SDA1907	Duple 320	C55F	1988	
E562MAC	Talbot Pullman	Talbot	B22F	1988	Ex Filer, Ilfracombe, 1995
179BUT	DAF SB2305DHS585	Van Hool Alizée	C55F	1988	Ex Hardings, Redditch, 1994
F232RNR	Toyota Coaster HB31R	Caetano Optimo	C21F	1989	Ex Dale Hire, Astwood Bank, 1994
G440NET	Leyland DAF400	Whittaker	M16	1990	
K550RJX	DAFSB3000DKV601	Van Hool Alizée	C49FT	1992	Ex Boon's, Boreham, 1996

Previous Registrations:
68BUT	A482FAU	179BUT	E442LNP, DSK594, E549MWP
83BUT	From new	BUT2B	From new

Livery: Turquoise, blue and red

Seen in Vauxhall, London is 83BUT, a Duple 340-bodied Leyland Tiger of Butler Brothers. The company is based in Kirkby-in-Ashfield from where they operate service B4. The service number is normally displayed at the bottom of the off side windscreen, a most unusual location. Services with numbers containing a prefix letter and a single service number was the norm for Mansfield and District and Butlers are keeping the practice alive. *Colin Lloyd*

The East Midland Bus Handbook

CAMMS

Camms of Nottingham Ltd, 273 Ilkeston Road, Radford, Nottingham, NG7 3FY

100	A100AVO	Leyland Tiger TRCTL11/3R	Duple Laser	C53FT	1983	
114	RJI1656	Volvo B10M-61	Plaxton Paramount 3500	C49FT	1983	Ex Watson, Annfield Plain, 1985
145	TFJ61X	AEC Reliance 6U2R	Duple Dominant IV	C53F	1981	Ex Watson, Annfield Plain, 1987
147	OGR51T	Leyland Leopard PSU3E/4R	Plaxton Supreme IV Express	C53F	1979	Ex Watson, Annfield Plain, 1987
148	WBR5V	Leyland Leopard PSU3E/4R	Plaxton Supreme IV	C53F	1980	Ex Watson, Annfield Plain, 1987
165	NNU128M	Daimler Fleetline CRL6-30	Roe	H42/29D	1973	Ex Chesterfield, 19??
178	XBF54S	Leyland Leopard PSU3E/4R	Duple Dominant I	C49F	1978	Ex PMT, 1992
180	XPK52T	AEC Reliance 6U2R	Duple Dominant II Express	C53F	1978	Ex Lively Marple, 1992
184	GHR302W	Leyland Leopard PSU3F/4R	Duple Dominant II Express	C53F	1981	Ex Thamesdown, 1993
185	RJI1657	Leyland Royal Tiger RT	Van Hool Alizée	C49F	1986	Ex Cosey, East Molesey, 1993
186	RJI1658	Leyland Royal Tiger RT	Van Hool Alizée	C49F	1986	Ex Cook, Biggleswade, 1993
187	TJI4698	Aüwaerter Neoplan N722/3	Plaxton Paramount 4000	CH55/20DT	1984	Ex Grey Green, 1995
188	TJI4699	Aüwaerter Neoplan N722/3	Plaxton Paramount 4000	CH55/20DT	1985	Ex Grey Green, 1995
189	LRB405W	Leyland Atlantean AN68A/1R	East Lancashire	H47/33D	1980	Ex Nottingham, 1995
190	LRB407W	Leyland Atlantean AN68A/1R	East Lancashire	H47/33D	1980	Ex Nottingham, 1995
191	LRB409W	Leyland Atlantean AN68A/1R	East Lancashire	H47/31D	1980	Ex Nottingham, 1995
192	YPL80T	AEC Reliance 6U2R	Duple Dominant II Express	C53F	1978	Ex Smithyman, Maltby, 1996
193	RKA886T	Leyland National 11351A/1R/SC		DP45F	1978	Ex Delta, Kirkby in Ashfield, 1996
194	UTX727S	Leyland National 10351A/1R		B41F	1978	Ex Delta, Kirkby in Ashfield, 1996
195	SKF12T	Leyland National 11351A/1R		B49F	1979	Ex Delta, Kirkby in Ashfield, 1996
196	MOD816P	Leyland National 11351/1R		B52F	1976	Ex Delta, Kirkby in Ashfield, 1996
197	FGE438X	Dennis Dominator DD137B	Alexander RL	H45/34F	1982	Ex Delta, Kirkby in Ashfield, 1996

Previous Registrations:

RJI1656	ANA403Y	TJI4698	B101XYH
RJI1657	D40HMT, RJI1656	TJI4699	B102XYH
RJI1658	C51CWX, HIL3474		

Livery: Orange and cream (buses) ; white, orange and red (coaches)

The Camms operation of bus services continues despite the sale of the Derby operations to what is now City Rider. Camms have recently acquired four Leyland Nationals from the Delta of Kirkby-in-Ashfield fleet which ran for under two years in competition with Trent, before closing down in early 1996. No.193 in the Camms fleet is RKA886T. *Tony Wilson*

CARNELL

Carnell Coaches, 72 Bridge Street, Sutton Bridge, Lincolnshire, PE12 9UA

Reg	Chassis	Body	Seating	Year	Notes
PCT596M	Bedford YRT	Plaxton Elite Express III	C53F	1974	Ex Delaine, Bourne, 1981
LCT980P	Bedford YRT	Duple Dominant Express	C53F	1976	
PAK690R	Bedford YMT	Plaxton Supreme III	C53F	1976	Ex Drabble, Sheffield, 1981
STA361R	Bedford YMT	Duple Dominant	C53F	1977	Ex National Travel (South West) 1980
CEC475S	Bedford YMT	Duple Dominant	C53F	1978	Ex Grey, Ely, 1992
AWE113T	Bedford YMT	Duple Dominant II	C45F	1979	Ex Bryan A Garratt, Syston, 1984
BGY595T	Bedford YMT	Duple Dominant II	C53F	1979	Ex National Travel (London) 1982
NPP328V	Bedford YLQ	Duple Dominant II Express	C45F	1980	Ex Redcar, Norwich, 1982
GTX755W	Bristol VRT/SL3/501	Eastern Coach Works	H43/31F	1980	Ex Red & White, 1994
SMY631X	Leyland Tiger TRCTL11/3R	Plaxton Supreme V	C50F	1982	Ex The Beeline, 1996
SMY632X	Leyland Tiger TRCTL11/3R	Plaxton Supreme V	C51F	1982	Ex The Beeline, 1996
SMY637X	Leyland Tiger TRCTL11/3R	Plaxton Supreme V	C50F	1982	Ex The Beeline, 1996
OHE270X	Volvo B10M-61	Duple Dominant IV	C50F	1982	Ex SUT 1987
PNL163Y	Bedford YMP	Duple Dominant IV	C35F	1982	Ex Red Arrow, Huddersfield, 1990
YPD121Y	Leyland Tiger TRCTL11/2R	Duple Dominant IV	C53F	1983	Ex Richardson, Midhurst, 1996
ENF572Y	Volvo B10M-61	Duple Dominant IV	C53F	1983	Ex Smith Shearings, 1989
ENF574Y	Volvo B10M-61	Duple Dominant IV	C53F	1983	Ex Smith Shearings, 1989
THL295Y	Volvo B10M-61	Duple Dominant IV	C51F	1983	Ex FHW, Willenhall, 1989
RDZ4275	DAF SB2300DHTD585	Plaxton Paramount 3200	C53F	1984	Ex AMR, Bedfont, 1995
FDZ4731	Volvo B10M-61	Van Hool Alizée	C53F	1984	Ex Shearings, 1990
B500SJL	Bedford YNT	Duple Laser	C53F	1985	
B290TCT	DAF MB2000DKVL600	Duple Caribbean	C55F	1985	
B526AHD	Mercedes-Benz L608D	Reeve Burgess	C19F	1985	Ex Euro Academy, Croydon, 1985
C210VCT	Bedford YNV Venturer	Plaxton Paramount 3200 II	C57F	1985	
C136DWT	Volvo B10M-61	Duple 340	C53F	1987	Ex Wallace Arnold, 1990
D811SGB	Volvo B10M-61	Plaxton Paramount 3500 III	C53F	1987	Ex Park's, 1988
E399DNR	Mercedes-Benz 609D	Reeve Burgess	C19F	1988	

Previous Registrations:
FDZ4731   A178MNE   RDZ4275   A80WHS

Livery: Cream and blue, and silver, red and orange

Carnell of Sutton Bridge operate a number of services in the south of Lincolnshire around The Wash. There is only one double deck in the fleet, the reaminder of the fleet are mostly 53-seat coaches. Seen in Kirton is Bodford AWE113T.
Steve Sanderson

CAVALIER

A D Ladbrook & C J Bloor, Seagate Road, Long Sutton, Spalding,
Lincolnshire, PE12 9AD

B428PJF	Ford Transit 190	Robin Hood	B16F	1985	Ex Bee Line Buzz, 1991
B469WTC	Ford Transit 190	Carlyle	B16F	1985	Ex Eastern National, 1995
C540TJF	Ford Transit 190	Rootes	B16F	1986	Ex Stevensons, 1992
C551TJF	Ford Transit 190	Rootes	B16F	1986	Ex Stevensons, 1992
C559TUT	Ford Transit 190	Rootes	B16F	1986	Ex Bee Line Buzz, 1991
C330SFL	Ford Transit 190	Carlyle	B16F	1986	Ex Cambus, 1995
C332SFL	Ford Transit 190	Carlyle	B16F	1986	Ex Cambus, 1995
D534HNW	Ford Transit 190	Carlyle	B16F	1986	Ex Sherrett, Cold Meece, 1995
D546SRM	Ford Transit 190	Cymric (1992)	M16	1986	
D519NDA	Freight Rover Sherpa	Carlyle	B20F	1986	Ex Silverwing, Keynsham, 1993
E726HBF	Freight Rover Sherpa	PMT	B20F	1987	Ex PMT, 1995
A20PSV	Mercedes-Benz 609D	?	C24F	1988	Ex ?, 1996
H742VHS	Mercedes-Benz 609D	Sparshatt	C24F	1990	Ex Staffordian, Stafford, 1996
K2CAV	Renault Master T35D	Cymric	M16	1992	
K3CAV	Renault Master T35D	Cymric	M16	1992	
K4CAV	Renault Master T35D	Cymric	M16	1992	
K5CAV	Renault Master T35D	Cymric	M16	1992	
K6CAV	Renault Master T35D	Cymric	M16	1992	

Livery: White and blue

Previous Registrations:
A20PSV   ?

Cavalier Small Party Travel operates minibuses from its base in the Lincolnshire village of Long Sutton. This operator has purchased five of the less-common Renault Master minibuses with Cymric bodywork. Also operated are a number of Ford Transits including C551TJF, shown here, which was originally a Midland Fox Cub though obtained by Cavalier from Stevensons. *Roy Marshall*

CITY RIDER

Derby City Transport Ltd, Ascot Drive, London Road, Derby, DE24 8ND

Part of the Cowie Group

21-26		Scania K92CRB		Alexander PS		B51F*	1988		*23/6 are B49F
21	E21ECH	23	E23ECH	24	E24ECH	25	E25ECH	26	E26ECH
27	F27JRC		Scania K93CRB		Alexander PS	B53F	1989		
28	F28JRC		Scania K93CRB		Alexander PS	B51F	1989		
29-33		Scania L113CRL		East Lancashire European		B51F	1996		
29	N429XRC	30	N430XRC	31	N431XRC	32	N432XRC	33	N433XRC
34-38		Dennis Dart 9.8SDL3040		East Lancashire EL2000		B40F	1994		
34	L34PNN	35	L35PNN	36	L36PNN	37	L37PNN	38	L38PNN
61	E181UWF		Renault-Dodge S56		Reeve Burgess	B25F	1987	Ex South Yorkshire, 1992	
62	E188UWF		Renault-Dodge S56		Reeve Burgess	B25F	1987	Ex SMC Travel, Garston, 1994	
63	E933UBO		Renault-Dodge S56		Northern Counties	B25F	1988	Ex Red & White, 1993	
65	D146RAK		Renault-Dodge S56		Reeve Burgess	B25F	1987	Ex SMC Travel, Garston, 1994	
66	D152RAK		Renault-Dodge S56		Reeve Burgess	B25F	1987	Ex SMC Travel, Garston, 1994	
67	D156RAK		Renault-Dodge S56		Reeve Burgess	B25F	1987	Ex SMC Travel, Garston, 1994	
68	K390NGG		Mercedes-Benz 811D		Dormobile Routemaker	DP33F	1992	Ex Avondale Coaches, Greenock, 1995	
70	G64SNN		Mercedes-Benz 709D		Carlyle	DP29F	1990	Ex Phil Anslow Travel, Blaenavon, 1995	
71	J401FNS		Mercedes-Benz 709D		Dormobile Routemaker	DP29F	1991	Ex Avondale Coaches, Greenock, 1995	
72-91		Mercedes-Benz 709D		Alexander Sprint		B27F	1996		
72	N472XRC	76	N476XRC	80	N480XRC	84	P484CAL	88	P489CAL
73	N473XRC	77	N477XRC	81	N481XRC	85	P485CAL	89	P489CAL
74	N474XRC	78	N478XRC	82	P482CAL	86	P486CAL	90	P490CAL
75	N475XRC	79	N479XRC	83	P483CAL	87	P487CAL	91	P491CAL
92-99		Renault-Dodge S56		Northern Counties		B23F*	1988	Ex Cleveland Transit, 1993-94	
								*97 is B20F; 99 is DP21F	
92	E326LHN	94	E328LHN	96	E330LHN	98	E332LHN	99	F334SPY
93	E327LHN	95	E329LHN	97	E331LHN				
109-121		Ailsa B55-10		Northern Counties		H38/35F	1982		
109	SRC109X	112	SRC112X	115	SRC115X	118	TCH118X	120	TCH120X
110	SRC110X	113	SRC113X	116	TCH116X	119	TCH119X	121	TCH121X
111	SRC111X	114	SRC114X	117	TCH117X				
122	STV122X		Ailsa B55-10		Marshall	H44/35F	1982		
123	STV123X		Ailsa B55-10		Marshall	H44/35F	1982		

Opposite: **City Rider** is the operating name of Derby City Transport and part of British Bus plc recently been taken over by Cowie, the north-eastern transport group better known for its car operation than buses. Here we see two single-deck buses that show the changes in style at East Lancashire in recent times. The upper picture shows 30, N430XRC, one of the new Scania saloons with the new European low-floor body style, while the lower picture shows 38, L38PNN with an EL2000 design applied to the Dennis Dart.

61 CHELLASTON
City Rider
City Rider
N430 XRC
SALE
7.99

C24 PERTH STREET
City Rider
City Rider
L38 PNN

Displaying the latest version of the City Rider livery is 140, B140GAU, a Marshall-bodied Volvo B10M Citybus. The blue and grey livery introduced by Derby has now been replaced by a brighter yellow incorporating a red roof and blue skirt panels. The fleetname has now been changed from Blue Bus Services to City Rider and the service to Sinfin is now C38 with the C reflecting the new image.
Tony Wilson

126	YAU126Y	Volvo Citybus B10M-50		Marshall		H45/33F	1983	
127	YAU127Y	Volvo Citybus B10M-50		Marshall		H45/33F	1983	
128	YAU128Y	Volvo Citybus B10M-50		Marshall		H43/33F	1983	
129-133		Volvo Citybus B10M-50		East Lancashire		H45/31F	1984	
129	A129DTO	130	A130DTO	131	A131DTO	132	A132DTO	133	A133DTO
134-143		Volvo Citybus B10M-50		Marshall		H45/33F	1984	
134	B134GAU	136	B136GAU	138	B138GAU	140	B140GAU	142	B142GAU
135	B135GAU	137	B137GAU	139	B139GAU	141	B141GAU	143	B143GAU
144-153		Volvo Citybus B10M-50		Northern Counties		H42/33F	1986/88	
144	C144NRR	146	C146NRR	148	C148NRR	150	E150BTO	152	E152BTO
145	C145NRR	147	C147NRR	149	E149BTO	151	E151BTO	153	E153BTO
160-164		Scania N113DRB		East Lancashire		H45/33F	1995	
160	N160VVO	161	N161VVO	162	N162VVO	163	N163VVO	164	N164VVO
165-169		Volvo Olympian YV3YNF215TC		Northern Counties Palatine I		H47/30F	1996	
165	N165XVO	166	N166XVO	167	P167BTV	168	P168BTV	169	P169BTV
298-315		Leyland Fleetline FE30AGR		Northern Counties		H43/30F	1978-81	
298	XRR298S	302w	GTO302V	306	GTO306V	310	MTV310W	313	MTV010W
299	GTO299V	304	GTO304V	307w	GTO307V	311	MTV311W	314	MTV314W
301	GTO301V	305	GTO305V	309	MTV309W	312	MTV312W	315	MTV315W

Livery: Yellow, blue and red.

Named Vehicles: 34, *John Barton* ; 35, *Peter Varley*

Volvo Olympians are again the latest double-deck buses for City Rider though the 1995 delivery saw the arrival of five Scania N113DRBs with East Lancashire bodywork. One of these, 161, N161VVO is seen in London Road when heading for Alvaston.
David Stanier

The British Bus group, now owned by Cowie, recently bought several batches of Alexander-bodied Mercedes-Benz 709D minibuses. One batch of ten was allocated to the City Rider fleet in early 1996 with more of the same type expected. Displayed in this view is 74, N474XRC.
David Stanier

For many years the standard Derby double deck bus was based on Volvo chassis. As well as a large number of front-engined Ailsas there are also underfloor engined, and aptly named, Volvo Citybuses in the fleet. This view shows 127, YAU127Y, a Volvo B10M Citybus seen operating the Blagreaves Lane service.
David Stanier

CONFIDENCE

K M Williams, 105 Coombe Rise, Oadby, Leicestershire, LE2 5TJ

Depots: Spalding Street, Leicester and Harrison Close, South Wigston.

13	AHA451J	Leyland Leopard PSU4B/4R	Plaxton Elite II	C40F	1971	Ex Midland Red East, 1983
15	WLT655	AEC Routemaster R2RH	Park Royal	H36/28R	1961	Ex London Buses, 1985
18	VWM83L	Leyland Atlantean AN68/1R	Alexander AL	H45/29D	1973	Ex Merseybus, 1988
19	VWM89L	Leyland Atlantean AN68/1R	Alexander AL	H45/29D	1973	Ex Merseybus, 1988
20	OTO540M	Leyland Atlantean AN68/1R	East Lancashire	H47/30D	1974	Ex Nottingham, 1990
21	GVO717N	Leyland Atlantean AN68/1R	East Lancashire	H47/31D	1974	Ex Nottingham, 1990
22	OTO570M	Leyland Atlantean AN68/1R	East Lancashire	H47/30D	1974	Ex Nottingham, 1990
23	HOR305N	Leyland Atlantean AN68/1R	Alexander AL	H45/30D	1975	Ex Portsmouth, 1991
24	HOR306N	Leyland Atlantean AN68/1R	Alexander AL	H45/30D	1975	Ex Portsmouth, 1991
25	KSA183P	Leyland Atlantean AN68A/1R	Alexander AL	H45/29D	1976	Ex Portsmouth Transit, 1991
26	OTO557M	Leyland Atlantean AN68/1R	East Lancashire	H47/30D	1974	Ex Nottingham, 1993
27	OTO551M	Leyland Atlantean AN68/1R	East Lancashire	H47/30D	1974	Ex Nottingham, 1992
28	OTO562M	Leyland Atlantean AN68/1R	East Lancashire	H47/30D	1974	Ex Nottingham, 1993
29	MNU625P	Leyland Atlantean AN68A/1R	East Lancashire	H47/31D	1976	Ex Nottingham, 1994
30	MNU631P	Leyland Atlantean AN68A/1R	East Lancashire	H47/31D	1976	Ex Nottingham, 1994
31	XRR616M	Leyland Leopard PSU3B/4R	Plaxton Elite III Express	C53F	1973	Ex Trent (Barton), 1994
32	UVO125S	Leyland Leopard PSU3E/4R	Duple Dominant	C49F	1977	Ex Trent (Barton), 1994
33	MNU632P	Leyland Atlantean AN68A/1R	East Lancashire	H47/31D	1976	Ex Nottingham, 1994
34	KAU564V	Leyland Leopard PSU3E/4R	Plaxton Supreme IV Express	C51F	1980	Ex Trent (Barton), 1996
35	LNU569W	Leyland Leopard PSU3E/4R	Plaxton Supreme IV Express	C53F	1980	Ex Trent (Barton), 1996

Livery: Black, grey and red

Confidence of Oadby, near Leicester, have a predominantly double-deck fleet. With the exception of the much rallied AEC Routemaster, all the double deck buses are Leyland Atlanteans, most of which are former-Nottingham vehicles. No30 in the Confidence fleet is MNU631P, an East Lancashire-bodied example that carries the black, grey and red livery. *Steve Sanderson*

CROPLEY

Cropley Bros Tours (Fosdyke) Ltd, The Laurels, Old Main Road,
Fosdyke, Lincolnshire, PE20 7BU

Depot : Main Road, Fosdyke.

CDH275T	Volvo B58-56	Plaxton Supreme III	C53F	1978	Ex Robinson, Willenhall, 1988
RIB2699	Volvo B58-61	Jonckheere Bermuda	C53F	1981	Ex Lever, East Knoyle, 1992
WJS200X	Volvo B58-56	Plaxton Supreme IV	C53F	1981	Ex WHM, Brentwood, 1992
WUY713	Volvo B10M-61	Berkhof Everest 365	C51F	1983	Ex James Bevan, Lydney, 1996
A81RGE	Mercedes-Benz L608D	Reeve Burgess	C21F	1983	Ex Airey, Arkholme, 1995
USK207	Volvo B10M-61	Plaxton Paramount 3500	C53F	1984	Ex Ralph, Langley, 1993
4506UB	Volvo B10M-61	Plaxton Paramount 3500	C53F	1984	Ex Ralph, Langley, 1993
XSV839	Volvo B10M-61	Plaxton Paramount 3500	C49FT	1984	Ex Epsom Coaches, 1993
EAZ4709	Volvo B10M-61	Plaxton Paramount 3500 II	C53F	1985	Ex Epsom Coaches, 1994
EAZ5347	Volvo B10M-61	Plaxton Paramount 3500 II	C53F	1985	Ex Epsom Coaches, 1994
8302NF	Volvo B10M-61	Plaxton Paramount 3500 II	C53F	1985	Ex Epsom Coaches, 1994

Previous Registrations:

4506UB	A518NCL	EAZ5347	B506CGP	WUY713	JJN179Y
8302NF	B508CGP	RIB2699	WNH145W	XSV839	A400WGH
EAZ4709	B505CGP	USK207	A521NCL		

Livery: White and Turquoise

The village of Fosdyke in the fenlands of Lincolnshire is home to Cropley Brothers. All the fleet carries the simple but distinctive turquoise and white livery. The only minicoach owned is **A81RGE**, a Reeve Burgess-converted Mercedes-Benz L608D seen here displaying the now mandatory school bus signs. *Steve Sanderson*

DAISY

Daisy Bus Service Ltd, 81A High Street, Broughton, Brigg, North Lincolnshire, DN20 0JR

LNX319L	Ford R192		Plaxton Elite III	C45F	1973	Ex Bowers, Chapel-en-le-Frith, 1994
OKY60R	Leyland Leopard PSU3C/4R		Duple Dominant	C53F	1977	Ex Hallam, Newthorpe, 1995
XYK766T	Leyland Leopard PSU3E/4R		Duple Dominant II	C53F	1978	Ex Bryan A Garratt, Leicester, 1995
KGY566Y	Bova EL26/581		Bova Europa	C53F	1982	Ex Hallam, Newthorpe, 1995
YPD114Y	Leyland Tiger TRCTL11/2R		Duple Dominant IV Express	C53F	1983	Ex London Country NE, 1989
DSV710	Volvo B10M-61		Berkhof Esprite 350	C49FT	1985	Ex Walton, Stockton, 1995
MIL2654	DAF MB230DKFL615		Jonckheere Deauville	C51FT	1987	Ex Holden, Great Harwood, 1995
TJI1700	Volvo B10M-61		Plaxton Paramount 3500 III	C49FT	1989	Ex Applegate, Newport (Glos), 1993
G208YDL	Mercedes-Benz 811D		Phoenix	B31F	1990	Ex Solent Blue Line, 1995
J715KBC	Toyota Coaster HDB30R		Caetano Optimo II	C21F	1991	Ex Britannia Travel, Otley, 1995
M332GFW	Volvo B10M-62		Caetano Algarve II	C49FT	1995	

Previous Registrations:

DSV710	From new		MIL2654	E222GNV
LXI9357	E589UHS		TJI1700	F471WAD

Livery: Cream and red

DEE WARD

F I Ward, Lutterworth Road, Gilmorton, Leicestershire, LE? ???

Depot: Station Road, Countesthorpe

TYJ394S	Bedford YMT		Duple Dominant II	C53F	1977	Ex Accord Coaches, Portslade, 1992
JGU943V	Bedford YMT		Duple Dominant II	C53F	1980	Ex Alan Smith, Kibworth, 1992
AFP440Y	Bedford YNT		Plaxton Paramount 3200	C53F	1982	Ex Evans, Tregaron, 1996
MJI7809	DAF MB200DKTL600		Plaxton Paramount 3500	C49FT	1983	Ex Eagle Line, Shipton Oliffe, 1995
B510BJO	DAF SB2300DHS585		Berkhof Esprite 340	C49FT	1985	Ex Gray Line, Bicester, 1993
B406VWX	Bedford YNT		Duple Laser	C53f	19??	Ex Mullover, Bedford, 1996
D850CNV	Bedford YNV		Caetano Algarve	C57F	1987	Ex Haywood & Prosser, Bedworth, 1995

Previous Registrations:

B510BJO	B683BTW, MJI1678	MJI7809	EM8488, DFP920Y

Livery: Varies ; most vehicles run in former owner's colours

Daisy Bus Service operates on the route from Scunthorpe to Brigg. Recently acquired for this service is G208YDL, photographed at the Scunthorpe terminus. This Phoenix-bodied Mercedes-Benz 811D is one of a batch disposed of by Solent Blue-Line during 1995. Daisy also operates a number of coaches under the Ermine International name. *Steve Sanderson*

Dee Ward have recently been awarded the tender to operate service 731 on behalf of Leicestershire County Council. This route runs only on Mondays and from Broughton Astley to Hinckley. During the period when the passengers are shopping in Hinckley, the vehicle rests in Hinckley bus station, the location of this view of B406VWX, a Duple Laser-bodied Bedford YNT. *Steve Sanderson*

THE DELAINE

The Delaine Bus Co Ltd, 8 Spalding Road, Bourne, Lincolnshire, PE10 9LE

45	KTL780	Leyland Titan PD2/20	Willowbrook	H35/28RD	1956	Privately preserved 1979-90
50	RCT3	Leyland Titan PD3/1	Yeates	H39/34RD	1960	
72	ACT540L	Leyland Atlantean AN68/2R	Northern Counties	H47/35F	1973	
93	KTL27Y	Leyland Tiger TRCTL11/2RZ	Duple Dominant	B62F	1983	
94	A24OVL	Leyland Tiger TRCTL11/2RZ	Duple Dominant	B62F	1983	
95	HFL672L	Leyland Atlantean AN68/2R	Northern Counties	H47/34F	1973	Ex Whippet, Fenstanton, 1984
98	C426MFE	Leyland Tiger TRCTL11/2RZ	Duple Dominant	B62F	1986	
99	GDB179N	Leyland Atlantean AN68/1R	Northern Counties	H43/32F	1975	Ex GM Buses, 1987
100	E100AFW	Leyland Tiger TRCTL11/2RZ	Duple Dominant	B62F	1987	
101	GDB180N	Leyland Atlantean AN68/1R	Northern Counties	H43/32F	1975	Ex GM Buses, 1987
102	GDB181N	Leyland Atlantean AN68/1R	Northern Counties	H43/32F	1975	Ex GM Buses, 1987
103	F603VEW	Leyland Tiger TRCTL11/2R	Duple 300	B62F	1988	
104	YPD104Y	Leyland Tiger TRCTL11/2R	Duple Dominant IV Express	C53F	1983	Ex London Country NE, 1988
105	YPD105Y	Leyland Tiger TRCTL11/2R	Duple Dominant IV Express	C53F	1983	Ex London Country NW, 1989
107	YPD107Y	Leyland Tiger TRCTL11/2R	Duple Dominant IV Express	C53F	1983	Ex London Country NE, 1989
108	YPD108Y	Leyland Tiger TRCTL11/2R	Duple Dominant IV Express	C53F	1983	Ex London Country NE, 1989
113	ALM59B	AEC Routemaster R2RH	Park Royal	H36/28R	1964	Ex Southampton, 1992
115	OTL3	Leyland Tiger TRBTL11/2R(Z)	East Lancashire EL2000 (1994)	B62F	1983	Ex Smith, Blairgowrie, 1992
116	M1OCT	Volvo Olympian YN2RV18Z4	East Lancashire	H51/35F	1995	
117	M2OCT	Volvo Olympian YN2RV18Z4	East Lancashire	H51/35F	1995	
118	N3OCT	Volvo Olympian YN2RV18Z4	East Lancashire	H51/35F	1995	
119	ANA224T	Leyland Atlantean AN68A/1R	Northern Counties	H43/32F	1978	Ex GMN, 1996
120	FVR256V	Leyland Atlantean AN68A/1R	Northern Counties	H43/32F	1979	Ex GMN, 1996
121	P1OTL	Volvo Citibus B10M-55	East Lancashire Flyte	B62F	1996	
122	P2OTL	Volvo Citibus B10M-55	East Lancashire Flyte	B62F	1996	

Previous Registrations:
KTL780   From new   RCT3   From new   OTL3   YPD125Y

Livery: Blue and cream

Delaine of Bourne added to its double deck fleet during 1996 with the acquisition of a trio of East Lancashire-bodied Volvo Olympians. All three vehicles are regular performers on The Delaine's trunk route from Bourne to Peterborough. The last vehicle to be delivered was No.118, N3OCT, seen here leaving Peterborough.
Tony Wilson

The 4th 'Vintage Running Day and Gathering' was organised by Delaine in 1996. This now annual event features half cab double deckers running on The Delaine service from Bourne to Peterborough operating every 15 minutes. Seen on the 1995 running day is 113, ALM59B, an AEC Routemaster restored to Delaine's high standard, after its purchase from Southampton in 1993. Though the vehicle carries The Delaine colours and is occasionally used by them it is privately owned. *Malc McDonald*

High capacity single deck buses have recently been favoured by Delaine. Sixty-two seats are contained in the Duple Dominant body of 98, C426MFE. This Leyland Tiger has a ZF manual gearbox rather than the more usual semi-automatic gearbox fitted to the majority of Tigers built. *Ralph Stevens*

DUNN-LINE

Monetgrange Ltd, 605 Nuthall Road, Cinderhill, Nottingham, NG8 6AF

OTO569M	Leyland Atlantean AN68/1R	East Lancashire	H47/30D	1974	Ex Nottingham, 1993	
MAU612P	Leyland Atlantean AN68A/1R	East Lancashire	H47/31D	1975	Ex Nottingham, 1994	
MAU614P	Leyland Atlantean AN68A/1R	East Lancashire	H47/31D	1975	Ex Nottingham, 1994	
MAU615P	Leyland Atlantean AN68A/1R	East Lancashire	H47/31D	1975	Ex Nottingham, 1994	
MAU616P	Leyland Atlantean AN68A/1R	East Lancashire	H47/31D	1975	Ex Nottingham, 1994	
MNU633P	Leyland Atlantean AN68A/1R	East Lancashire	H47/31D	1976	Ex Nottingham, 1994	
MNU635P	Leyland Atlantean AN68A/1R	East Lancashire	H47/31D	1976	Ex Nottingham, 1994	
UES274S	Volvo B58-56	Plaxton Supreme III	C53F	1978	Ex Crawley Luxury Coaches, 1994	
ARC641T	Leyland Atlantean AN68A/1R	East Lancashire	H47/33D	1978	Ex Nottingham, 1995	
ARC643T	Leyland Atlantean AN68A/1R	East Lancashire	H47/33D	1978	Ex Nottingham, 1995	
ARC645T	Leyland Atlantean AN68A/1R	East Lancashire	H47/33D	1978	Ex Nottingham, 1995	
BTV648T	Leyland Atlantean AN68A/1R	East Lancashire	H47/33D	1979	Ex Nottingham, 1995	
BTV651T	Leyland Atlantean AN68A/1R	East Lancashire	H47/33D	1979	Ex Nottingham, 1995	
BTV653T	Leyland Atlantean AN68A/1R	East Lancashire	H47/32D	1979	Ex Nottingham, 1995	
ARC668T	Leyland Atlantean AN68A/1R	East Lancashire	H47/32D	1979	Ex Nottingham, 1996	
BBT513V	Volvo B58-61	Unicar	C53F	1980	Ex Skills, Nottingham, 1994	
WJF8X	Ford Transit 160	Yeates	M12	1982	Ex Lewis, Coventry, 1994	
YFR649Y	Ford Transit 160	Dormobile	M8L	1982	Ex Lancashire CC, 1993	
MIL1054	Volvo B10M-61	Plaxton P'mount 3500 III(1987)	C51F	1982	Ex Harrison, Morecambe, 1996	
2191RO	Volvo B10M-61	Van Hool Astral	CH48/10DT	1984	Ex Express Travel, Perth, 1994	
ASV247	DAF SB2300DHS585	Jonckheere Jubilee	C50FT	1984	Ex Wood, Billericay, 1996	
FIL7615	DAF SB2300DHS585	Plaxton Paramount 3200	C57F	1984	Ex Dudley, Inkberrow, 1996	
B101BYS	Leyland Cub CU435	Duple Dominant	B31F	1985	Ex Collinson, Stonehouse, 1995	
B102BYS	Leyland Cub CU435	Duple Dominant	B31F	1985	Ex Collinson, Stonehouse, 1995	
C543TJF	Ford Transit 190D	Rootes	B16F	1986	Ex Nottingham, 1995	
C353SVV	Scania K92CRB	Jonckheere Transcity	B47D	1986	Ex Cairngorm Chairlift, Aviemore, 1995	
FIW567	Leyland Tiger TRCTL11/3RZ	Plaxton Paramount 3500 II	C49F	1986	Ex Rennie, Dunfermline, 1994	
OIW5036	Leyland Tiger TRCTL11/3RZ	Plaxton Paramount 3500 II	C49F	1986	Ex Rennie, Dunfermline, 1994	
D498NYS	Volvo B10M-61	Duple Dominant	B55F	1986	Ex Hutchison, Overtown, 1992	
D390PYS	Volvo B10M-55	Duple Dominant	B55F	1986	Ex Hutchison, Overtown, 1995	
D391PYS	Volvo B10M-55	Duple Dominant	B55F	1986	Ex Hutchison, Overtown, 1995	
D52TLV	Freight Rover Sherpa	Carlyle	B20F	1987	Ex Torkard, Hucknall, 1996	
D521WNV	DAF SB2300DHS585	Caetano Algarve	C53F	1987	Ex Miller, Foxton, 1993	
PJI3748	Volvo B10M-61	Van Hool Alizée	C49F	1987	Ex Sinclair, Greenhead, 1994	
IIW363	Volvo B10M-61	Van Hool Alizée	C53F	1987	Ex Allander, Milngavie, 1995	
HSK833	Volvo B10M-61	Jonckheere Deauville	C49FT	1988	Ex Supreme, Hadleigh, 1995	
A3BOB	Volvo B10M-61	Van Hool Alizée	C53F	1988	Ex Park's, 1995	
A5BOB	Volvo B10M-53	Plaxton Paramount 4000 III	CH55/12DT	1989	Ex Flights, Birmingham, 1995	
A4BOB	Volvo B10M-53	Plaxton Paramount 4000 III	CH55/12DT	1989	Ex Flights, Birmingham, 1994	
MIL1057	Volvo B10M-60	Plaxton Paramount 3500 III	C53F	1990	Ex Wallace Arnold, 1993	

The Dunn Line fleet contains a number of former City of Nottingham vehicles. MNU633P is an East Lancashire-bodied Leyland Atlantean which was acquired in 1994. Dunn Line service buses now carry a green and white colour scheme as illustrated here.
Steve Sanderson

The Dunn line coach livery recently changed to a predominantly white scheme that incorporates the dramatic use of purple, turquoise and pink. Demonstrating this scheme is M732KJU, one of six Volvo B10M coaches purchased in 1995. All feature the Belgian-built Jonckheere Deauville 45 coachwork.
Colin Lloyd

J6BOB	Volvo B10M-60	Jonckheere Deauville P599	C25FT	1991	
J9DLT	Bova FHD12.290	Bova Futura	C51F	1992	
K293GDT	Bova FHD12.290	Bova Futura	C55F	1993	
K3RAD	Bova FHD12.290	Bova Futura	C33FT	1993	
K295GDT	Bova FHD12.290	Bova Futura	C51FT	1993	
L6BOB	Volvo B10M-60	Van Hool Alizée	C53F	1993	Ex Collinson, Stonehouse, 1995
M730KJU	Volvo B10M-62	Jonckheere Deauville 45	C49FT	1995	
M731KJU	Volvo B10M-62	Jonckheere Deauville 45	C49FT	1995	
M732KJU	Volvo B10M-62	Jonckheere Deauville 45	C49FT	1995	
M733KJU	Volvo B10M-62	Jonckheere Deauville 45	C49FT	1995	
M734KJU	Volvo B10M-62	Jonckheere Deauville 45	C49FT	1995	
M735KJU	Volvo B10M-62	Jonckheere Deauville 45	C49FT	1995	
N997BWJ	Toyota Coaster HZB50R	Caetano Optimo III	C21F	1996	
N998BWJ	Volvo B10M-62	Van Hool Alizée	C49FT	1996	
N751DAK	Bova FHD12.340	Bova Futura	C49FT	1996	
N97ACH	Bova FHD12.340	Bova Futura	C51FT	1996	

Previous Registrations:

2191RO	A156XSF, A817FSF, MSP333, A871FSF	IIW363	D565MVR, GIL1684, D696OSJ
A3BOB	E965CGA, LSK965, E648UNE	K3RAD	K294GDT
A4BOB	F704COA	L6BOB	KSK952, L544YUS, TXI2426
A5BOB	F701COA	MIL1054	JNV627Y, 8850WU, WEC761Y
ASV247	A134XNH	MIL1057	G501LWU
FIL7615	7391MH, A334FRB	OIW5036	C424WFH
FIW567	C422WFH	PJI3748	D846KVE
HSK833	E695NNH	UES274S	BGS160S, BSK744

Livery: White and green (buses) ; White, purple, pink and turquoise (coaches)

The East Midland Bus Handbook

Eagre Coaches have a pair of Park Royal-bodied Leyland Atlanteans that were formerly with Greater Manchester. The newer of the two is BNC952T which is seen here at the depot at Morton, near Gainsborough. The depot backs onto the River Trent and the tidal bore of this river gives the company its name. *Mark Bailey*

The Eagre coach fleet contains a myriad of body styles with a number built to high specifications. 6077RE is a LAG Panoramic, photographed in Llanberis when on tour in North Wales. The index mark reflects the proprietor's initials. *Ralph Stevens*

EAGRE

R H Eaglen, Crooked Billet Street, Morton, Gainsborough, Lincolnshire, DN21 3AG

AFE610A	Leyland National 1151/1R/0402		B49F	1974	Ex Alder Valley South, 1988
AFE595A	Leyland National 11351/1R		B49F	1974	Ex Alder Valley South, 1988
HHH272N	Bristol VRT/SL2/6G	Eastern Coach Works	H43/34F	1974	Ex Cumberland, 1990
LRA799P	Bristol VRT/SL3/501	Eastern Coach Works	H43/31F	1975	Ex Trent, 1990
TRR814R	Volvo-Ailsa B55-20	Alexander AV	H44/35F	1975	Ex Derby, 1989
1878R	Leyland Leopard PSU3D/4R	Duple 320 (1987)	C53F	1977	Ex National Travel East, 1987
UNA864S	Leyland Atlantean AN68A/1R	Park Royal	H43/32F	1978	Ex GM Buses, 1991
CFE782S	Bedford YMT	Willowbrook Warrior (1989)	B61F	1978	Ex Blue Triangle, Bootle, 1993
BNC952T	Leyland Atlantean AN68A/1R	Park Royal	H43/32F	1978	Ex GM Buses, 1991
KSU479	Leyland Leopard PSU5C/4R	Duple Dominant IV	C53FT	1981	Ex Hallam, Newthorpe, 1994
UWY85X	Leyland Leopard PSU3E/4R	Duple Dominant IV Express	C53F	1981	Ex Yorkshire Rider, 1995
FGE435X	Dennis Dominator DD137B	Alexander RL	H45/34F	1982	Ex KCB, 1996
2160RE	Van Hool T815	Van Hool Acron	C48FT	1982	Ex Belmont, Askern, 1983
KSK957	MAN 16.280	Ayatts Apollo	C53F	1983	Ex John Smith & Sons, Thirsk, 1995
9962R	Leyland Leopard PSU3E/4R	Plaxton Paramount 3200	C49F	1983	
KAZ3253	Dennis Falcon HC SDA406	East Lancashire	B44D	1983	Ex Ipswich, 1996
KAZ3254	Dennis Falcon HC SDA406	East Lancashire	B44D	1983	Ex Ipswich, 1996
HHJ380Y	Leyland Tiger TRCTL11/2R	Alexander TE	DP53F	1983	Ex Eastern National, 1995
HFU531	Leyland Tiger TRCTL11/3RZ	Wadham Stringer Vanguard	DP54F	19..	Ex M.O.D, 1996
ROI876	Leyland Tiger TRCTL11/3R	Berkhof Everest	C51FT	199	Ex
7126RE	DAF SB2300DHS585	Jonckeere Jubilee P50	C49FT	1984	Ex Young, Rampton, 1986
7980R	Bova EL28/581	Duple Calypso	C53F	1984	Ex Classical, Beeston, 1988
3064RE	Van Hool T815	Van Hool Alicron	C53F	1984	Ex Lock, Surrey Docks, 1989
NIB4887	Leyland Tiger TRCTL11/3R	Plaxton Paramount 3500 II	C51F	1985	Ex Skills, Nottingham, 1995
A10RHE	Leyland Tiger TRCTL11/3R	Plaxton Paramount 3500 II	C51F	19	Ex
3653RE	Hestair-Duple SDA1512	Duple 425	C53FT	1987	Ex Classic, Annfield Plain, 1993
6510RE	DAF SB2300DHS585	Duple 340	C53FT	1987	Ex Ian's Nuneaton, 1994
6077RE	LAG G355Z	LAG Panoramic	C49FT	1988	Ex Silver Coach Lines, Edinburgh, 1990
F757SPU	Sanos S315.21	Sanos Charisma	C49FT	1989	Ex Hardings, Huyton, 1994

Previous Registrations:

1878R	OKY57R	7980R	A372ERR	KAZ3253	YDX103Y
2160RE	PWG148X, AFE80A	9962R	LVL727Y, TFE1R	KAZ3254	YDX105Y
3064RE	ROI876, A501VGP	AFE595A	TBL177N	KSU479	SAL921X
3653RE	D526BBV, KSU479	A10RHE	ROI876	KSX957	WJV980
6077RE	E673NNV	AFE805A	GPC733N	NIB4887	B56DKW
6510RE	D612YCX, CEC62, D332GVC	CFE782S	TER5S	TRR814R	RTO1R
7126RE	A133TFL	HFU531	?		

Livery: Red and cream (buses) ; white, red and yellow (coaches).

EAST MIDLAND

East Midland Motor Services Ltd, Grimsby Cleethorpes Transport Ltd,
Chesterfield Transport Ltd, New Street, Chesterfield, Derbyshire, S40 2LQ

Depots : Stonegravels, Chesterfield ; Flinthouse Garage, Calver ; Victoria Street, Grimsby ; Sutton Road, Mansfield and Hardy Street, Worksop.

A member of the Stagecoach group

1-9
		Dennis Lance 11SDA3106*		East Lancashire EL2000		B45F	1993	1-7 ex Grimsby Cleethorpes, 1993 *5-9 are type 11SDA3111	
1	K701NDO	3	K703NDO	5	L705HFU	7	L707HFU	9	L709HFU
2	K702NDO	4	K704NDO	6	L706HFU	8	L708HFU		

12-19
		Mercedes-Benz 811D		Alexander Sprint		B33F	1992	Ex Chesterfield, 1995	
12	J213AET	15	J215AET	17	J217AET	18	J218AET	19	J219AET
14	J214AET	16	J216AET						

21	EKY21V	Leyland National 2 NL116L11/1R	B52F	1980	Ex Chesterfield, 1995
22	EKY22V	Leyland National 2 NL116L11/1R	B52F	1980	Ex Chesterfield, 1995
23	EKY23V	Leyland National 2 NL116L11/1R	B52F	1981	Ex Chesterfield, 1995

24-29
		Leyland National 2 NL106L11/1R				B44F	1980	Ex Chesterfield, 1995	
24	EKY24V	26	EKY26V	27	EKY27V	28	EKY28V	29	EKY29V
25	EKY25V								

30-34
		Leyland National 2 NL116AL11/1R				B52F	1981	Ex Chesterfield, 1995	
30	OWB30X	31	OWB31X	32	OWB32X	33	OWB33X	34	OWB34X

35	SKY31Y	Leyland Tiger TRCTL11/3R	Eastern Coach Works B51	C51F	1983	
36	SKY32Y	Leyland Tiger TRCTL11/3R	Eastern Coach Works B51	C51F	1983	
37	PJI4316	Leyland Tiger TRCTL11/2R	Duple Dominant IV	C47F	1983	
38	PJI4317	Leyland Tiger TRCTL11/2R	Duple Dominant IV	C47F	1983	

39-44
		Leyland Tiger TRCTL11/2R		Alexander TE		DP45F*	1983-84	*42/3 are DP49F	
39	A39XHE	41	A41XHE	42	A42XHE	43	A43XHE	44	A44XHE

49	B49DWE	Leyland Tiger TRCTL11/2RH	Alexander TE	DP49F	1984	

50-55
		Leyland National 2 NL116HLXCT/1R				B52F*	1984	Ex Chesterfield, 1995 *50/1 are DP47F	
50	B150DHL	52	B152DHL	53	B153DHL	54	B154DHL	55	B155DHL
51	B151DHL								

54c	B54DWJ	Leyland Tiger TRCTL11/2RH	Alexander TE	DP49F	1985	
56	RHL174X	Leyland Tiger TRCTL11/3R	Duple Dominant IV	C53F	1982	Ex Chesterfield, 1995
57	YPD129Y	Leyland Tiger TRCTL11/2R	Duple Dominant IV Express	DP53F	1983	Ex Chesterfield, 1995
58	YPD133Y	Leyland Tiger TRCTL11/2R	Duple Dominant IV Express	DP53F	1983	Ex Chesterfield, 1995

Opposite: Two double-deck buses illustrate the East Midlands colour section. The upper picture shows one of the former Grimsby-Cleethorpes Leyland Fleetlines that featured dual-door bodywork and centre staircase built by Roe. Many of the type have now been replaced in Grimsby by the 1995 delivery of Volvo Olympians, all of which are allocated to the coastal town. The lower picture shows former Chesterfield 162, TWF202Y, also bodied by Roe. The recent renumbering of the fleet has led to a reduction in the duplicated fleet numbers, this vehicle gaining number 300.

Talbots
AMERICAN CLASSIC CLOTHING
NOW IN MEADOWHALL.
Stagecoach
Sorry Not in Service
126
Stagecoach
126
XFU 126V

39
HOLME HALL
Stagecoach
162
162
TWF 202Y

59	B52DWE	Leyland Tiger TRCTL11/2RH	Alexander TE	DP49F	1984		
60	B53DWJ	Leyland Tiger TRCTL11/2RH	Alexander TE	DP49F	1985		
62	AYR322T	Leyland National 10351A/2R		B38D	1979	Ex Haven Coaches, Newhaven, 1993	
63	VKU72S	Leyland National 11351A/1R		B49F	1978	Ex Chesterfield, 1995	
64	E60WDT	Leyland Lynx LX112TL11ZR1	Leyland Lynx	DP45F	1987	Ex Chesterfield, 1995	
65	E61WDT	Leyland Lynx LX112TL11ZR1	Leyland Lynx	DP45F	1987	Ex Chesterfield, 1995	
71	A71GEE	Leyland Olympian ONTL11/1R	Eastern Coach Works	H45/31F	1983	Ex Grimsby Cleethorpes, 1993	
72	A72GEE	Leyland Olympian ONTL11/1R	Eastern Coach Works	H45/31F	1983	Ex Grimsby Cleethorpes, 1993	
73	A73GEE	Leyland Olympian ONTL11/1R	Eastern Coach Works	H47/28D	1983	Ex Grimsby Cleethorpes, 1993	
74	A74GEE	Leyland Olympian ONTL11/1R	Eastern Coach Works	H47/28D	1983	Ex Grimsby Cleethorpes, 1993	
75	F75TFU	Dennis Dominator DDA1021	Alexander RH	H45/33F	1989	Ex Grimsby Cleethorpes, 1993	
76	F76TFU	Dennis Dominator DDA1021	Alexander RH	H45/33F	1989	Ex Grimsby Cleethorpes, 1993	
77c	VKU77S	Leyland National 11351A/1R		B49F	1978	Ex Chesterfield, 1995	
77	F77TFU	Dennis Dominator DDA1021	Alexander RH	H45/33F	1989	Ex Grimsby Cleethorpes, 1993	
78	F78TFU	Dennis Dominator DDA1022	Alexander RH	H45/33F	1989	Ex Grimsby Cleethorpes, 1993	
79c	VKU79S	Leyland National 11351A/1R		B49F	1978	Ex Chesterfield, 1995	
79	G79VFW	Dennis Dominator DDA1028	Alexander RH	H45/33F	1990	Ex Grimsby Cleethorpes, 1993	
80	G80VFW	Dennis Dominator DDA1028	Alexander RH	H45/33F	1990	Ex Grimsby Cleethorpes, 1993	
81	G81VFW	Dennis Dominator DDA1029	Alexander RH	H45/33F	1990	Ex Grimsby Cleethorpes, 1993	
82c	RBU180R	Leyland National 11351A/1R		B49F	1978	Ex Chesterfield, 1995	

82-89		Dennis Dominator DDA1034*	East Lancashire		H45/33F	1991-92	Ex Grimsby Cleethorpes, 1993 *86-9 are DDA1036	
82	H482BEE	84	H484BEE	86	J91DJV	88	J93DJV	89	J94DJV
83	H483BEE	85	H485BEE	87	J92DJV				

90-98		Mercedes-Benz 709D		Alexander Sprint		B25F*	1988	Ex Chesterfield, 1995 *97/8 are DP25F
90	E90YWB	92	E92YWB	94	E94YWB	96	E96YWB	98	E98YWB
91	E91YWB	93	E93YWB	95	E95YWB	97	E97YWB		
99	H257THL	Mercedes-Benz 709D		Reeve Burgess Beaver		B25F	1991	Ex Chesterfield, 1995

101-109		Volvo Olympian YN2RV18Z4		Northern Counties Palatine		H47/29F	1993	
101	K101JWJ	103	K103JWJ	105	K105JWJ	107	K107JWJ	109	L109LHL
102	K102JWJ	104	K104JWJ	106	K106JWJ	108	L108LHL		
103w	BJV103L	Daimler Fleetline CRG6LX		Roe		O45/29D	1973	Ex Grimsby Cleethorpes, 1993
113w	MBE613R	Leyland Fleetline FE30AGR		Roe		O45/29D	1976	Ex Grimsby Cleethorpes, 1993

117-129		Leyland Fleetline FE30AGR	Roe		H45/29D	1979-80	Ex Grimsby Cleethorpes, 1993
117	TFU61T	119	WFU467V	120	OJV120S	126	XFU126V	129	XFU129V
118	WFU466V								

130-144		Volvo Olympian YN2RV18Z4		Alexander RL		H47/29F	1995	
130	N130AET	133	N133AET	136	N136AET	139	N139AET	142	N142AET
131	N131AET	134	N134AET	137	N137AET	140	N140AET	143	N143AET
132	N132AET	135	N135AET	138	N138AET	141	N141AET	144	N144AET
146	NKY146R	Leyland Fleetline FE30ALR		Roe		H42/29D	1977	

150-159		Leyland Fleetline FE30AGR		Roe		H42/29D	1978	Ex Chesterfield, 1995
150	UWA150S	154	UWA154S	155	UWA155S	157	UWA157S	159	UWA159S
151	UWA151S								

This Duple Laser-bodied Leyland Tiger was new to the Midland Red North fleet and operated as a Midland Express vehicle. It is now operating for the main East Midland fleet, on longer distance routes which, in line with group policy, are branded Stagecoach Express. Number 193, A354BHL is seen about to leave the Derbyshire village of Wirksworth bound for Meadowhall, near Sheffield. *Andrew Bagshaw*

159G	BFW136W	Ford R1114	Plaxton Supreme IV	C53F	1981	Ex Grimsby Cleethorpes, 1993
165	PTD641S	Leyland Fleetline FE30AGR	Northern Counties	H43/32F	1977	Ex Chesterfield, 1995
172	XGS736S	Leyland Leopard PSU3E/4R	Plaxton Supreme III	C53F	1978	Ex Grimsby Cleethorpes, 1993
173	BHO441V	Leyland Leopard PSU5C/4R	Duple Dominant II	C55F	1980	Ex Grimsby Cleethorpes, 1993
174	MRJ270W	Leyland Leopard PSU5C/4R	Plaxton Supreme IV	C41DL	1980	Ex Grimsby Cleethorpes, 1993
175	EFU935Y	Leyland Leopard PSU5C/4R	Duple Dominant I	C53F	1983	Ex Grimsby Cleethorpes, 1993
176	OJL823Y	Leyland Leopard PSU5C/4R	Duple Dominant III	C53F	1983	Ex Grimsby Cleethorpes, 1993
177	OJL822Y	Leyland Leopard PSU5C/4R	Duple Dominant III	C49F	1983	Ex Grimsby Cleethorpes, 1993
183	PJI4314	Leyland Tiger TRCTL11/2R	Plaxton Paramount 3200 E	C47F	1983	
187	PYE841Y	Leyland Tiger TRCTL11/3R	Duple Laser	C53F	1983	Ex Grimsby Cleethorpes, 1993
188	PYE842Y	Leyland Tiger TRCTL11/3R	Duple Laser	C53F	1983	Ex Grimsby Cleethorpes, 1993
189	PSU764	Leyland Tiger TRCTL11/3R	Duple Laser	C53F	1983	Ex Grimsby Cleethorpes, 1993
190	PSU443	Leyland Tiger TRCTL11/3R	Duple Laser	C53F	1983	Ex Grimsby Cleethorpes, 1993
191	A243YGF	Leyland Tiger TRCTL11/3RH	Duple Laser	C57F	1984	Ex Grimsby Cleethorpes, 1993
192	PS2743	Leyland Tiger TRCTL11/3RH	Duple Laser	C57F	1984	Ex Grimsby Cleethorpes, 1993
193	A354BHL	Leyland Tiger TRCTL11/3RH	Duple Laser	C57F	1984	Ex Grimsby Cleethorpes, 1993
201	GOL398N	Leyland National 11351/1R		B49F	1975	Ex Midland Red West, 1990
202	JAO477V	Leyland National 10351A/2R		B44F	1980	Ex Leyland demonstrator, 1984
203	ABA25T	Leyland National 11351A/1R		B49F	1979	Ex GM Buses, 1990
205	URA605S	Leyland National 11351A/1R(Volvo)		B49F	1977	Ex Chesterfield, 1995
206	VKE566S	Leyland National 11351A/1R(Volvo)		B49F	1977	Ex Chesterfield, 1995
207	RAU597R	Leyland National 11351A/1R(Volvo)		B49F	1976	Ex Chesterfield, 1995
208	VKU73S	Leyland National 11351A/1R(Volvo)		B49F	1978	Ex Chesterfield, 1995

This Dennis Dominator carries an East Lancashire body which has a remarkable similarity to the Stagecoach favoured Alexander type. No.84, H484BEE is seen operating the busy 3F service which serves both Grimsby and Cleethorpes. *Tony Wilson*

209-224		Bristol VRT/SL3/6LXB*		Eastern Coach Works		H43/31F	1980-81 *218 is model 6LXC	
209	EWE203V	211	JAK211W	218	KWA218W	223	KWA223W	224	KWA224W
210	EWE206V	214	KWA214W	221	KWA221W				

231	EJV31Y	Dennis Falcon H SDA411	Wadham Stringer Vanguard	B42F	1983	Ex Grimsby Cleethorpes, 1993
232	EJV32Y	Dennis Falcon H SDA411	Wadham Stringer Vanguard	B42F	1983	Ex Grimsby Cleethorpes, 1993
233	EJV33Y	Dennis Falcon H SDA411	Wadham Stringer Vanguard	B42F	1983	Ex Grimsby Cleethorpes, 1993
234	EJV34Y	Dennis Falcon H SDA411	Wadham Stringer Vanguard	B42F	1983	Ex Grimsby Cleethorpes, 1993
299	TWF201Y	Leyland Olympian ONLXB/1R	Roe		H47/29F	1982	Ex Chesterfield, 1995
300	TWF202Y	Leyland Olympian ONLXB/1R	Roe		H47/29F	1982	Ex Chesterfield, 1995

301-325		Leyland Olympian ONLXB/1R		Eastern Coach Works		H45/32F	1981-84	
301	NHL301X	306	SHE306Y	311	SHE311Y	316	A316XWG	321	A321YWJ
302	NHL302X	307	SHE307Y	312	UDT312Y	317	A317XWG	322	A322AKU
303	NHL303X	308	SHE308Y	313	UDT313Y	318	A318XWG	323	A323AKU
304	NHL304X	309	SHE309Y	314	A314XWG	319	A319YWJ	324	A324AKU
305	NHL305X	310	SHE310Y	315	A315XWG	320	A320YWJ	325	A325AKU

326-330		Leyland Olympian ONLXB/1R		Eastern Coach Works		CH40/32F	1985	
326	C326HWJ	327	C327HWJ	328	C328HWJ	329	C329HWJ	330	C330HWJ

331-336		Leyland Olympian ONLXB/1R		Eastern Coach Works		H45/32F	1986	
331	C331HWJ	333	C333HWJ	334	C334HWJ	335	C335HWJ	336	C336HWJ
332	C332HWJ								

337	GSO8V	Leyland Olympian ONLXB/1RV	Alexander RL	H45/32F	1987	Ex United Counties, 1992

339-343		Leyland Olympian ON6LXB/2RZ		Alexander RL		DPH51/31F	1989	
339	G339KKW	340	G340KKW	341	G341KKW	342	G342KKW	343	G343KKW

344-353
Leyland Olympian ON25R6G13Z4 Alexander RL DPH51/31F* 1990-91 *349-353 are DPH47/27F

344	H344SWA	346	H346SWA	348	H348SWA	350	J350XET	352	J352XET
345	H345SWA	347	H347SWA	349	J349XET	351	J351XET	353	J353XET

354-358
Leyland Olympian ON2R50G13Z4 Northern Counties Palatine H47/29F 1992

354	K354DWJ	355	K355DWJ	356	K356DWJ	357	K357DWJ	358	K358DWJ

359-363
Leyland Olympian ON2R54G13Z4 Alexander RL DPH43/27F 1992

359	K359DWJ	360	K360DWJ	361	K361DWJ	362	K362DWJ	363	K363DWJ

412	DWF22V	Leyland Leopard PSU3E/4R	Duple Dominant(1985)	B55F	1979		
413	DWF23V	Leyland Leopard PSU3E/4R	Duple Dominant(1985)	B51F	1979		
414	DWF24V	Leyland Leopard PSU3E/4R	Alexander P(1985)	B52F	1979		
416	DWF26V	Leyland Leopard PSU3E/4R	Duple Dominant(1985)	B55F	1980		
421	E927PBE	Leyland Tiger TRBLXCT/2RH	Alexander P	DP51F	1987	Ex Grimsby Cleethorpes, 1993
422	E928PBE	Leyland Tiger TRBLXCT/2RH	Alexander P	DP51F	1987	Ex Grimsby Cleethorpes, 1993
423	E929PBE	Leyland Tiger TRBLXCT/2RH	Alexander P	DP51F	1987	Ex Grimsby Cleethorpes, 1993
424	E930PBE	Leyland Tiger TRBLXCT/2RH	Alexander P	DP51F	1987	Ex Grimsby Cleethorpes, 1993

425-433
Leyland Tiger TRCTL11/2RH Alexander P B52F 1985

425	B625DWF	427	B627DWF	429	B629DWF	431	B631DWF	433	B633DWF
426	B626DWF	428	B628DWF	430	B630DWF	432	B632DWF		

435-453
Volvo B6-9.9M Alexander Dash B40F 1993

435	L435LWA	439	L439LWA	443	L443LWA	448	L448LWA	451	L451LWA
436	L436LWA	440	L440LWA	445	L445LWA	449	L449LWA	452	L452LWA
437	L437LWA	441	L441LWA	446	L446LWA	450	L450LWA	453	L453LHJ
438	L438LWA	442	L442LWA	447	L447LWA				

591-600
Volvo B10M-55 Alexander PS DP48F 1994 Ex Ribble, 1995

591	L341KCK	593	L343KCK	595	L339KCK	597	M411RRN	599	M413RRN
592	L342KCK	594	L344KCK	596	L340KCK	598	M412RRN	600	M414RRN

601-609
Volvo B10M-55 Alexander PS DP48F 1995

601	M601VHE	603	M603VHE	605	M605VHE	607	M607VHE	609	M609WET
602	M602VHE	604	M604VHE	606	M606VHE	608	M608WET		

The Chesterfield Transport fleet contained a large number of Leyland Nationals, most of which were secondhand. While many have now been withdrawn from service, those fitted with Volvo engines seem destined for a longer life as they have been numbered in a new series. 201, GOL398N came from Midland Red West.
Tony Wilson

614	EKW614V	Leyland National 2 NL106L11/1R			B44F	1980		
615	EKW615V	Leyland National 2 NL106L11/1R			B44F	1980		
616	EKW616V	Leyland National 2 NL106L11/1R			B44F	1980		

617-621

		Leyland National 2 NL116L11/1R			B49F	1980		
617	GWE617V	618	GWE618V	619	GWE619V	620	HWJ620W	621	HWJ621W

622	MWG622X	Leyland National 2 NL116AL11/1R	B49F	1981	
623	MWG623X	Leyland National 2 NL116AL11/1R	B49F	1981	
624	MWG624X	Leyland National 2 NL116AL11/1R	B49F	1981	
625	LAG188V	Leyland National 2 NL116L11/1R	B49F	1980	Ex East Yorkshire, 1988
626	LAG189V	Leyland National 2 NL116L11/1R	B49F	1980	Ex East Yorkshire, 1988
627	NRP580V	Leyland National 2 NL116L11/1R	B49F	1980	Ex United Counties, 1992
628	SVV586W	Leyland National 2 NL116L11/1R	B49F	1981	Ex United Counties, 1992
634	VWA34Y	Leyland National 2 NL116HLXB/1R	DP47F	1983	
635	VWA35Y	Leyland National 2 NL116HLXB/1R	DP47F	1983	
636	VWA36Y	Leyland National 2 NL116HLXB/1R	DP47F	1983	

637-643

		Volvo B10M-62		Plaxton Premiére Interurban	DP51F	1993		
637	L637LDT	639	L639LDT	641	L641LDT	642	L642LDT	643	L643LDT
638	L638LDT	640	L640LDT					

652	HSV196	Volvo B10M-61	Plaxton Paramount 3500 III	C53F	1987	Ex Premier Travel Services, 1996
653	HSV195	Volvo B10M-61	Plaxton Paramount 3500 III	C50F	1988	Ex Premier Travel Services, 1996
654	HSV194	Volvo B10M-61	Plaxton Paramount 3500 III	C50F	1988	Ex Premier Travel Services, 1996
655	H402DEG	Volvo B10M-60	Plaxton Paramount 3500 III	C53F	1990	Ex Premier Travel Services, 1996

700-710

		Mercedes-Benz L608D	Reeve Burgess	B20F*	1986	Ex Cumberland, 1995
						*702/6/8-10 are DP19F

700	D34UAO	702	D504RCK	705	D518RCK	707	D522RCK	709	D547RCK
701	D503RCK	703	D511RCK	706	D519RCK	708	D539RCK	710	D561RCK

720-727

		Mercedes-Benz 811D	Reeve Burgess Beaver	B31F	1989-90	

720	G820KWF	722	G822KWF	724	G824KWF	726	G826KWF	727	G827KWF
721	G821KWF	723	G823KWF	725	G825KWF				

728	E721BVO	Mercedes-Benz 811D	Optare StarRider	B33F	1988	Ex Maun, Mansfield, 1990
729	E880DRA	Mercedes-Benz 811D	Optare StarRider	B33F	1988	Ex Maun, Mansfield, 1990
730	E481DAU	Mercedes-Benz 811D	Optare StarRider	B33F	1988	Ex Maun, Mansfield, 1990

731-751

		Mercedes-Benz 709D	Alexander Sprint	B25F	1993	

731	L731LWA	735	L735LWA	739	L739LWA	743	L743LWA	748	L748LWA
732	L732LWA	736	L736LWA	740	L740LWA	744	L744LWA	749	L749LWA
733	L733LWA	737	L737LWA	741	L741LWA	745	L745LWA	750	L750LWA
734	L734LWA	738	L738LWA	742	L742LWA	746	L746LWA	751	L751LHL

752-776

		Mercedes-Benz 709D	Alexander Sprint	B25F	1995-96	

752	N752CKU	757	N757CKU	762	N762EWG	767	N767EWG	772	N772EWG
753	N753CKU	758	N758CKU	763	N763EWG	768	N768EWG	773	N773EWG
754	N754CKU	759	N759CKU	764	N764EWG	769	N769EWG	774	N774EWG
755	N755CKU	760	N760CKU	765	N765EWG	770	N770EWG	775	N775EWG
756	N756CKU	761	N761CKU	766	N766EWG	771	N771EWG	776	N776EWG

Previous Registrations:

A243YGF	A601HVT, PS2045	PJI4316	UHE37Y
GSO8V	D378XRS	PJI4317	UHE38Y
HSV194	E904UNW	PS2743	A602HVT
HSV195	E905UNW	A354BHL	PS3696, A603HVT
HSV196	E315OEG	PSU443	A844SYR
OJL822Y	SSG321Y, PS2945	PSU764	PYE843Y
OJL823Y	EJV419Y, P32743	RHL174X	OHE278X, 503UM
PJI4314	UWJ33Y		

Livery: Stagecoach corporate - White, red, orange and blue.

ELSEY

A W Elsey Ltd, High Street, Gosberton, Spalding, Lincolnshire, PE11 4NA

WSV418	Leyland Leopard PSU3E/4R	Plaxton Supreme IV	C53F	1980	Ex Bailey, Toton, 1992
SLJ386X	Leyland Leopard PSU5C/4R	Plaxton Supreme V	C57F	1981	Ex Midland, Auchterarder, 1992
E333EVH	DAF MB230LB615	Van Hool Alizée	C55F	1988	
E112YNM	Scania K112CRS	Van Hool Alizée	C49FT	1987	Ex Ace, Enfield, 1992
G849VAY	Dennis Javelin 11SDL1905	Duple 300	B55F	1989	
G997KJX	DAF SB2305DHS585	Duple 320	C57F	1990	
G998KJX	DAF SB2305DHS585	Duple 320	C53F	1990	
K120OCT	Kässbohrer Setra S215HD	Kässbohrer	C49F	1992	Ex Ebdon, Sidcup, 1996
K519RJX	DAF SB3000DKVF601	Van Hool Alizée	C49FT	1993	
K529EHE	Scania K113CRB	Van Hool Alizée	C53F	1993	
L907RDO	Ford Transit VE6	Ford	M8	1994	
M290OUR	Iveco Turbo City 480-10-21	Wadham Stringer Vanguard	B47F	1994	

Previous Registrations:
WSV418   KBH847V

Livery: White, red and grey

Elseys Coaches of Gosberton operate a service between Boston and Spalding. Purchased for this route in 1995 was M290OUR, one of only six Iveco Turbo City single decks imported from Italy the previous year, this pair carry bodywork by Wadham Stringer. The Elsey example was previously demonstrated to a number of operators by importer AW of Ratby. *Steve Sanderson*

EMMERSON

OM & AG Stocks and Brumby, Bluestone Lane, Immingham, North East Lincolnshire, DN40 2EL

Depots: Gilbey Road, Pyewipe, Grimsby & Bluestone Lane, Immingham.

Reg	Chassis	Body	Seating	Year	Notes
ABA21T	Leyland National 11351A/1R		B49F	1979	Ex GM Buses, 1987
NLO857V	Bedford YMT	Plaxton Supreme IV	C53F	1980	Ex McLernon, Grimsby, 1985
173LYB	DAF MB200DKTL550	Plaxton Supreme IV	C53F	1980	Ex McLernon, Grimsby, 1985
WFU561V	Ford R1114	Duple Dominant II	C53F	1980	
MKP179W	Bedford YMT	Wadham Stringer Vanguard	B61F	1981	Ex Boro'line, Maidstone, 1987
VBH40W	Ford R1114	Duple Dominant IV	C53F	1981	Ex The Londoners, Nunhead, 1986
VBH50W	Ford R1114	Duple Dominant IV	C53F	1981	Ex The Londoners, Nunhead, 1986
VNH155W	Leyland Leopard PSU3F/4RT	Duple Dominant IV	C53F	1981	Ex Camms, Nottingham, 1993
EFU613Y	Ford R1114	Duple Dominant IV	C53F	1983	
MIB648	Volvo B10M-61	Duple Laser	C57F	1983	Ex Coachman, Cowplain, 1995
A575GJV	Bedford YNT	Duple Laser	C51F	1984	
XFC486	Bova EL28/581	Duple Calypso	C53F	1984	Ex Supreme, Coventry, 1987
NSU180	Scania K112CRS	Plaxton Paramount 3200 II	C53F	1985	Ex Supreme, Hadleigh, 1993
217MYB	Bedford YNV Venturer	Plaxton Paramount 3200 III	C53F	1988	Ex Bibby, Ingleton, 1990
XFK173	Volvo B10M-61	Ikarus Blue Danube	C49F	1988	
RJI4578	Van Hool T815H	Van Hool Alizée	C49FT	1988	Ex Tellings-Golden Miller, Cardiff, 1993
G979APJ	Mercedes-Benz 408D	Crystals	M15	1990	

Previous Registrations:

173LYB	JDU902V		NSU180	B546CHJ	XFC486	A313JRW
217MYB	E391KCW		RJI4578	E446MMM	XFK173	From new
MIB648	MCR333Y, 710VCV, 800GTR					

Livery: Orange, black and white

Emmersons of Immingham operate from bases in both Immingham and Grimsby. The location of this view is the main garage. VBH50W, is one of two Ford R1114 coaches purchased from The Londoners in 1986 and, ten years on, still giving good service. *Steve Sanderson*

ENTERPRISE & SILVER DAWN

M D Gallagher, The Mill, Grantham Road, Waddington, Lincolnshire, LN5 9NA

2140	MAL795P	Bristol VRT/SL3/6LX	Eastern Coach Works	H43/31F	1976	Ex Trent, 1993
2143	MFN45R	Bristol VRT/SL3/6LXB	Eastern Coach Works	H43/31F	1976	Ex East Kent, 1993
2146	JYG431V	Bristol VRT/SL3/6LXB	Eastern Coach Works	H43/31F	1979	Ex Yorkshire Buses, 1994
2147	VCU400T	Leyland Fleetline FE30AGR	MCW	H43/32F	1979	Ex Darlington, 1995
2148	VUA473X	Bristol VRT/SL3/6LXB	Eastern Coach Works	H43/31F	1981	Ex West Riding, 1995
2149	LMS162W	Leyland Fleetline FE30AGR	Alexander AD	H44/31F	1980	Ex Clydeside, 1995
2202	E433PFU	Bedford YNV Venturer	Duple 320	C57F	1988	
2255	YFC19V	Leyland Leopard PSU3E/4R	Duple Dominant II Express	C49F	1979	Ex The Oxford Bus Company, 1992
2258	PGA833V	Leyland Leopard PSU3F/4R	Alexander AT	C49F	1980	Ex KCB Network, 1996

Livery: Cream and brown

Enterprise and Silver Dawn provide several bus services in Lincoln with the fleet carrying a brown and cream livery. In recent times, the Bristol VRT and Leyland Fleetline have been the choice for double deck purchases. Seen leaving Lincoln during the famous weekend of the famous Christmas Market is 2146, JYG431V, a Bristol bound for RAF Waddington. *Bill Potter*

EVERETT

J D Everett, The Garage, Atterby, Lincolnshire, LN2 3BD

OTL633V	Bedford YMT	Plaxton Supreme IV Express	C53F	1980	
XPP281X	Bedford YMT	Duple Dominant II	C53F	1982	Ex Hodgkinson, Gainsbrough, 1996
C35FEC	Bedford YNT	Plaxton Paramount 3200 II	C53F	1986	Ex Bibby, Ingleton, 1992
D800KSE	Bedford YNT	Plaxton Paramount 3200 II	C53F	1987	Ex Mayne, Buckie, 1988

Livery: Cream and blue

EXPRESS MOTORS

P Brown, 10 Rutland, Kirkby in Ashfield, Nottinghamshire, NG17 9PQ

Depot: Hulland Motors, Hulland, Derbyshire

KJD421P	Bristol LH6L	Eastern Coach Works	B43F	1976	Ex Robson, Thornaby, 1994
OJD66R	Bristol LH6L	Eastern Coach Works	B39F	1976	Ex Shaftesbury & District, 1995
OJD89R	Bristol LH6L	Eastern Coach Works	B45F	1977	Ex Coombs, Weston-super-Mare, 1995
UPB311S	Leyland National 10351A/1R		B41F	1977	Ex London & Country, 1995
YVW902S	Bristol LHS6L	Plaxton Supreme III	C33F	1978	Ex Somerbus, Paulton, 1995
FBV271W	Bristol LHS6L	Eastern Coach Works	B35F	1980	Ex Blandford Bus, 1993
F109YVP	MCW MetroRider MF158/16	MCW	B28F	1988	Ex Stagecoach East London, 1996

Livery: Blue and white

FELIX

Felix Bus Services Ltd, 157 Station Road, Stanley, Ilkeston, Derbyshire, DE7 6FJ

WRC826S	Bedford YMT	Duple Dominant II	C53F	1978	
GRF264V	Leyland Leopard PSU3E/4R	Duple Dominant II Express	C53F	1979	Ex Tillingbourne, 1988
BES270V	Leyland Leopard PSU3E/4R	Plaxton Supreme IV Express	C53F	1978	Ex Earnside, Glenfarg, 1987
DTN958W	Leyland Leopard PSU3E/4R	Plaxton Supreme IV Express	C53F	1980	Ex Holmes, Clay Cross, 1986
F697HNU	Leyland Tiger TRBTL11/2R	Plaxton Derwent	B54F	1988	
G698PRR	Dennis Javelin 12SDA1907	Duple 320	C57F	1990	
G699PRR	Dennis Javelin 12SDA1907	Duple 320	C57F	1990	
J564URW	Leyland Lynx LX2R11C15245	Leyland Lynx 2	B51F	1992	Ex Volvo demonstrator, 1992
L701MRA	Dennis Javelin 12SDA2117	Plaxton Premiére 320	C53F	1993	
L702MRA	Dennis Javelin 12SDA2117	Plaxton Premiére 320	C53F	1993	
M21UUA	Dennis Lance 11SDA3113	Optare Sigma	B47F	1994	Ex Optare demonstrator, 1995
M301KRY	Volvo B10B-58	Alexander Strider	B51F	1995	
N703AAL	Dennis Javelin 12SDA2117	Plaxton Premiére 320	C53F	1996	

Previous Registrations:
FHA609Y   YPD137Y, GJI2223

Livery: Red and maroon

Lincoln Cathedral dominates the city's skyline. Everett of Atterby operate into the city from several villages to the north. D800KSE is a Plaxton Paramount bodied Bedford YNT which has been in the Everett fleet since 1988, having been new to Scottish operator Mayne of Buckie.
Tony Wilson

Express Motors have their offices in Kirkby-in-Ashfield, Nottinghamshire though the operating base is at Hulland in Derbyshire. The Bristol LHS is the dominant type in this small fleet. FBV271W was one of two vehicles which, in 1980, started on the Clitheroe-based 'Betty's Bus' network of rural services for Ribble. It was photographed in Ashbourne.
Tony Wilson

Felix Bus Services has been the operator of a service from Ilkeston to Derby via Stanley and West Hallam for many years. Seen on the service is M21UUA, an Optare Sigma-bodied Dennis Lance. This vehicle had previously been a demonstrator and is now a regular performer on the service.
Tony Wilson

47

FOWLER'S TRAVEL

W H Fowler & Sons (Coaches) Ltd, Dog Drove, Holbeach Drove, Lincolnshire, PE12 0SD

Reg	Chassis	Body	Seating	Year	Notes
519SLG	Bedford SB3	Plaxton Embassy	C41F	1961	Ex Miller, Foxton, 1992
CJN441C	Leyland Titan PD3/6	Massey	H38/32R	1965	Ex Lincoln City, 1993
FRA521L	AEC Reliance 6U3ZR	Plaxton Elite III	C51F	1973	Ex Butler, Kirkby-in-Ashfield, 1990
SHH85M	AEC Reliance 6MU4R	Plaxton Elite III	C41F	1973	Ex Hall, Waterbeck, 1995
LUG81P	Leyland Atlantean AN68/1R	Roe	H43/33F	1975	Ex Yorkshire Rider, 1993
LUG88P	Leyland Atlantean AN68/1R	Roe	H43/33F	1975	Ex Yorkshire Rider, 1995
OEG283P	Bedford YRT	Plaxton Supreme III	C53F	1976	Ex Grey, Ely, 1995
SFL438R	Bedford YMT	Plaxton Supreme III	DP53F	1977	Ex Catchpole, Tydd St Giles, 1991
DWU293T	Bristol VRT/SL3/6LXB	Eastern Coach Works	H43/31F	1978	Ex Keighley & District, 1991
NUB93V	AEC Reliance 6U2R	Plaxton Supreme IV	C53F	1980	Ex Kemp, Chillenden,1996
JDO241W	Bedford YMT	Plaxton Supreme IV Express	C53F	1981	
UFP236X	DAF MB200DKFL600	Plaxton Supreme V	C57F	1982	Ex Winterbourne Pioneer, 1993
YPD136Y	Leyland Tiger TRCTL11/2R	Duple Dominant IV Express	DP53F	1983	Ex Kentish Bus, 1990
A131EPA	Leyland Tiger TRCTL11/2RH	Plaxton Paramount 3200 E	C53F	1984	Ex London Buses, 1993
D823UBH	Bedford YMT	Plaxton Derwent II	B55F	1986	Ex Rover Bus Service, Chesham, 1993
D601RGJ	Bedford YMT	Plaxton Derwent II	B53F	1987	Ex Epsom Buses, 1994
D604RGJ	Bedford YMT	Plaxton Derwent II	B53F	1987	Ex Epsom Buses, 1995
D154HML	Leyland Tiger TRCTL11/3RZ	Plaxton Paramount 3200 III	C53F	1987	Ex Armchair, Brentford, 1993
F259CEW	Scania N113DRB	Alexander RH	H47/33F	1989	
A10WHF	Volvo B10M-61	Van Hool Alizée	C48DT	1989	Ex Kenzie, Shepreth, 1996
G601XMD	Leyland Tiger TRCL10/3ARZA	Plaxton Paramount 3200 III	C53F	1990	Ex London Coaches, 1994
706STT	Scania K113CRB	Plaxton Premiére 320	C53F	1992	Ex Harry Shaw, 1995
L31ORC	Dennis Javelin 12SDA2125	Plaxton Premiére 350	C53F	1994	Ex Skills, Nottingham, 1995
N691AHL	Scania L113CRL	Northern Counties Paladin	B51F	1995	
N692AHL	Scania L113CRL	Northern Counties Paladin	B51F	1995	
N693AHL	Scania L113CRL	Northern Counties Paladin	B51F	1995	

Previous Registrations:

519SLG	From new	FRA521L	WVA290L, 20VWC
706STT	J36UHP	OEG283P	OFM728P, ESU369, ESU320
A10WHF	F36DAV	SFL438R	SBD56R, 706STT
D823UBH	D620PWA, 760BUS	SHH85M	SGT360L

Named Vehicles: 706STT, *Jackie* ; A131EPA, *Amy* ; DWU293T, *Hayley* ; G601XMD ,*Ella May* ; D601RGJ, *Tinker* ; D604RGJ, *Ross* ; D823UBH, *George*

Livery: Cream and orange

The Kings Lynn to Spalding via Holbeach service is operated every hour by Fowlers Travel. The trio of Plaxton Derwent-bodied Scania K92 vehicles were sold to RoadCar and have been replaced by three new Scania L113CRL 51-seaters fitted with Northern Counties Paladin bodies. The last of the batch, N693AHL is seen in Kings Lynn bus station.
Phillip Stephenson

GLOVERS

Glovers Coaches Ltd, 56 Walton Crescent, Ashbourne, Derbyshire, DE6 1FZ

Depot: Moor Farm Road East, Ashbourne Ind Est.

HRB932V	Bedford YMT	Duple Dominant II	C53F	1980	
NNU71W	Leyland Leopard PSU3E/4R	Duple Dominant IV	C53F	1981	
URA481X	Bedford YMP	Duple Dominant IV	C45F	1982	
YNN396Y	Leyland Tiger TRCTL11/3R	Duple Dominant III	C53F	1983	
A506FSS	Dennis Lancet SDA516	Alexander P	B53F	1984	Ex Northern Scottish, 1991
A281FAL	Mercedes-Benz L307D	Reeve Burgess	M12	1984	
B252KTO	Volvo B10M-61	Plaxton Paramount 3200 II	C53F	1985	
D776WVO	Bedford YNT	Plaxton Paramount 3200 III	C53F	1987	
E964SVU	Freight Rover Sherpa	Made-to-Measure	B18FL	1987	Ex Filer, Ilfracombe, 1991
G699OCH	Volvo B10M-60	Plaxton Paramount 3200 III	C53F	1989	
G700OCH	Mercedes-Benz 609D	Reeve Burgess Beaver	C25F	1989	
N381EAK	Volvo B10M-62	Plaxton Première 350	C53F	1996	
N382EAK	Volvo B10M-62	Plaxton Première 350	C53F	1996	

Livery: Cream and blue

Glovers are based in the Derbyshire village of Ashbourne. The fleet contains a Dennis Lancet which was one of a batch delivered to Alexander Northern back in 1984. Now in this operator's cream and blue livery, A506FSS is seen about to load at a school in Ashbourne. *Tony Wilson*

GRAYSCROFT

Grayscroft Bus Services Ltd, 15A Victoria Road, Mablethorpe, Lincolnshire, LN12 2AF

AFE719A	AEC Reliance 2MU3RV	Weymann	OB40F	1962	Ex London & Country, 1995
MCO257H	Leyland Atlantean PDR2/1	Park Royal	H47/30D	1970	Ex Clayton, Leicester, 1990
ATH108T	Bristol LHS6L	Plaxton Supreme IV	C33F	1979	Ex Oxon Travel, Bicester, 1995
MGR914T	Leyland Leopard PSU3E/4R	Duple Dominant	B55F	1979	Ex Translinc, Lincoln, 1994
VJG810T	Leyland Leopard PSU3E/4R	Duple Dominant II	C49F	1979	Ex East Kent, 1989
XJG815V	Leyland Leopard PSU5C/4R	Duple Dominant II	C53F	1980	Ex East Kent, 1989
AJV555W	Bedford YMT	Plaxton Supreme IV	C53F	1980	
NBZ1670	Leyland Leopard PSU5D/5R	Plaxton Supreme IV	C49F	1981	Ex Yelloway, 1987
TJI1679	Leyland Leopard PSU3F/4R	Plaxton Supreme IV	C53F	1981	Ex Wallace Arnold, 1986
RJI1653	Bedford YNT	Plaxton Paramount 3200	C53F	1984	
RJI1654	Leyland Tiger TRCTL11/3R	Duple Laser	C50F	1984	Ex Brighton & Hove, 1991
RJI1655	Leyland Tiger TRCTL11/3RZ	Duple 340	C53F	1986	Ex Shearings, 1992
D131OWG	Renault-Dodge S56	Reeve Burgess	DP25F	1987	Ex Chesterfield, 1993
TJI1676	Dennis Javelin SDA1907	Duple 320	C57F	1988	
TJI1677	Volvo B10M-60	Plaxton Expressliner	C49F	1990	Ex Premier Travel, 1996
TJI1678	Dennis Javelin SDA1907	Plaxton Paramount 3200 III	C53F	1990	

Previous Registrations:

AFE719A	325NKT	RJI1654	A810CCD	TJI1677	G382REG
ATH108T	FTW133T, 10OOX	RJI1655	C343DND	TJI1678	G961WNR
NBZ1670	MRJ100W	TJI1676	E760HJF	TJI1679	PNW305W
RJI1653	A506HBE				

Livery: White, blue and orange

Grayscroft Travel operate the Mablethorpe town service from the shopping centre to North End. AFE719A was purchased in 1995 to operate this route which serves several caravan sites in the summer. Built in 1962 the Weymann-bodied AEC Reliance was converted to open top by Maidstone and District, its previous owner. *Tony Wilson*

HAIL AND RIDE

R C & G A Marsh (5555 Taxis), 28 Seathorne Road, Skegness, Lincolnshire, PE25 1RP

UTV213S	Leyland Fleetline FE30AGR	Northern Counties	H47/31D	1977	Ex Nottingham, 1995
SVM378W	Bedford YMT	Plaxton Supreme IV	C53F	1980	Ex Byley Garage, Byley, 1995
WUG532X	Ford R1114	Plaxton Supreme IV	C53F	1981	Ex Smith, Coupar Angus, 1995
GFO754X	Bedford YMQ	Duple Dominant II	C35F	1981	Ex Evans, Prenton, 1993
D404EFA	Ford Transit	Ford	M8	1987	Ex private owner, 1993
D758WRR	Ford Transit	Ford	M8	1987	Ex private owner, 1993
D323CLB	Ford Transit	Ford	M8	1987	Ex private owner, 1993
D756PTU	Freight Rover Sherpa	Dormobile	B16F	1986	Ex PMT, 1992
D552HNW	Iveco Daily 49.10	Robin Hood City Nippy	B16F	1986	Ex Sussex Bus, Pagham, 1996
D861LWR	Freight Rover Sherpa	Dormobile	B20F	1987	Ex Ambuskill, Tividale, 1994
E90OUH	Freight Rover Sherpa	Carlyle Citybus 2	B20F	1987	Ex Shamrock, Pontypridd, 1994
F218AKG	Freight Rover Sherpa	Carlyle Citybus 2	B20F	1988	Ex Walsh, Alkrington, 1994
G274HDW	Freight Rover Sherpa	Carlyle Citybus 2	B20F	1990	Ex Burke, Reddish, 1994

Previous Registrations:
SVM378W   62BYL, EDK349W

Livery: Blue and white

There is intense competition in the holiday resort of Skegness with three companies plying for passengers. Four Fives taxis started their competitive operation in 1992 and now operate under the Hail and Ride name. UTV213S is a former Nottingham Fleetline seen loading in Skegness for Butlins Funcoast World. *David Longbottom*

HAINES

N E & F E Haines, Ralphs Lane, Frampton West, Boston, Lincolnshire, PE20 1QU

FMO841V	Bedford YMT	Duple Dominant II	C45F	1980	Ex Station, Wokingham, 1988
JPM815V	Volvo B58-61	Plaxton Supreme IV	C53F	1980	Ex Warren, Alton, 1991
OHL912X	Renault-Dodge S46	Rootes	B21F	1982	Ex Ambuskill, Warley, 1991
MMW49X	Bedford YNT	Duple Dominant IV	C53F	1982	Ex O'Brien, Ratcliffe, 1989
FIL4032	Leyland Leopard PSU5D/5R	Duple Dominant III	C53F	1982	Ex Beeston, Hadleigh, 1994
KAX714	Leyland Tiger TRCTL11/3R	Plaxton Paramount 3500	C49FT	1983	Ex Bryan A Garratt, Leicester, 1992
XSU978	Leyland Tiger TRCTL11/3R	Plaxton Paramount 3500	C49FT	1983	Ex Staffordian, Stafford, 1994
D854KWR	Freight Rover Sherpa	Dormobile	B20F	1987	Ex Yorkshire Rider, 1991
E250ADO	Mercedes-Benz 609D	Coachcraft	C21F	1988	
G218EOA	Iveco Daily 49-10	Carlyle Dailybus	DP12F	1989	Ex British Midland, Heathrow, 1995
G232GOJ	Leyland-DAF 400	Crystals	M16	1990	Ex van, 1993
G704EOX	Leyland-DAF 400	Crystals	M16	1990	Ex van, 1990
H633GHA	Leyland-DAF 400	Crystals	M16	1990	Ex van, 1994
J328ONE	Leyland-DAF 400	Jubilee (1992)	M16	1991	Ex van, 1992

Previous Registrations:
FIL4032	WGV863X	KAX714	RNY312Y
JPM815V	NNS937V, JHF682	XSU978	BAJ635Y

Livery: Cream

HODSON

Hodson's Coaches Ltd, Chapel Lane, Navenby, Lincolnshire, LN5 0ER.

VTL358	Bedford YMT	Plaxton Supreme IV	C53F	1979	Ex Whittle, Highley, 1982
CIB9152	Kässbohrer Setra S215HD	Kässbohrer	C49FT	1986	Ex Chisholm, Swanley, 1995
E211ETN	DAF SB2300DHS585	Duple 340	C53F	1988	Ex Craiggs, Radcliffe, 1992
H284HLM	Mercedes-Benz 814L	North West Coach Sales	C24F	1991	Ex Byley Stores, Byley, 1994
L4HOD	Mercedes-Benz 814D	TBP	C29FL	1994	
L5HOD	Mercedes-Benz 410D	Crystals	M15	1994	
A19HOD	Mercedes-Benz 814D	Autobus Classique Nouvelle	C25F	1996	

Previous Registrations:
CIB9152	4777EL	VTL358	AUJ744T

Livery: Cream, pink and maroon.

The Phil Haines fleet contains minibuses and coaches. FIL4032 is a 12-metre Leyland Leopard which carries a Duple Dominant III body featuring the 'Greyhound' style parallelogram windows that were briefly popular in the early 1980s *Steve Sanderson*

On three days a week, Hodson's of Navenby operate a service from Coleby to Newark. L4HOD is the regular performer on this route and is a Mercedes-Benz 814D version of Mercedes-Benz chassis. It is fitted with a body manufactured by the TBP company which was more closely associated with tri-axle Peugeot minibuses. *Steve Sanderson*

HOLLOWAYS

Holloways Coaches Ltd, Cottage Beck Road, Scunthorpe, North Lincolnshire, DN16 1TP

Depot: Kettering Road, Scunthorpe

XWG653T	Leyland Atlantean AN68A/1R	Roe	H45/29D	1978	Ex South Yorkshire's Transport, 1990
XWG655T	Leyland Atlantean AN68A/1R	Roe	H45/29D	1978	Ex South Yorkshire's Transport, 1990
YSU906	Bedford YLQ	Plaxton Supreme III	C41F	1978	
CWG681V	Leyland Atlantean AN68A/1R	Alexander AL	H45/29D	1979	Ex South Yorkshire's Transport, 1991
CWG684V	Leyland Atlantean AN68A/1R	Alexander AL	H45/29D	1979	Ex South Yorkshire's Transport, 1991
CWG699V	Leyland Atlantean AN68A/1R	Alexander AL	H45/29D	1979	Ex South Yorkshire's Transport, 1991
CWG746V	Leyland Atlantean AN68A/1R	Alexander AL	H45/29D	1979	Ex Bygone Buses, Biddenden, 1994
PSV436	Leyland Tiger TRCTL11/2R	Plaxton Paramount 3200	C53F	1983	
PSV389	Leyland Tiger TRCTL11/2R	Plaxton Paramount 3200	C53F	1984	
E692UNE	Leyland Tiger TRCTL11/3RZ	Plaxton Paramount 3200 II	C53F	1988	Ex Hague, Sheffield, 1995
F201HSO	Leyland Tiger TRCTL11/3ARZ	Plaxton Paramount 3200 III	C53F	1988	Ex Park's, 1992
F774GNA	Leyland Tiger TRCL10/3ARZ	Plaxton Paramount 3200 III	C53F	1989	Ex Hanson Coach, Halifax, 1995
F597HYC	Dennis Javelin 8.5SDL1903	Plaxton Paramount 3200 III	C35F	1989	Ex Taylor, Sutton Scotney, 1996
F92WFA	Dennis Javelin 12SDA1907	Plaxton Paramount 3200 III	C57F	1989	Ex Robin Hood, Rudyard, 1994
H231FFE	Dennis Javelin 11SDA1906	Plaxton Paramount 3200 III	C53F	1991	

Previous Registrations:
F92WFA	9595RU	PSV436	A513LPP
PSV389	B224ATL	YSU906	DFW295T

Livery: Yellow and red (buses) ; white, blue and red (coaches)

Holloways of Scunthorpe is predominantly a contract operator but also runs a number of shopping services to the Freshney Place shopping centre in Grimsby. Plaxton Paramount 3200 bodies are favoured for the coaches in the fleet, typified by F92WFA, based on a Dennis Javelin. *Richard Belton*

HULLEY'S

Henry Hulley & Sons Ltd, Derwent Garage, Calver Road, Baslow, Derbyshire, DE45 1RF

1	F62XRP	Mercedes-Benz 609D	Reeve Burgess Beaver	C23F	1988	Ex Gibbs, Milton Keynes, 1992
2	D850PWN	Mercedes-Benz 609D	Reeve Burgess	B20F	1987	Ex Thomas Bros, Llandeilo, 1994
3	F24HGG	Volvo B10M-60	Plaxton Paramount 3500 III	C53F	1989	Ex Stagecoach East London, 1995
4	E289MMM	Van Hool T815	Van Hool Alizée	C49FT	1988	Ex Whites Coaches, Heathfield, 1995
5	A53HRE	Leyland Tiger TRCTL11/2R	Plaxton Paramount 3200 E	C53F	1984	Ex Midland, Auchterarder, 1993
6	E691UNE	Leyland Tiger TRCTL11/3RZ	Plaxton Paramount 3200 III	C53F	1988	Ex Shearings, 1992
7	E753HJF	Bedford YNT	Duple 320	C53F	1988	Ex Horton, Ripley, 1991
8	TJI4702	DAF MB230DKFL615	Plaxton Paramount	C50FT	1987	Ex Grangeburn, Motherwell, 1996
9	D451CNR	Bedford YNT	Duple 320	C53F	1987	Ex Horton, Ripley, 1990
10	G945JPW	Volvo B10M-60	Plaxton Paramount 3500 III	C53F	1989	Ex Express Travel, Perth, 1995
11	WCK143V	Leyland Leopard PSU3E/4R	Duple Dominant II Express	C51F	1980	Ex Midland, 1993
12	JMB329T	Leyland Leopard PSU3E/4R	Duple Dominant II	C49F	1979	Ex Happy Als, Birkenhead, 1992
14	Q364FVT	Leyland Leopard PSU3A/4RT	Willowbrook(1992)	B52F	1970	Ex Border, Burnley, 1995
15	CKC627X	Leyland Tiger TRCTL11/2R	Duple Dominant IV Express	C49F	1982	Ex Knotty Bus, Chesterton, 1995
16	YPD112Y	Leyland Tiger TRCTL11/2R	Duple Dominant IV Express	C53F	1983	Ex Whitelaw, Stonehouse, 1990
17	MCS404W	Leyland Leopard PSU3F/4R	Plaxton Supreme IV Express	C53F	1981	Ex Silver Service, Darley Dale, 1989
17	B873YYX	Leyland Tiger TRCTL11/3R	Duple Laser	C53F	1985	Ex KMJ Coaches, Golcar, 1991
18	ODM499V	Leyland Leopard PSU3E/4R	Duple Dominant II	C49F	1979	Ex Happy Al's, Birkenhead, 1992
19	WCK137V	Leyland Leopard PSU3E/4R	Duple Dominant II Express	C49F	1980	Ex Midland, 1993
20	OCY907R	Bristol VRT/SL3/501(6LXB)	Eastern Coach Works	H43/31F	1977	Ex Trent, 1994
21	D571VBV	Freight Rover Sherpa	Dormobile	B16F	1986	Ex Bakewell Coaches, 1996

Previous Registration:
Q364FVT   LJX817H   TJI4702   D63UKB, A19ALS, AKG231A, D627YCX

Named vehicle ; G945JPW, *Lady Diana II*

Livery: Blue and white

Hulley's and the former Silver Service local bus operations were merged under the Hulley's name some time ago with vehicles painted in the Silver Service white and blue colours. This second-hand Leyland Leopard was built for the Halifax municipal company in 1970 and gained the unusual 'Q' registration Q364FVT when re-bodied by Willowbrook. *Tony Wilson*

HORNSBY

Hornsby Travel Services Ltd, 51 High Street, Ashby, Scunthorpe,
North Lincolnshire, DN15 6EN

B1	KUC179P	Daimler Fleetline CRL6	Park Royal	H44/28D	1976	Ex London Transport, 1984
B2	KUC181P	Daimler Fleetline CRL6	Park Royal	H44/27D	1975	Ex London Transport, 1981
B3	SUA141R	Leyland Atlantean AN68/1R	Roe	H43/33F	1977	Ex Yorkshire Rider, 1994
B4	WNW160S	Leyland Atlantean AN68/1R	Roe	H43/33F	1977	Ex Yorkshire Rider, 1994
B5	XFW983S	Leyland Atlantean AN68/1R	Roe	H43/33F	1978	
B6	THX542S	Leyland Fleetline FE30ALRSp	Park Royal	H44/27D	1977	Ex London Buses, 1992
B7	THX173S	Leyland National 10351A/2R		B44F	1977	Ex London Buses, 1992
B8	FDC414V	Leyland Leopard PSU3E/4R	Plaxton Supreme IV Express	DP53F	1979	Ex Cleveland Transit, 1994
B12	3730RH	Leyland Tiger TRCTL11/3R	Plaxton Paramount 3500	C49FT	1984	
B13	7455RH	Leyland Tiger TRCTL11/3RZ	Plaxton Paramount 3500 II	C49FT	1985	
B14	RJI8583	Dennis Javelin 12SDA1908	Plaxton Paramount 3200 III	C57F	1988	Ex Bakers, Weston-super-Mare, 1994
B16	WUK155	Renault PR100.2	Northern Counties	B47F	1989	Ex Northern Counties, 1991
B17	RJI8608	Dennis Javelin 12SDA1907	Plaxton Paramount 3200 III	C53F	1989	Ex Bakers, Weston-super-Mare, 1994
B18	8955RH	Leyland Tiger TRCL10/3ARZM	Plaxton Paramount 3500 III	C49F	1989	
B19	G276VML	Renault PR100.2	Northern Counties	B48F	1989	Ex Parfitt's, Rhymney Bridge, 1994
B20	G365FOP	Mercedes-Benz 811D	Carlyle	B31F	1990	
B21	G366FOP	Mercedes-Benz 811D	Carlyle	B31F	1990	
B22	G409NAK	Renault Master T35D	Coachcraft	M15	1990	
B23	H898LOX	Mercedes-Benz 811D	Carlyle	B31F	1991	
B24	2732RH	Dennis Javelin 12SDA1929	Plaxton Paramount 3200 III	C53F	1991	
B25	L591CJW	Renault Trafic T35D	Jubilee	M12	1993	
B26	L804YTL	Mercedes-Benz 811D	Reeve Burgess Beaver	B31F	1994	
B27	971OHT	MAN 11.190	Caetano Algarve II	C35F	1994	
B28	8227RH	Volvo B10M-62	Plaxton Excalibur	C49F	1994	
B29	6053RH	Dennis Javelin 12SDA1929	Plaxton Première 350(1995)	C53F	1990	
B30	J718MFE	Toyota HiAce	Toyota	M8	1992	Ex van, 1995
B31	KUC997P	Leyland Fleetline FE30ALR	MCW	H44/29F	1976	Ex Garratt, Ashby, 1995
B32	J693AWB	Toyota HiAce	Toyota	M8	1992	Ex van, 1995
B33	G316XEE	Ford Transit VE6	Ford	M8	1990	Ex van, 1995
B34	N661OFE	Iveco Daily 59-12	Mellor	B27F	1996	
B35	1642RH	Dennis Javelin 12SDA2155	Plaxton Première 320	C55F	1996	

Previous Registrations:

1642RH	From new	7455RH	C248CKH	RJI8583	E503JWP
2732RH	H299GVL	8227RH	M21GAT	RJI8608	F908UPR
3730RH	From new	8955RH	From new	WUK155	F100AKB
6053RH	G414YAY	971OHT	From new		

Livery: Blue and red

Service 337 operates from Ashby to Scunthorpe in a joint operation with RoadCar. Seen leaving Scunthorpe bus station on this route is SUA141R is one of two Roe-bodied Leyland Atlanteans purchased in 1994 from Yorkshire Rider. *Tony Wilson*

Hornsby midibuses also carry the Bustlers brand name. G365FOP is one of three Carlyle-bodied Mercedes-Benz 811D vehicles in the fleet. It is seen in Hull when operating the Sunday tendered service 350 between the Humber port and Scunthorpe which is joint with Applebys. The Monday to Saturday service is also a joint operation, but between RoadCar and East Yorkshire.
David Longbottom

A fire at the Hornsby depot in 1994 caused the loss of a number of vehicles. While most were sent to the breakers as a result, one Dennis Javelin was less seriously damaged and the chassis saved for re-bodying. 6053RH emerged from Plaxtons in 1995 with a new Premiére body. *Richard Belton*

HUNT'S

F Hunt (Coach Hire) Ltd, 18 Market Place, Alford, Lincolnshire, LN13 9EB

w	NDX579	Leyland Leopard PSU3C/4R	Plaxton Supreme III Express	C47F	1976	Ex Chase, Chasetown, 1991
	HDL406N	Bristol VRT/SL2/6LX	Eastern Coach Works	H39/31F	1975	Ex Southern Vectis, 1991
	XFW951S	Bristol LH6L	Eastern Coach Works	B43F	1977	Ex Derby Blue Bus, 1995
	GMS289S	Leyland Leopard PSU3D/4R	Alexander AY	B53F	1978	Ex Tame Valley, Birmingham, 1993
	XFP502S	Bedford YMT	Plaxton Supreme III	C53F	1978	Ex Moor Dale, Newcastle, 1981
	DVL940T	Bedford YMT	Plaxton Supreme IV Express	C53F	1978	
	PNW308W	Leyland Leopard PSU3F/4R	Plaxton Supreme IV	C53F	1981	Ex Silverwing, Hedon, 1994
	5611FH	Leyland Tiger TRCTL11/3R	Plaxton Paramount 3500	C53F	1983	Ex The Londoners, Nunhead, 1986
	TWJ340Y	Dennis Falcon SDA410	East Lancashire	B52F	1983	Ex Ipswich, 1995
	TWJ341Y	Dennis Falcon SDA410	East Lancashire	B52F	1983	Ex Ipswich, 1995
	TWJ342Y	Dennis Falcon SDA410	East Lancashire	B52F	1983	Ex Ipswich, 1995
	9882FH	Leyland Tiger TRCTL11/3R	Van Hool Alizée	C51F	1984	Ex Travellers, Hounslow, 1988
	3613FH	Leyland Tiger TRCTL11/3RZ	Van Hool Alizée	C53F	1987	Ex Travellers, Hounslow, 1990
	3275FH	Volvo B10M-61	Van Hool Alizée	C53F	1987	Ex Lochview, Gourock, 1993
	E404EPE	Renault-Dodge S46	Northern Counties	B22F	1987	Ex McConnachie, Port Glasgow, 1994
	7683FH	Mercedes-Benz 609D	Whittaker Europa	C21F	1989	Ex Stockdale, Selby, 1995

Previous Registrations:
3275FH	D559MVR	5611FH	KGS492Y	9882FH	A140RMJ
3613FH	D230HMT	7683FH	F569EWJ	NDX579	JOX447P

Livery: White, red and grey

Hunt's started their Alford to Skegness service at de-regulation and have recently bought three Dennis Falcons for the route. Seen in Skegness is TWJ340Y. This East Lancashire-bodied Falcon was built for the Chesterfield fleet but has since been owned by the municipal company in Ipswich. It was on loan for a period to Warrington who painted it in their scheme and whose 'Welcome aboard' sign is retained. *Richard Belton*

HYLTON & DAWSON

A E Hylton, Chestnut Road, Glenfield, Leicester, LE3 8DB

Depots: Chestnut Road, Glenfield and West Street, Glenfield

WKE65S	Bedford YMT	Duple Dominant	B61F	1978	Ex Boro'line, Maidstone, 1984
CAX14V	Bedford YMT	Duple Dominant II	C53F	1980	Ex Bailey, Kirkby in Ashfield, 1988
HRO985V	Bedford YMT	Duple Dominant II	C53F	1979	Ex Kirby, Bushey Heath, 1983
CKN332Y	Bedford YMQ/S	Lex Maxeta	B37F	1982	Ex Vickers, Worksop, 1995
HD9923	Bedford YNT	Duple Laser	C53F	1984	
C321UFP	Bedford YNT	Duple 320	C53F	1986	
E760JAY	Bedford YNT	Duple 320	C55F	1988	
G424YAY	Dennis Javelin SDA1906	Duple 320	C53F	1990	

Previous Registrations:
HD9923   A705TEW

Livery: White, maroon and blue (buses) ; cream and maroon (coaches).

Hylton and Dawson are the established operator on the Leicester to Glenfield service. While coaches are often utilised a service bus was acquired for the route in 1995. CKN332Y is a short Bedford YMP fitted with the less common Lex Maxeta body. *Tony Wilson*

ISLE COACHES

C & J Bannister, 97 High Street, Owston Ferry,
North Lincolnshire, DN9 1RC

	NTV730M	Leyland National 1151/2R/0101		B28DL	1973	Ex South Yorkshire's Transport, 1992
	TET745S	Leyland Fleetline FE30AGR	Roe	H43/33F	1977	Ex South Yorkshire's Transport, 1986
w	SHE557S	Leyland Fleetline FE30AGR	Alexander AL	H45/33F	1978	Ex Astons, Kempsey, 1991
	GSC857T	Leyland Fleetline FE30AGR	Eastern Coach Works	H43/32F	1978	Ex Mayne, Manchester, 1995
	FSD89V	Leyland Leopard PSU3E/4R	Plaxton Supreme IV Express	C53F	1979	Ex Adamson, Edinburgh, 1986
	FWA472V	Leyland National NL106L11/1R		B44F	1980	Ex South Yorkshire's Transport, 1990
	FWA475V	Leyland National NL106L11/1R		B44F	1980	Ex South Yorkshire's Transport, 1991
	KWA24W	Leyland National NL116L11/1R		B52F	1980	Ex South Yorkshire's Transport, 1991
	LMS153W	Leyland Fleetline FE30AGR	Alexander AL	H44/31F	1980	Ex MTL Heysham, 1995
	GIJ9093	Volvo B10M-61	Van Hool Alizée	C49FT	1984	Ex Daisy, Broughton, 1992
	B152ALG	Leyland Tiger TRCTL11/2RH	Duple Laser 2	C49F	1984	Ex Andy James, Sherston, 1993
	B673EHL	Mercedes-Benz L307D	Reeve Burgess	M12	1985	
	D500RWF	Leyland Tiger TRCTL11/3RZ	Plaxton Paramount 3200 II	C57F	1987	Ex Wood's Coaches, Barnsley, 1992

Previous Registrations:
GIJ9093   A195MNE

Livery: Cream and blue

Bannister of Owston Ferry trades as Isle Coaches, the company name having its origin in the location of the operator's base in the Isle of Axeholme, an area to the west of the River Trent. Isle Coaches operates from the Island into Doncaster, and this photograph KWA24W is seen leaving the Owston Ferry terminus for the Yorkshire town. This Leyland National 2 was purchased from SYT in 1991.
Steve Sanderson

JOHNSON'S

Johnson's Coaches, Ashlea, Thornton Road, Goxhill, Barrow-upon-Humber,
North Lincolnshire, DN19 7HN

ARB527T	Bedford YMT	Plaxton Supreme III Express	C49F	1978	Ex Barton, 1988
NLG909T	Leyland Leopard PSU5C/4R	Plaxton Supreme IV	C53F	1979	Ex Meredith, Malpas, 1995
LUA251V	Volvo B58-61	Plaxton Supreme IV	C53F	1980	Ex Amport & District, Thruxton, 1992
HAX6W	Bedford YMT	Duple Dominant	C53F	1980	Ex Carnell, Sutton Bridge, 1996
B496UNB	Leyland Tiger TRCTL11/3RZ	Plaxton Paramount 3500 II	C53F	1985	Ex Shearings, 1992
C329PEW	Leyland Tiger TRCTL11/3RZ	Plaxton Paramount 3200 II	C53F	1986	Ex Premier Travel Services, 1995
D956WJH	Freight Rover Sherpa	Dormobile	B16F	1986	Ex Hampshire Bus, 1993

Previous Registrations:
NLG909T   EDF270T, MIB614, ARF930T, 469KNP

Livery: Cream

Johnson's of Goxhill operate a market day service from Barton-on-Humber to Scunthorpe. Seen at the Scunthorpe terminus of this route is ARB525T. This Plaxton Supreme-bodied Bedford YMT was sold to Johnson's in 1988 after only ten years service with its original owner Barton, the major transport company whose buses are now part of Trent. *Phillip Stephenson*

JOHNSON BROS

C B & C A Johnson, Green Lane Garage, Green Acres, Green Lane, Hodthorpe,
Derbyshire, S80 4XR

	OSF305G	Bristol VRT/SL/6LX	Eastern Coach Works	H43/31F	1969	Ex Southern Vectis, 1986
	OSF307G	Bristol VRT/SL/6LX	Eastern Coach Works	H43/31F	1969	Ex Southern Vectis, 1986
w	NGM168G	Bristol VRT/SL/6LX	Eastern Coach Works	H43/31F	1969	Ex Southern Vectis, 1986
	PKE810M	Bristol VRT/SL/6LX	Eastern Coach Works	H43/34F	1974	Ex Maidstone & District, 1988
	HTU155N	Bristol VRT/SL2/6LX	Eastern Coach Works	H43/31F	1975	Ex Crosville, 1989
	JWL993N	Bristol VRT/SL2/6LX	Eastern Coach Works	H43/34F	1975	Ex Moffat & Williamson, Gauldry, 1994
	JWL997N	Bristol VRT/SL2/6LX	Eastern Coach Works	H43/31F	1975	Ex Moffat & Williamson, Gauldry, 1994
	HWE826N	Bristol VRT/SL2/6LX	Eastern Coach Works	H43/34F	1975	Ex Yorkshire Traction, 1993
	KKY833P	Bristol VRT/SL3/501	Eastern Coach Works	H43/34F	1976	Ex Yorkshire Traction, 1993
	KKY835P	Bristol VRT/SL3/501	Eastern Coach Works	H43/34F	1976	Ex RoadCar, 1994
	OWE854R	Bristol VRT/SL3/501	Eastern Coach Works	H43/31F	1977	Ex Yorkshire Traction, 1993
	OWE857R	Bristol VRT/SL3/501	Eastern Coach Works	H43/31F	1977	Ex Yorkshire Traction, 1993
	OWE858R	Bristol VRT/SL3/501	Eastern Coach Works	H43/31F	1977	Ex Yorkshire Traction, 1993
	RWA859R	Bristol VRT/SL3/501	Eastern Coach Works	H43/31F	1977	Ex RoadCar, 1994
	RWT544R	Bristol VRT/SL3/6LX	Eastern Coach Works	H43/31F	1977	Ex Moffat & Williamson, Gauldry, 1994
	RWT546R	Bristol VRT/SL3/6LX	Eastern Coach Works	H43/31F	1977	Ex Moffat & Williamson, Gauldry, 1994
	TDT864S	Bristol VRT/SL3/501	Eastern Coach Works	H43/31F	1977	Ex Yorkshire Traction, 1993
	MIW2422	Bristol VRT/SL3/501	Eastern Coach Works	H43/31F	1978	Ex Clarkson, South Elmsall, 1994
	VPP957S	Bedford YMT	Plaxton Supreme III	C53F	1978	
	ASP281T	Leyland Leopard PSU5C/4R	Plaxton Supreme IV	C57F	1979	Ex Moffat & Williamson, Gauldry, 1993
	JTU131V	Volvo B58-56	Plaxton Supreme	C57F	1980	Ex ????, 1994
	LHE601W	Volvo B58-56	Plaxton Supreme IV	C53F	1981	
	B833KRY	Volvo B10M-61	Plaxton Paramount 3500	C53F	1984	
	C446SJU	Ford Transit 190D	Robin Hood	B16F	1985	Ex Glenvic, Bristol, 1995
	C509TJF	Ford Transit 190D	Alexander	B16F	1985	Ex Midland Fox, 1994
	JBT16S	Volvo B10M-61	Plaxton Paramount 3500 III	C53F	1987	
	E911EAY	Volvo B10M-61	Plaxton Paramount 3500 III	C57F	1989	
	E43MMT	Mercedes-Benz L307D	Reeve Burgess	M12	1987	Ex WHM, Hutton, 1990
	F238MVS	Volvo B10M-61	Van Hool Alizée	C57F	1989	Ex Sworder, Walkern, 1992
	G39HKY	Scania K113CRB	Van Hool Alizée	C49FT	1989	Ex Top Deck, Horsell, 1992
	JBT3S	Volvo B10M-60	Van Hool Alizée	C53F	1990	
	H4JBT	Scania K93CRB	Duple 320	C59F	1990	Ex Snell, Newton Abbott, 1995
	J1JBT	Scania K113CRB	Van Hool Alizée	C51FT	1991	
	L3JBT	Scania K113CRB	Van Hool Alizée	C49FT	1994	
	M2JBT	Toyota Coaster HZB50R	Caetano Optimo II	C21F	1994	
	N1JBT	Scania K113CRB	Van Hool Alizée	C46FT	1995	
	N2JBT	Scania K113CRB	Van Hool Alizée	C46FT	1996	

Previous Registrations:
ASP281T   EDF261T, FSU375   JBT3S   G378NHL   MIW2422   VHB679S
H4JBT   H79COD   JBT16S   D366CBC

Named vehicles: B833KRY, *Euroliner I* ; JBT16S, *Euroliner III* ; E911EAY, *Eurocruiser I* ; JBT3S, *Euromaster I* ;
J1JBT, *Euromaster II* ; F238MVS, *Eurotourer I* ; L3JBT, *Eurostar I* ; M2JBT, *Minitourer II* ; N1JBT, *Eurostar II* ;
N2JBT, *Euroclass I*.

Livery: Blue and gold

Johnson Bros of Worksop operate a substantial fleet of Eastern Coach Works-bodied Bristol VR double-deckers primarily on contract work. Many of these vehicles were obtained from Yorkshire Traction group companies though HTU155N was purchased from Crosville in 1989. *Steve Sanderson*

Johnson Bros also operate a varied coach fleet including a number of recently built Scanias. This example carries one of the last Duple 320 bodies produced before the Blackpool factory closed. The 320 indicates that the coach is 3.20 metres high. H4JBT was photographed in London. *Colin Lloyd*

London Buses purchased a large number of dual-door Leyland Nationals most of which have long since left the capital. Kettlewell's of Retford have removed the middle door from THX120S and as a result the seating capacity has been increased from 36 to 44. This vehicle is shown entering Retford bus station. *Tony Wilson*

The largest vehicle in the Kettlewell's fleet is HIL4619. This is a Neoplan Skyliner coach which was built to carry 75 passengers. Some of Kettlewell's vehicles run on the licence of associated company Pegasus Coachways though all carry Kettlewell fleet names. *Tony Wilson*

KETTLEWELL'S

Kettlewell (Retford) Ltd, Grove Street, Retford, Nottinghamshire, DN22 6LA
Pegasus Coachways Ltd, Grove Street, Retford, Nottinghamshire, DN22 6LA

NEV678M	Leyland National 1151/1R/0402		B52F	1973	Ex Constable, Long Melford, 1995
GHV67N	Daimler Fleetline CRL6	Park Royal	H45/32F	1975	Ex Cutting, Brockley, 1986
JOV701P	Bristol VRT/SL2/6LX	MCW	H43/33F	1975	Ex West Midlands, 1986
JOV777P	Volvo-Ailsa B55-10	Alexander AV	H44/35F	1976	Ex London Buses, 1991
JOV780P	Volvo-Ailsa B55-10	Alexander AV	H44/35F	1976	Ex London Buses, 1991
THX120S	Leyland National 10351A/2R		B44F	1978	Ex London Buses, 1991
THX196S	Leyland National 10351A/2R		B36D	1978	Ex London Buses, 1991
AYR315T	Leyland National 10351A/2R		B44F	1979	Ex London Buses, 1991
HAL598R	Volvo B58-56	Irizar	C53F	1980	
JRR359Y	Ford R1014	Plaxton Supreme IV	C45F	1980	
LVO46W	Volvo B58-56	Plaxton Supreme IV	C53F	1980	
BFU909W	Volvo B58-56	Plaxton Supreme IV	C57F	1980	
670PUO	Van Hool T815	Van Hool Alizée	C40FT	1982	Ex Moore, Sleaford, 1990
WRA688Y	Leyland Leopard PSU3E/4R	Duple Dominant IV	C53F	1982	
WXH612	Aüwaerter Neoplan N216H	Aüwaerter Jetliner	C49FT	1983	
KXI7014	Aüwaerter Neoplan N216H	Aüwaerter Jetliner	C49FT	1983	
XFP1Y	DAF SB2005DHU585	Smit Euroliner	C53F	1983	
XFP2Y	DAF SB2005DHU585	Smit Euroliner	C53F	1983	
JIL7899	Volvo B10M-61	Jonckheere Jubilee P90	CH49/9F	1983	
LIL2837	Scania K112CLS	Jonckheere Jubilee P50	C49FT	1983	Ex Slatterys, Kentish Town, 1991
A254LLL	Scania K112CLS	Jonckheere Jubilee P50	C49FT	1983	Ex Slatterys, Kentish Town, 1991
KET6	Scania K112CRS	Ajokki Deltaplan	C49FT	1984	
KXI6744	Scania K112CLS	Jonckheere Jubilee P50	C51F	1984	Ex Slatterys, Kentish Town, 1991
B429DDT	Bedford YNT	Duple Laser 2	C53F	1984	Ex Morbey, Tickhill, 1988
B493UNB	Leyland Tiger TRCTL11/3RZ	Plaxton Paramount 3500 II	C53F	1985	Ex Rosemary, Terrington St Clement, 1993
C181KET	DAF SB2005DHU585	Smit Orionliner	C53F	1986	
C167JVL	Mercedes-Benz L307D	Coachwork	C12F	1985	
D538VRR	Renault-Dodge S56	East Lancashire	B29F	1987	
D169VRA	Renault-Dodge S56	East Lancashire	B29F	1987	
HIL4619	Aüwaerter Neoplan N122/3	Aüwaerter Skyliner	CH75F	1987	Ex Bestall, Loxley, 1994
E861URH	Mercedes-Benz 407D	Coachcraft	C15F	1988	
G704HPW	Leyland Tiger TRCTL11/3ARZM	Plaxton Paramount 3500 III	C53F	1989	Ex Rosemary, Terrington St Clement, 1993
P6KET	Scania K113CRB	Van Hool Alizée	C49FT	1996	

Previous Registrations:

670PUO	WDG750X	JIL7899	A147JTA	LIL2837	6520ZX, A253LLL
A254LLL	6461ZX	KET6	A60WVL	WXH612	MUL606Y
BFU909W	LVO47W, KET6	KXI6744	6519ZX, B728RLM		
HIL4619	D327NWG	KXI7014	TWG560Y		

Livery: White, black and light brown

KIME'S

J R & SR Kime, The Garage, Sleaford Road, Folkingham, Sleaford, Lincolnshire, NG34 0SB

Fleet No	Chassis	Body	Seating	Year	Notes
SJI3696	Daimler Fleetline CRG6LXB-33	Alexander J	H48/34F	1971	Ex Moffat & Williamson, Gauldry, 1985
SJI6321	Leyland Fleetline FE30ALR	MCW	H43/33F	1976	Ex West Midlands Travel, 1989
SJI6322	Leyland Fleetline FE30AGR	Roe	H45/29D	1977	Ex Grimsby-Cleethorpes, 1993
GMS283S	Leyland Leopard PSU3E/4R	Alexander AY	B53F	1978	Ex Kelvin Scottish, 1988
SJI6323	Leyland Fleetline FE30ALR(AGR)	MCW	H44/24D	1978	Ex London Buses, 1992
SJI6567	Leyland Fleetline FE30AGR	Northern Counties	H43/31F	1978	Ex Cleveland Transit, 1990
SJI6568	Leyland Fleetline FE30AGR	Northern Counties	H43/31F	1978	Ex Cleveland Transit, 1990
SJI6569	Bristol VRT/SL3/501(6LXB)	Eastern Coach Works	H43/31F	1978	Ex Nottingham Omnibus, 1994
FCT703V	Bedford YMT	Plaxton Supreme IV Express	C53F	1980	
SJI6571	Bristol VRT/SL3/501	Eastern Coach Works	H43/31F	1980	Ex Red and White, 1994
JCT257W	Bedford YMT	Plaxton Supreme IV Express	C53F	1981	
SJI6570	Leyland Atlantean AN68B/1R	Alexander AL	H45/29D	1981	Ex Mainline, 1993
KVL442Y	Bedford YNT	Plaxton Paramount 3200 E	C53F	1983	
B193DVL	Bedford YNT	Plaxton Paramount 3200	C53F	1985	
B705GFE	Bedford YNT	Plaxton Paramount 3200	C53F	1985	
C925WFO	Bedford YNT	Plaxton Paramount 3200 II	C53F	1986	
DAZ4300	Volvo B10M-61	Van Hool Alizée	C53F	1987	Ex Cambridge Coach Services, 1993
DAZ4301	Volvo B10M-61	Plaxton Paramount 3200 III	C53F	1987	
DAZ4302	Dennis Javelin 12SDA1907	Plaxton Paramount 3200 III	C53F	1988	

Previous Registrations:

DAZ4300	D345KVE	SJI6322	MBE612R	SJI3696	PRG122J
DAZ4301	E686BTL	SJI6323	THX524S	SJI6569	LHG439T
DAZ4302	E174FFW	SJI6567	YVN515T	SJI6570	JKW299W
SJI6321	KON306P	SJI6568	YVN518T	SJI6571	GTX749W

Livery: Green and cream

Kime's are based at Folkingham, near Sleaford, in the heart of rural Lincolnshire, but Kime's buses can be seen some distance from their home base. Spalding is the location of this view of SJI6569, one of many double deck vehicles in the fleet to acquire Northern Irish number plates. This Bristol VRT was new to Ribble but obtained by Kime's from the short lived Nottingham Omnibus operation.
Roy Marshall

66

KINCH

Kinchline Ltd, G K Kinch, 13-21 Hayhill Industrial Estate, Sileby Road, Barrow-upon-Soar, Leicestershire, LE12 8LD

Depots : Sileby Road, Barrow-upon-Soar, Bishops Meadow, Loughborough.

EFN178L	Leyland National 1151/1R/2402		B44FL	1973	Ex East Kent, 1989
TVP852S	Leyland National 11351A/1R		DP45F	1978	Ex Frontline, Tamworth, 1993
STK132T	Leyland Atlantean AN68/1R	Roe	H43/31F	1979	Ex Citybus, Plymouth, 1996
STK135T	Leyland Atlantean AN68/1R	Roe	H43/31F	1979	Ex Citybus, Plymouth, 1996
BAU674T	Leyland Atlantean AN68/1R	Northern Counties	H47/31D	1979	Ex Nottingham, 1996
BAU675T	Leyland Atlantean AN68/1R	Northern Counties	H47/31D	1979	Ex Nottingham, 1996
BRC677T	Leyland Atlantean AN68/1R	Northern Counties	H47/31D	1979	Ex Nottingham, 1996
BRC678T	Leyland Atlantean AN68/1R	Northern Counties	H47/31D	1979	Ex Nottingham, 1996
BRC679T	Leyland Atlantean AN68/1R	Northern Counties	H47/31D	1979	Ex Nottingham, 1996
FDC419V	Leyland Leopard PSU3E/4R	Plaxton Supreme IV Express	DP55F	1980	Ex Cleveland Transit, 1994
FDC420V	Leyland Leopard PSU3E/4R	Plaxton Supreme IV Express	DP55F	1980	Ex Cleveland Transit, 1994
RGS820V	Leyland National NL116L11/1R		B22FL	1980	Ex Fife Scottish, 1996
RGS822V	Leyland National NL116L11/1R		B52F	1980	Ex Fife Scottish, 1996
MSO15W	Leyland National NL116L11/1R		B52F	1980	Ex Fife Scottish, 1996
PNW599W	Leyland National NL116L11/1R		B52F	1980	Ex Yorkshire Rider, 1995
PNW600W	Leyland National NL116L11/1R		B52F	1980	Ex Yorkshire Rider, 1995

T51	WYV51T	Leyland Titan TNLXB/2RRSp	Park Royal	H44/22D	1979	Ex London Buses, 1994
T53	WYV53T	Leyland Titan TNLXB/2RRSp	Park Royal	H44/22D	1979	Ex London Buses, 1994
T54	WYV54T	Leyland Titan TNLXB/2RRSp	Park Royal	H44/24D	1979	Ex London Buses, 1994
T62	WYV62T	Leyland Titan TNLXB/2RRSp	Park Royal	H44/24D	1979	Ex London Buses, 1994
T81	CUL81V	Leyland Titan TNLXB/2RRSp	Park Royal	H44/31F	1980	Ex Nottingham, 1995
T119	CUL119V	Leyland Titan TNLXB/2RRSp	Park Royal	H44/31F	1980	Ex Nottingham, 1995

In recent times Kinch have had a major presence on the Nottingham to Clifton Estate route, though the operations in this area were discontinued in the spring of 1996. Photographed in Leicester St Margaret's Street are WYV54T and KYV342X, two of the many Leyland Titans purchased by Kinch from London Buses when the Nottingham services were expanding, though this type will shortly become extinct with the arrival of new Dennis Darts. *Malc McDonald*

Kinch is now the major operator in Loughborough with operations expanding as a result of the acquisition of a number of routes previously worked by Midland Fox. Investment in new vehicles for the Loughborough services has seen six Plaxton Pointer-bodied Dennis Darts enter service with another six low-floor versions due. L404CJF is seen bound for Shelthorpe Road. *Malc McDonald*

401	L401CJF	Dennis Dart 9.8SDL3035	Plaxton Pointer	B40F	1994	
402	L402CJF	Dennis Dart 9.8SDL3035	Plaxton Pointer	B40F	1994	
403	L403CJF	Dennis Dart 9.8SDL3035	Plaxton Pointer	B40F	1994	
404	L404CJF	Dennis Dart 9.8SDL3035	Plaxton Pointer	B40F	1994	
405	M405HFP	Dennis Dart 9.8SDL3035	Plaxton Pointer	B40F	1994	
406	M406HFP	Dennis Dart 9.8SDL3035	Plaxton Pointer	B40F	1994	
407	P407	Dennis Dart SLF	Plaxton Pointer	B40F	1996	
408	P408	Dennis Dart SLF	Plaxton Pointer	B40F	1996	
409	P409	Dennis Dart SLF	Plaxton Pointer	B40F	1996	
410	P410	Dennis Dart SLF	Plaxton Pointer	B40F	1996	
411	P411	Dennis Dart SLF	Plaxton Pointer	B40F	1996	
412	P412	Dennis Dart SLF	Plaxton Pointer	B40F	1996	
	P	Optare Excel L1070	Optare	B45F	1996	
	P	Optare Excel L1070	Optare	B45F	1996	
471	HIL7771	Leyland Leopard PSU3E/4R	Willowbrook Warrior (1991)	B48F	1980	Ex Tees & District, 1991
473	HIL7773	Leyland Leopard PSU3E/4R	Willowbrook Warrior (1991)	B48F	1980	Ex Tees & District, 1991
807	L807YBC	Mercedes-Benz 709D	Dormobile Routemaker	B27F	1993	
809	L809CJF	Mercedes-Benz 709D	Marshall C19	B27F	1994	
810	L810CJF	Mercedes-Benz 709D	Marshall C19	B27F	1994	
811	L811CJF	Mercedes-Benz 709D	Marshall C19	B27F	1994	
812	L812CJF	Mercedes-Benz 709D	Marshall C19	B27F	1994	
813	L813DJU	Mercedes-Benz 709D	Marshall C19	B27F	1994	
814	L814DJU	Mercedes-Benz 709D	Marshall C19	B27F	1994	
815	M815KJU	Mercedes-Benz 709D	Plaxton Beaver	B27F	1995	
816	N816PJU	Mercedes-Benz 709D	Plaxton Beaver	B27F	1995	
817	N817PJU	Mercedes-Benz 709D	Plaxton Beaver	B27F	1995	
818	N818RFP	Mercedes-Benz 709D	Plaxton Beaver	B27F	1996	
819	N819RFP	Mercedes-Benz 709D	Plaxton Beaver	B27F	1996	
820	N820RFP	Mercedes-Benz 709D	Plaxton Beaver	B27F	1996	
821	N821RFP	Mercedes-Benz 811D	Plaxton Beaver	B31F	1996	
821	P822	Mercedes-Benz 711D	Plaxton Beaver	B27F	On order	

Previous Registrations:
HIL7771 TUP582V   HIL7773 AGR227W

Livery: Two-tone blue and yellow

*Opposite:*The Kinch fleet has seen a major influx of new vehicles in thelast three years so that by the end of september 1996, when all the new Dart SLFs have arrived, all 28 front line vehicles will be less than three years old. The Leyland nationals, Leopard and Atlanteans will then form a reserve fleet solely used for contract work. Shown here are new minibus 817, N817PJU and Leopard 471, HIL7771.

121 LEICESTER
KINCHBUS
KINCHBUS
N817 PJU

70 SCHOOL SERVICE
KINCHBUS
KINCHBUS
KINCHBUS
WILLOWBROOK
WARRIOR
HIL 7771

LAMCOTE

Lamcote Motors (Radcliffe) Ltd, Main Road, Radcliffe on Trent,
Nottinghamshire, NG12 2BG

A subsidiary of Dunn Line

w	YHA361J	Ford R312	Plaxton Derwent	DP21F	1971	Ex Midland Red, 1983
	232ENX	Bristol VRT/SL2/6LX	Eastern Coach Works	H43/34F	1974	Ex Yorkshire Traction, 1990
	MTX458	Volvo B58-61	Duple Dominant	C45DL	1976	Ex Birkett, Sabden, 1995
	UCK956R	Volvo B58-56	Duple	C53F	1976	Ex Dunn Line, 1996
	WOI8022	Bristol VRT/SL3/501	Eastern Coach Works	H43/31F	1977	Ex Trent, 1991
	38FGC	Leyland Leopard PSU3E/4R	Duple Dominant II	C53F	1978	Ex National Travel East, 1987
	FXI7116	Ford R1114	Plaxton Supreme III	C47DL	1978	Ex Copeland, Meir, 1995
	FDO802	Leyland Leopard PSU5C/4R	Plaxton Supreme IV	C25FL	1979	Ex Winged Fellowship Trust, 1992
	7822VW	Ford R1114	Plaxton Supreme IV	C53F	1979	Ex Nash, Smethwick, 1984
	KCH472V	Ford R1114	Duple Dominant II	C49F	1979	Ex Ford, Warley, 1981
	577TVO	Ford R1014	Wadham Stringer Vanguard	DP29F	1982	Ex London Borough of Greenwich, 1993
	SIA4683	Volvo B10M-61	Duple Goldliner	C49FT	1982	Ex McColl, Balloch, 1996
	EUG125Y	DAF MB200DKTL600	Caetano Alpha	C53F	1982	Ex Hallam, Newthorpe, 1996
	YIA6276	DAF MB200DKFL600	Plaxton Paramount 3200	C49F	1983	Ex Carryden, Catchgate, 1991
	20VWC	Leyland Royal Tiger B54	Roe Doyen	C49FT	1984	Ex Kentish Bus, 1989
	326WAL	Leyland Royal Tiger B54	Roe Doyen	C49FT	1984	Ex Kentish Bus, 1989
	A168OHJ	DAF SB2300DHS585	Berkhof Esprite 340	C53F	1984	Ex Wakefield, Saltburn, 1996
	966GXP	DAF SB2300DHS585	Berkhof Esprite 340	C49FT	1985	Ex Bolton, Farnham, 1991
	C538TJF	Ford Transit 190D	Rootes	B16F	1986	Ex Dunn Line, 1996
	WRC419	Van Hool T815	Van Hool Acron	C53F	1988	Ex Poole, Wormley, 1994
	J4KEC	Plaxton 425	Lorraine	C53FT	1993	Ex Abbeyways, Halifax, 1995

Previous Registrations:

20VWC	A653EMY	7822VW	AOB825T	A168OHJ	A168OHJ, 7326KF
232ENX	PHE816M	966GXP	B677BTW	MTX458	MDW194P
326WAL	A652EMY	FDO802	DRB62T	SIA4683	FHS753X
38FGC	UWA96S	FXI7116	WLJ223S, SDK765, TDK443S	WOI8022	PVO818R
577TVO	OHV194Y	J4KEC	L414FVH	WRC419	E999DGS
				YIA6276	ANA460Y

Livery: Silver/White, green and black

The Lamcote business was purchased by Dunn Line of Nottingham in early 1996. Livery changes are taking place to bring in the Dunn Line scheme but using Lamcote's green and black. The fleet contains a pair of Leyland Royal Tigers with Roe Doyen bodies. They were part of the National Travel London fleet before joining Kentish Bus. 326WAL, one of the pair is in a silver livery with green and black stripes that sweep over the rear wheel.
Tony Wilson

LEICESTER CITYBUS

Leicester Citybus Ltd, Abbey Park Road, Leicester, LE4 5AH

A subsidiary of FirstBus plc

5	RJI5704	LAG G355Z	LAG Panoramic	C49F	1988	Ex Durbin Coaches, 1996	
6	RJI5706	LAG G355Z	LAG Panoramic	C49F	1987	Ex Durbin Coaches, 1996	
7	XDU178	Volvo B10M-61	Van Hool Alizée	C49FT	1985	Ex Mair's Coaches, 1995	
8	542GRT	Volvo B10M-61	Jonckheere Jubilee P599	C51FT	1987	Ex The Londoners, 1995	
19	FFK312	Leyland Tiger TRCTL11/2R	Plaxton Paramount 3200 E	C49F	1983		
20	A14SMT	Leyland Tiger TRCTL11/3RZ	Duple Caribbean 2	C51F	1984	Ex SMT, 1996	
21	B569LSC	Leyland Tiger TRCTL11/3RH	Duple Caribbean 2	C49F	1985	Ex SMT, 1996	
22	EGB50T	Leyland Leopard PSU3E/4R	Alexander AYS	DP53F	1978	Ex KCB Network, 1995	
23	B160WRN	Leyland Tiger TRCTL11/3RH	Duple Laser 2	C53F	1985	Ex Ribble, 1988	
24	B165WRN	Leyland Tiger TRCTL11/3RH	Duple Laser 2	C53F	1985	Ex Ribble, 1988	

31-35   MCW Metrobus DR102/35   Alexander RL   H45/33F   1983

31	AUT31Y	32	AUT32Y	33	AUT33Y	34	AUT34Y	35	AUT35Y

40-56   Dennis Dominator DDA142*   East Lancashire   H43/33F   1981-82 *49-52 are DDA141
                                                                                                                                         53-56 are DDA146

40	TBC40X	44	TBC44X	48	TBC48X	51	TBC51X	54	TBC54X
41	TBC41X	45	TBC45X	49	TBC49X	52	TBC52X	55	TBC55X
42	TBC42X	46	TBC46X	50	TBC50X	53	TBC53X	56	TBC56X
43	TBC43X	47	TBC47X						

57-78   Dennis Dominator DDA155*   East Lancashire   H43/33F   1982-83 *70 is DDA160,
                                                                                                                                         71-4 are DDA173, 75-8 are DDA168

57	VAY57X	62	XJF62Y	67	XJF67Y	71	A71FRY	75	A75FRY
58	VAY58X	63	XJF63Y	68	XJF68Y	72	A72FRY	76	A76FRY
59	VAY59X	64	XJF64Y	69	XJF69Y	73	A73FRY	77	A77FRY
60	XJF60Y	65	XJF65Y	70	AUT70Y	74	A74FRY	78	A78FRY
61	XJF61Y	66	XJF66Y						

The Leicester Citybus fleet contains a small number of MCW Metrobuses fitted with Alexander RL bodies. Some came from fellow First Bus subsidiary Midland Bluebird but 34, AUT34Y is one of five indigenous examples.
Phillip Stephenson

79-86			Dennis Dominator DDA1102*		East Lancashire	H43/33F	1984-85	*81-3 are DDA1002	
								*84-86 are DDA901	
79	B79MJF	81	B81MJF	83	B83MJF	85	B85MRY	86	B86MRY
80	B80MJF	82	B82MJF	84	B84MRY				
87-99			Dennis Dominator DDA1015		East Lancashire	H46/33F	1988		
87	E87HNR	90	E90HNR	93	E93HNR	96	E96HNR	98	E98HNR
88	E88HNR	91	E91HNR	94	E94HNR	97	E97HNR	99	E99HNR
89	E89HNR	92	E92HNR	95	E95HNR				
143-152			Dennis Dominator DDA1024		East Lancashire	H46/33F	1989		
143	F143MBC	149	F149MBC	150	F150MBC	151	F151MBC	152	F152MBC
146	F146MBC								
154	FJF193		Leyland Titan PD2/1		Leyland	H33/29R	1950		
179-200			Dennis Dominator DDA120*		East Lancashire	H43/33F	1978-80	*188/98 are DDA110	
								200 is DDA110A	
179	FUT179V	184	FUT184V	187	FUT187V	198	YRY198T	200	YRY200T
182	FUT182V	185	FUT185V	188	YRY188T				
205	NFP205W		Dennis Dominator DDA131		East Lancashire	H43/33F	1980		
206	MUT206W		Dennis Dominator DDA131		East Lancashire	H43/33F	1980		
233	UFP233S		Dennis Dominator DDA101		East Lancashire	H43/31F	1977		
240-264			Dennis Dominator DDA120		East Lancashire	H43/33F	1978-81		
240	FUT240V	245w	FUT245V	252	MUT252W	257	MUT257W	260w	MUT260W
241w	FUT241V	250	FUT250V	256w	MUT256W	259	MUT259W	264	MUT264W
265	ULS637X		MCW Metrobus DR102/28		Alexander RL	H45/33F	1982	Ex Midland Bluebird, 1994	
266	ULS642X		MCW Metrobus DR104/10		Alexander RL	H45/33F	1982	Ex Midland Bluebird, 1994	
267	BLS423Y		MCW Metrobus DR102/33		Alexander RL	H45/33F	1983	Ex Midland Bluebird, 1994	
268	BLS432Y		MCW Metrobus DR102/33		Alexander RL	H45/33F	1983	Ex Midland Bluebird, 1994	
269	BLS443Y		MCW Metrobus DR102/33		Alexander RL	H45/33F	1983	Ex Midland Bluebird, 1994	
270	ULS636X		MCW Metrobus DR102/28		Alexander RL	H45/33F	1982	Ex Midland Bluebird, 1994	
401-407			Leyland Tiger TRBL10/3ARZA*		Alexander N	B55F	1988-89	Ex Timeline, 1996	
								401/7 are TRBCL10/3ARZA	
401	F50ENF	403	G53RND	405	G55RND	406	G56RND	407	F37ENF
402	F38ENF	404	G54RND						
501-510			Mercedes-Benz O405		Optare Prisma	B49F	1995		
501	M501GRY	503	M503GRY	505	M505GRY	507	M507GRY	509	M509GRY
502	M502GRY	504	M504GRY	506	M506GRY	508	M508GRY	510	M510GRY
611-619			Dennis Falcon SDA422		East Lancashire EL2000	B48F	1991-92		
611	H611EJF	613	H613EJF	615	H615EJF	617	K617SBC	619	K619SBC
612	H612EJF	614	H614EJF	616	H616EJF	618	K618SBC		

Opposite top: Leicester Citybus, the FirstBus operation in the East Midlands shares several of the management tasks with the Northampton operation. Both were county towns of neighbouring counties. The fleet has been painted in the GRT-style with cream and two-tone red liveries. The upper picture shows one of the remaining Dennis Dominators, a type which Leicester pioneered. The majority featured East Lancashire bodywork similar to that carried by 184, FUT184V, though a variant on the style can be seen on another example in the background.
Opposite bottom: An interesting acquisition by Leicester Citybus in 1995 was a batch of seven Leyland Tiger buses previously with Timeline and new to Shearings. These carry the Alexander N-type body which was only built at the Belfast plant where the new low-floor Ultra is now built. Pictured in the city shortly after repaint is 401, F50ENF.

184
Leicester citybus
22
Evington
A fab-tabulous new release.
Leicester citybus
184
FUT 184V
L563 YNR
Leicester citybus

HEADLINES
YRES·MONSELL
Leicester Citybus
401
Leicester Citybus
401
F50 ENF

As part of a commitment to upgrade its bus fleet, the GRT Group was placing air conditioned Mercedes-Benz buses into service when First Bus was formed. This vehicle, 509, M509GRY, is one of ten Optare Prisma-bodied O405 vehicles allocated to the Leicester Citybus fleet that carry the predominantly cream 'GRT Advance' livery. *Tony Wilson*

620-626　　Dennis Falcon HC SDA422　　Northern Counties Paladin　　B48F　　1993

620	K620SBC	622	K622SBC	624	L624XFP	625	L625XFP	626	L626XFP
621	K621SBC	623	L623XFP						

718-737　　Iveco Daily 49-10　　Carlyle Dailybus　　B25F　　1989

718w	F718PFP	724w	F724PFP	728	G728WJU	732	G732WJU	735	G735WJU
720u	F720PFP	725w	F725PFP	729	G729WJU	733	G733WJU	736	G736WJU
721w	F721PFP	726w	F726PFP	730	G730WJU	734	G734WJU	737	G737WJU
723	F723PFP	727	G727WJU	731	G731WJU				

746-761　　Renault-Dodge S56　　Northern Counties　　B25F*　　1991-93　*753/4 are DP25F

746	K746VJU	750	K750VJU	753	J753MFP	756	J756MFP	759	J759NNR
748	K748VJU	751	H751ENR	754	J754MFP	757	J757MFP	760	K760SBC
749	K749VJU	752	H752ENR	755	J755MFP	758	J758NNR	761	K761SBC

763	D321REF	Renault-Dodge S56	Northern Counties	B19F	1986	Ex Cleveland Transit, 1992	
767u	G257LWF	Renault-Dodge S56	Reeve Burgess Beaver	B23F	1989	Ex Rider Group, 1996	
768	G258LWF	Renault-Dodge S56	Reeve Burgess Beaver	B23F	1989	Ex Rider Group, 1996	
769	G253LWF	Renault-Dodge S56	Reeve Burgess Beaver	B23F	1989	Ex Rider Group, 1996	
770	G255LWF	Renault-Dodge S56	Reeve Burgess Beaver	B23F	1989	Ex Rider Group, 1996	
771	G256LWF	Renault-Dodge S56	Reeve Burgess Beaver	B23F	1989	Ex Rider Group, 1996	
772	G252LWF	Renault-Dodge S56	Reeve Burgess Beaver	B23F	1989	Ex Rider Group, 1996	
773	E443JSG	Renault-Dodge S56	Alexander	B25F	1987	Ex SMT, 1996	
774	E444JSG	Renault-Dodge S56	Alexander	B25F	1987	Ex SMT, 1996	
775	G254LWF	Renault-Dodge S56	Reeve Burgess Beaver	B23F	1989	Ex Rider Group, 1996	

Livery: Cream, red and maroon　**Note:** 185 and 250 are on long term hire to Barton

Previous Registrations:

542GRT	E219GNV	RJI5704	E135KRP	XDU178	From new
FFK312	BUT19Y	RJI5706	F23WNH	A14SMT	B466WRN

MACPHERSON

MacPherson Coaches Ltd, The Garage, Hill Street, Donisthorpe, Leicestershire, DE12 7PL

XSJ647T	Leyland Fleetline FE30AGR	Northern Counties	H44/31F	1979	Ex Western Scottish, 1992
XSJ649T	Leyland Fleetline FE30AGR	Northern Counties	H44/31F	1979	Ex Western Scottish, 1992
XSJ650T	Leyland Fleetline FE30AGR	Northern Counties	H44/31F	1979	Ex Western Scottish, 1992
A330VHB	Ford R1115	Plaxton Paramount 3200	C53F	1984	Ex Hoyland, Willenhall, 1994
B921GUX	Ford R1115	Plaxton Paramount 3200	C53F	1985	Ex Lakeside, Ellesmere, 1996
C58USS	Ford R1115	Plaxton Paramount 3200 II	C53F	1986	Ex Mayne, Buckie, 1994
PIB2459	Ford R1115	Plaxton Paramount 3200 II	C35F	1986	Ex Messenger, Aspatria, 1996
E346EVH	DAF SB3000DKV601	Van Hool Alizée	C53FT	1987	Ex Smith, Alcester, 1989
F249RJX	DAF MB230LT615	Plaxton Paramount 3500 III	C53F	1989	
J33MCL	Mercedes-Benz 0303/15R	Plaxton Paramount 3500 III	C51FT	1992	
J55MCL	Mercedes-Benz 0303/15R	Plaxton Paramount 3500 III	C51FT	1992	
M22MCL	Eos E180Z	Eos 90	C53F	1995	
M44MCL	Eos E180Z	Eos 90	C53F	1995	
N66MCL	Eos E180Z	Eos 90	C53F	1996	
N77MCL	Eos E180Z	Eos 90	C53F	1996	

Previous Registrations:
C58USS   C643LKU, XXI8950   KYA839T   MCG990T, XFJ379   PIB2459   C296LVH

Named vehicles: E747JAY, *Clan Chieftan* ; E346EVH, *Daniel Jame*s ; XSJ647T, *Fat Boab* ; XSJ649T, *Wee Eck* ; XSJ650T, *Soapy Souter* ; J33MCL, *Hauf Two* ; J55MCL, *Amy Jade*.   **Livery:** Cream

MacPherson of Donisthorpe operate a number of vehicles formerly with the Scottish Bus Group, including three fom Western Scottish. All three of the Northern Counties-bodied Fleetlines are in this view showing the names of characters from the 'Oor Wullie' comic strip carried by these vehicles. XSJ647T is 'Fat Boab'. *Steve Sanderson*

MARSHALL

J A Marshall, 11 Main Street, Sutton-on-Trent, Newark, Nottinghamshire, NG23 6PF

DD10	RAL795	Daimler CVG6	Massey	H33/28RD	1954	Ex Gash, Newark, 1987
B30	RAU624R	Bedford YLQ	Plaxton Supreme III	C45F	1976	Ex Gash, Newark, 1988
B31	B675EWE	Bedford YNT	Plaxton Paramount 3200 II	C53F	1985	Ex Wainfleet, Nuneaton, 1990
DF34	A15DAF	DAF SB2300DHS585	Plaxton Paramount 3200	C53F	1984	Ex Sykes, Appleton Roebuck, 1992
MR37	G228FJX	MCW MetroRider MF154/4	MCW	C26F	1989	Ex Warrington, Ilam, 1993
VH38	YRR3	Van Hool T815H	Van Hool Alizée	C49FT	1988	Ex Tellings-Golden Miller, Cardiff, 1993
L39	DNK585Y	Leyland Tiger TRCTL11/2R	Plaxton Supreme V	C57F	1982	Ex Ingleby, York, 1994
DD40	VRC479S	Leyland Fleetline FE30ALR	Northern Counties	H44/31F	1978	Ex Nottingham, 1994
DD41	VRC480S	Leyland Fleetline FE30ALR	Northern Counties	H44/31F	1978	Ex Nottingham, 1994
VL42	H3YRR	Volvo B10M-60	Plaxton Paramount 3500 III	C49F	1991	Ex Westerham Coaches, 1995
DD43	BTV654T	Leyland Atlantean AN68A/1R	East Lancashire	H47/33D	1979	Ex Nottingham, 1995
DD44	OYJ68R	Leyland Atlantean AN68A/1R	East Lancashire	H44/29D	1977	Ex Nottingham, 1996

Previous Registrations:
A15DAF	A462HJF	RAL795	From new
H3YRR	H836AHS	YRR3	E447MMM

Livery: Blue and cream

The Marshalls of Sutton on Trent fleet includes a Daimler CVG6 previously by Gash. The Gash livery inspired a two-tone blue and cream layout now adopted for this fleet. BTV654T, however, still carries its former owner's colours and is one of four double deckers in the fleet that have come from Nottingham. The Gash fleet numbering scheme has also been adopted. *Steve Sanderson*

MAUN CRUSADER

Maun International Travel Consultants Ltd, 151 Outram Street, Sutton-in-Ashfield,
Nottinghamshire, NG17 4FU

Depot: Westfield Site, Bellamy Rd, Mansfield.

NNU124M	Daimler Fleetline CRL6-30	Roe	H42/29F	1973	Ex Camms, Nottingham, 1993
OTO548M	Leyland Atlantean AN68/1R	East Lancashire	H47/30D	1974	Ex Nottingham, 1992
JOV754P	Volvo-Ailsa B55-10	Alexander AV	H44/35F	1976	Ex Skills, Nottingham, 1996
BKR945T	AEC Reliance 6U2R	Duple Dominant II	C53F	1979	Ex Bird, North Hykeham, 1996
SXF319	DAF MB200DKL600	Plaxton Supreme IV	C53F	1979	Ex Copeland, Meir, 1996
WCK141V	Leyland Leopard PSU3E/4R	Duple Dominant II Express	C49F	1980	Ex Eve Coaches, Dunbar, 1993
FKM303V	Dennis Dominator DD129	Willowbrook	H44/31F	1980	Ex Maidstone & District, 1995
FKM304V	Dennis Dominator DD129	Willowbrook	H44/31F	1980	Ex Maidstone & District, 1995
276EPX	Volvo B58-61	Jonckheere Bermuda	C53FT	1981	Ex Reynolds, Watford, 1995
FGE440X	Dennis Dominator DD137B	Alexander RL	H45/34F	1982	Ex Delta, Kirkby in Ashfield, 1996
PJI8334	DAF MB200DKTL600	Caetano Alpha	C53F	1981	Ex Barry, Weymouth, 1996
LIL4799	Ford A0610	Moseley Faro	C25F	1982	Ex King & Taylor, Rochdale, 1995
899DXV	DAF MB230DKFL615	Duple 320	C52FT	1987	
470WYA	DAF MB230DKFL615	Duple 340	C53FT	1987	
HIL6253	Leyland Tiger TRCTL11/3RH	Duple 340	C53FT	1987	Ex Goodwin, Eccles, 1996
G870YDU	DAF MB230DKFL615	Caetano Algarve	C49FT	1989	Ex Supreme, Coventry, 1992

Previous Registrations:

276EPX	WNV818W		HIL6253	D323RNS	PJI8334	TWW175W
470WYA	E317EVH		LIL4799	XNC580X	SXF319	KVS174V
899DXV	E318EVH					

Livery: Ivory, red, green, yellow and orange.

Maun Crusader are active in the operation of tendered bus services. Seen arriving in Newark from Southwell on such a Nottinghamshire County Council service is FKM304V one of two Willowbrook-bodied Dennis Dominators obtained from Maidstone and District. The livery on this vehicle is multicoloured. *Steve Sanderson*

MIDLAND FOX

Midland Fox Ltd, 30 Millstone Lane, Leicester, LE1 5RN

Depots : Ashby Road, Coalville; Dodwells Bridge, Hinckley; Peacock Lane, Leicester; Sandacre Lane, Leicester; Springfield Street, Market Harborough; Burton Street, Melton Mowbray; Duke Street, Melton Mowbray and Station Street, South Wigston.

1	URH657	Leyland Tiger TRCTL11/3R	Plaxton Paramount 3200	C51F	1983	
2	FAZ2784	Leyland Tiger TRCTL11/3RH	Plaxton Paramount 3200 E	C53F	1985	Ex Crosville Wales, 1996
4	FIL3452	Leyland Tiger TRCTL11/3RH	Plaxton Paramount 3200 II	C50FT	1985	
8	A108EPA	Leyland Tiger TRCTL11/2R	Plaxton Paramount 3200 E	C53F	1983	Ex London Country NE, 1989
9	A125EPA	Leyland Tiger TRCTL11/2R	Plaxton Paramount 3200 E	C53F	1983	Ex London Country NE, 1989
19	109CRC	Leyland Tiger TRCTL11/3R	Plaxton Paramount 3200	C46FT	1983	Ex London & Country, 1990
20	LJI5632	Leyland Tiger TRCTL11/3R	Plaxton Paramount 3200	C48FT	1983	Ex London & Country, 1990
21	111XKT	Leyland Tiger TRCTL11/3R	Plaxton Paramount 3200	C46FT	1983	Ex London & Country, 1990
22	JDE972X	Leyland Tiger TRCTL11/3R	Plaxton Supreme VI Express	C57F	1982	Ex Hills, Nuneaton, 1991
23	BPR103Y	Leyland Tiger TRCTL11/3R	Duple Laser	C53F	1983	Ex London & Country, 1990
24	A37SMA	Leyland Tiger TRCTL11/2R	Duple Laser	C49F	1984	Ex Crosville Wales, 1993
25	A38SMA	Leyland Tiger TRCTL11/2R	Duple Laser	C49F	1984	Ex Crosville Wales, 1993
26	B146ALG	Leyland Tiger TRCTL11/2RH	Duple Laser 2	C49F	1984	Ex Crosville Wales, 1993
27	B151ALG	Leyland Tiger TRCTL11/2RH	Duple Laser 2	C49F	1985	Ex Crosville Wales, 1993
28	BPR108Y	Leyland Tiger TRCTL11/3R	Duple Laser	C50F	1983	Ex London & Country, 1990
29	BPR99Y	Leyland Tiger TRCTL11/3R	Duple Laser	C57F	1983	Ex London & Country, 1990
71	81SVO	Leyland Leopard PSU5D/4R	Plaxton Supreme IV	C57F	1981	Ex Bedminster Coaches, 1983
75	YCF826	Leyland Leopard PSU5/4R	Plaxton Elite III	C57F	1975	Ex Orsborn, Wollaston, 1989
86	LJI8156	DAF MB200DKFL600	Van Hool Alizée	C53F	1984	Ex Orsborn, Wollaston, 1989
87	LJI8157	DAF MB200DKFL600	Van Hool Alizée	C53F	1984	Ex Orsborn, Wollaston, 1989
153	662NKR	DAF MB200DKFL615	Plaxton Supreme VI	C57F	1982	Ex Bland, Stamford, 1990
192	C632PAU	DAF MB230DKFL615	Plaxton Paramount 3200 II	C53F	1986	Ex Trent, 1991
193	C633PAU	DAF MB230DKFL615	Plaxton Paramount 3200 II	C53F	1986	Ex Trent, 1991
211	N211TBC	Volvo B10M-62	Plaxton Expressliner II	C49FT	1996	
212	N212TBC	Volvo B10M-62	Plaxton Expressliner II	C49FT	1996	
213	FIL3451	Volvo B10M-60	Van Hool Alizée	C52F	1989	Ex Tellings-Golden Miller, Byfleet, 1992
214	XPA110	Volvo B10M-60	Van Hool Alizée	C52F	1989	Ex Tellings-Golden Miller, Byfleet, 1992
236	F406DUG	Volvo B10M-60	Plaxton Paramount 3500 III	C50F	1989	Ex Wallace Arnold, 1992
237	F407DUG	Volvo B10M-60	Plaxton Paramount 3500 III	C50F	1989	Ex Wallace Arnold, 1992
246	J246MFP	Volvo B10M-60	Plaxton Paramount 3500 III	C46FT	1992	Ex Express Travel, Liverpool, 1995
247	J247MFP	Volvo B10M-60	Plaxton Paramount 3500 III	C46FT	1992	Ex Express Travel, Liverpool, 1995
317	TVC402W	Leyland Leopard PSU5C/4R	Plaxton Supreme IV	C53F	1981	Ex Hills, Nuneaton, 1991
329	MPL129W	Leyland Leopard PSU3E/4R	Duple Dominant II	C49F	1981	Ex Bland, Stamford, 1990
387	ONN287M	Leyland Leopard PSU3B/4R	Plaxton Elite III Express	C53F	1974	Ex Fen Travel, Syston, 1993
388	YCS92T	Leyland Leopard PSU3D/4R	Alexander AY	DP53F	1978	Ex ?, 1995
612	796UHT	Leyland Leopard PSU5D/5R	Plaxton Supreme IV	C50F	1981	Ex Fen Travel, Syston, 1992
784	BVP784V	Leyland Leopard PSU3E/4R	Plaxton Supreme IV	C53F	1980	Ex Midland Red, 1981
785	BVP785V	Leyland Leopard PSU3E/4R	Plaxton Supreme IV	C53F	1980	Ex Midland Red, 1981
805	BVP805V	Leyland Leopard PSU3E/4R	Willowbrook 003	C53F	1980	Ex Midland Red, 1981
839	LOA839X	Leyland Leopard PSU3F/4R	Willowbrook 003	C53F	1982	Ex Midland Red Coaches, 1986
2155	GNV656N	Leyland National 11351/1R		B49F	1974	Ex The Shires, 1996
2156	JIL2156	Leyland National 11351/1R		B49F	1974	Ex National Welsh, 1989
2157	JIL2157	Leyland National 1151/1R/0402	East Lancs Greenway (1994)	B49F	1973	Ex Kinch, Barrow-on-Soar, 1989
2158	JIL2158	Leyland National 11351A/1R	East Lancs Greenway (1994)	B49F	1977	Ex Midland Red, 1981
2159	JIL2159	Leyland National 11351A/1R	East Lancs Greenway (1994)	B49F	1977	Ex Midland Red, 1981
2160	JIL2160	Leyland National 11351/1R	East Lancs Greenway (1994)	B49F	1975	Ex London & Country, 1994
2161	JIL2161	Leyland National 11351/1R	East Lancs Greenway (1994)	B49F	1974	Ex Kinch, Barrow-on-Soar, 1989
2162	JIL2162	Leyland National 1151/1R/0102	East Lancs Greenway (1994)	B49F	1974	Ex Kinch, Barrow-on-Soar, 1989
2163	JIL2163	Leyland National 11351/1R	East Lancs Greenway (1994)	B49F	1974	Ex National Welsh, 1989
2164	JIL2164	Leyland National 11351A/1R	East Lancs Greenway (1994)	B49F	1978	Ex London & Country, 1994
2165	JIL2165	Leyland National 11351A/1R	East Lancs Greenway (1994)	B49F	1976	Ex London & Country, 1994

2166-2179

		Scania L113CRL	East Lancashire European	B51F	1996	
2166	N166PUT	2169	N169PUT	2172	N172PUT	2175	N175PUT	2178	N178PUT
2167	N167PUT	2170	N170PUT	2173	N173PUT	2176	N176PUT	2179	N179PUT
2168	N168PUT	2171	N171PUT	2174	N174PUT	2177	N177PUT		

Midland Fox 87, LJI8157, carries the white and blue Foxhound livery which has been adopted for the coach operation. This Van Hool Alizée-bodied DAF is seen in London when operating on behalf of National Express. It was acquired by Midland Fox with the Orsborn business in 1989. *Colin Lloyd*

In the early 1990s Midland Fox purchased several MCW Metrobus double-deck buses to replace elderly Daimler Fleetlines. Around twenty are still in service with bodywork mixed between Alexander and MCW styles. Photographed in Leicester was 2488, EWF488V, one of four to operate in dual-door configuration. *Malc McDonald*

2445	JHE145W	MCW Metrobus DR104/6		MCW	H46/31F	1981	Ex Stevensons, 1994	
2453	JHE153W	MCW Metrobus DR104/6		MCW	H46/31F	1981	Ex South Yorkshire's Transport, 1991	
2460	JHE160W	MCW Metrobus DR104/6		MCW	H46/31F	1981	Ex South Yorkshire's Transport, 1991	
2467	JHE167W	MCW Metrobus DR104/6		MCW	H46/31F	1981	Ex South Yorkshire's Transport, 1991	
2474	EWF474V	MCW Metrobus DR102/13		MCW	H46/27D	1980	Ex Stevensons, 1988	
2477	JHE177W	MCW Metrobus DR104/6		MCW	H46/31F	1981	Ex South Yorkshire's Transport, 1991	
2478	ULS618X	MCW Metrobus DR102/28		Alexander RL	H45/33F	1982	Ex North Western, 1992	
2479	JHE179W	MCW Metrobus DR104/6		MCW	H46/31F	1981	Ex South Yorkshire's Transport, 1991	
2480	JHE189W	MCW Metrobus DR104/6		MCW	H46/31F	1981	Ex Stevensons, 1994	
2481	CKS391X	MCW Metrobus DR102/24		Alexander RL	H45/33F	1981	Ex Midland Red North, 1993	
2482	JHE192W	MCW Metrobus DR104/6		MCW	H46/31F	1981	Ex Stevensons, 1994	
2483	JHE193W	MCW Metrobus DR104/6		MCW	H46/31F	1981	Ex Stevensons, 1994	
2484	EWF484V	MCW Metrobus DR102/13		MCW	H46/27D	1980	Ex Stevensons, 1988	
2485	ULS615X	MCW Metrobus DR102/28		Alexander RL	H45/33F	1982	Ex Midland Red North, 1993	
2486	CKS386X	MCW Metrobus DR102/24		Alexander RL	H45/33F	1981	Ex North Western, 1992	
2488	EWF488V	MCW Metrobus DR102/13		MCW	H46/27D	1980	Ex Stevensons, 1988	
2489	CKS389X	MCW Metrobus DR102/24		Alexander RL	H45/33F	1981	Ex North Western, 1992	
2490	CKS390X	MCW Metrobus DR102/24		Alexander RL	H45/33F	1981	Ex Midland Red North, 1993	
2491	EWF491V	MCW Metrobus DR102/13		MCW	H46/27D	1980	Ex Stevensons, 1988	
2493	JWF493W	MCW Metrobus DR102/13		MCW	H46/30F	1980	Ex ?, 1996	
2494	JWF494W	MCW Metrobus DR102/13		MCW	H46/30F	1980	Ex ?, 1996	

2531-2560

Leyland Fleetline FE30AGR — Alexander AL — H45/29D — 1977-78 Ex South Yorkshire's Transport, 1990

2531	PWE531R	2545	SHE545S	2549	SHE549S	2553	SHE553S	2559	SHE559S
2534	PWE534R	2546	SHE546S	2552	SHE552S	2555	SHE555S	2560	SHE560S

4151	E701XKR	Scania N112DRB	Alexander RH	H47/31F	1988	Ex Kentish Bus, 1996
4152	E702XKR	Scania N112DRB	Alexander RH	H47/31F	1988	Ex Kentish Bus, 1996

4153-4158

Scania N113DRB — Alexander RH — H47/33F — 1989 Ex BTS, Borehamwood, 1993

4153	F153DET	4155	F155DET	4156	F156DET	4157	F157DET	4158	F158DET
4154	F154DET								

4159-4178

Scania N113DRB — East Lancashire — H47/33F — 1994-95

4159	M159GRY	4163	M163GRY	4167	M167GRY	4171	M171GRY	4175	M175GRY
4160	M160GRY	4164	M164GRY	4168	M168GRY	4172	M172GRY	4176	M176GRY
4161	M161GRY	4165	M165GRY	4169	M169GRY	4173	M173GRY	4177	M177GRY
4162	M162GRY	4166	M166GRY	4170	M170GRY	4174	M174GRY	4178	M178GRY

4478	D80UTF	Leyland Olympian ONLXCT/1RH	Eastern Coach Works	CH39/27F	1986	Ex Reading, 1994
4479	D81UTF	Leyland Olympian ONLXCT/1RH	Eastern Coach Works	CH39/27F	1986	Ex Reading, 1994
4480	C42HHJ	Leyland Olympian ONLXCT/1RH	Eastern Coach Works	H47/31F	1985	Ex Colchester, 1994
4481	D44RWC	Leyland Olympian ONLXCT/1RH	Eastern Coach Works	H47/31F	1986	Ex Colchester, 1994
4482	C286BBP	Leyland Olympian ONLXB/1R	East Lancashire	DP43/27F	1986	Ex Sheffield Omnibus, 1993
4483	A280ROW	Leyland Olympian ONLXB/1R	East Lancashire	H45/31F	1984	Ex Sheffield Omnibus, 1993
4484	A278ROW	Leyland Olympian ONTL11/1R	East Lancashire	H47/29F	1984	Ex Sheffield Omnibus, 1993

4485-4489

Leyland Olympian ONT11/1R — Eastern Coach Works — H46/31 — 1981-82 Ex Merseybus, 1993

4485	ACM705X	4486	ACM706X	4487	ACM707X	4488	ACM710X	4489	ACM711X

4490-4494

Leyland Olympian ONLXB/1R — Eastern Coach Works — H45/32F — 1983 Ex Crosville Wales, 1989

4490	MTU116Y	4491	MTU117Y	4492	MTU118Y	4493	MTU119Y	4494	MTU121Y

4501-4514

Leyland Olympian ONLXB/1R — Eastern Coach Works — H45/32F — 1983-84

4501	A501EJF	4504	A504EJF	4508	A508EJF	4511	A511EJF	4513	B513LFP
4502	A502EJF	4505	A505EJF	4509	A509EJF	4512	A512EJF	4514	B514LFP
4503	A503EJF	4507	A507EJF	4510	A510EJF				

Opposite: **For some years Midland Fox have used a red and yellow livery divided vertically, with the leading portion yellow. Fleetnames have been Midland Fox for the full-size buses with Fox Cub for the minibuses. Shown here are Scania N113DRB 4151, E701XKR, which carries an Alexander RH body and N354OBC from the minibus fleet. This too carries bodywork by Alexander and was one of many of the Sprint bodystyle to be supplied to British Bus subsidiaries during 1995.**

49
Wigston Harcourt
via Royal Infirmary
midland fox
4151
E701 XKR
Smiths

27
Pendlebury Drive
fox cub
fox cub
M354
N354 OBC

The majority of the Leyland Nationals in the Midland Fox fleet form a batch re-built by East Lancashire during 1994. A number of these vehicles have recently been re-painted in an experimental dark blue livery complete with *Urban Fox* branding, as carried by 2163, JIL2163, and seen here. *Tony Wilson*

4516	A132SMA	Leyland Olympian ONLXB/1R	Eastern Coach Works	H45/32F	1983	Ex Crosville Wales, 1989	
4517	A133SMA	Leyland Olympian ONLXB/1R	Eastern Coach Works	H45/32F	1983	Ex Crosville Wales, 1989	
4518	A134SMA	Leyland Olympian ONLXB/1R	Eastern Coach Works	H45/32F	1983	Ex Crosville Wales, 1989	
4519	A135SMA	Leyland Olympian ONLXB/1R	Eastern Coach Works	H45/32F	1983	Ex Crosville Wales, 1989	
4520	C30EUH	Leyland Olympian ONTL11/2R	East Lancashire	H47/31F	1985	Ex ?, 19	

4521-4525   Leyland Olympian ONCL10/1RZ   Alexander RL   H45/30F   1989

4521	G521WJF	4522	G522WJF	4523	G523WJF	4524	G524WJF	4525 G525WJF

4526	B186BLG	Leyland Olympian ONLXB/1RZ	Eastern Coach Works	H45/32F	1984	Ex Crosville Wales, 1990
4527	B187BLG	Leyland Olympian ONLXB/1RZ	Eastern Coach Works	H45/32F	1984	Ex Crosville Wales, 1990
4528	B190BLG	Leyland Olympian ONLXB/1RZ	Eastern Coach Works	H45/32F	1984	Ex Crosville Wales, 1990

4529-4533   Leyland Olympian ONCL10/1RZ   Northern Counties   H47/30F   1989   Ex Kentish Bus, 1992

4529	G506SFT	4530	G508SFT	4531	G509SFT	4532	G512SFT	4533 G513SFT

7014	DTL382X	Ford R1114	Plaxton Supreme IV	C53F	1982	Ex Fen Travel, Syston, 1993
8006	LJI5631	DAF MB200DKFL600	Plaxton Paramount 3500	C49F	1985	Ex Welsh, Upton, 1988
M75	C475TAY	Ford Transit 190D	Robin Hood	B16F	1985	

M201-M218   Iveco Daily 49.10   Carlyle Dailybus 2   B25F   1988

M201	E201HRY	M205	E205HRY	M209	E209HRY	M213	E213HRY	M216 E216HRY
M202	E202HRY	M206	E206HRY	M210	E210HRY	M214	E214HRY	M217 E217HRY
M203	E203HRY	M207	E207HRY	M212	E212HRY	M215	E215HRY	M218 E218HRY
M204	E204HRY	M208	E208HRY					

Twenty new Scania N113DRB double decks with East Lancashire bodies were purchased for 1994-95. One of the type, 4168, M168GRY is seen in the centre of Leicester. The fleet also contains Scania double deckers transferred from BTS and Kentish Bus. *Tony Wilson*

M219-M240   Iveco Daily 49.10   Carlyle Dailybus 2   B25F*   1988-89 *M219-21/3-5 are DP25F

M219	F519TOV	M224	F24XVP	M229	F29XVP	M233	G233EOA	M237	G237EOA
M220	F520TOV	M225	F25XVP	M230	G230EOA	M234w	G234EOA	M238	G238EOA
M221	F21XVP	M226	F26XVP	M231	G231EOA	M235	G235EOA	M239	G239EOA
M222	F22XVP	M227	F27XVP	M232	G232EOA	M236	G236EOA	M240	G240EOA
M223	F23XVP	M228	F28XVP						

M242	F242SJU	Iveco Daily 49.10	Robin Hood City Nippy	B25F	1989	
M243	E183BNN	Iveco Daily 49.10	Robin Hood City Nippy	B25F	1987	Ex Stevensons, 1990
M244	E184BNN	Iveco Daily 49.10	Robin Hood City Nippy	B25F	1987	Ex Stevensons, 1990
M245	H245MOE	Iveco Daily 49.10	Carlyle Dailybus 2	B25F	1990	
M246	H246MOE	Iveco Daily 49.10	Carlyle Dailybus 2	B25F	1990	
M247	H247MOE	Iveco Daily 49.10	Carlyle Dailybus 2	B25F	1990	
M249	C517DYM	Iveco Daily 49.10	Robin Hood City Nippy	B21F	1986	Ex London Buses, 1991
M250	D520FYL	Iveco Daily 49.10	Robin Hood City Nippy	B21F	1986	Ex London Buses, 1991

M253-M257   Iveco Daily 49.10   Carlyle Dailybus   B25F   1989   Ex Bee Line Buzz, 1990

M253	G83OTU	M254	G84OTU	M255	G85OTU	M256	G86OTU	M257	G87OTU

M258	E188CNE	Iveco Daily 49.10	Northern Counties	B22F	1988	Ex Bee Line Buzz, 1990
M259	E250ACC	Iveco Daily 49.10	Robin Hood City Nippy	B21F	1988	Ex Crosville Wales, 1994
M260	G238GCC	Iveco Daily 49.10	Carlyle Dailybus 2	B25F	1989	Ex North Western, 1994
M261	G239GCC	Iveco Daily 49.10	Carlyle Dailybus 2	B25F	1989	Ex North Western, 1994
M262	G244GCC	Iveco Daily 49.10	Carlyle Dailybus 2	B25F	1989	Ex North Western, 1994
M263	G245GCC	Iveco Daily 49.10	Carlyle Dailybus 2	B25F	1989	Ex North Western, 1994
M264	G247GCC	Iveco Daily 49.10	Carlyle Dailybus 2	B25F	1989	Ex North Western, 1994
M265	G249GCC	Iveco Daily 49.10	Carlyle Dailybus 2	DP25F	1989	Ex North Western, 1994
M266	G250GCC	Iveco Daily 49.10	Carlyle Dailybus 2	B25F	1989	Ex North Western, 1994
M268	F263CEY	Iveco Daily 49.10	Robin Hood City Nippy	B21F	1988	Ex Crosville Wales, 1994
M269	F264CEY	Iveco Daily 49.10	Robin Hood City Nippy	B21F	1988	Ex Crosville Wales, 1994
M270	F260CEY	Iveco Daily 49.10	Robin Hood City Nippy	B21F	1988	Ex Crosville Wales, 1994
M271	F262CEY	Iveco Daily 49.10	Robin Hood City Nippy	B21F	1988	Ex Crosville Wales, 1994

The East Midland Bus Handbook

M272	E254ACC	Iveco Daily 49.10		Robin Hood City Nippy	B21F	1988	Ex Crosville Wales, 1994		
M273	F261CEY	Iveco Daily 49.10		Robin Hood City Nippy	B21F	1988	Ex Crosville Wales, 1994		
M274	F274CEY	Iveco Daily 49.10		Robin Hood City Nippy	B21F	1988	Ex Crosville Wales, 1994		
M289	F379UCP	Mercedes-Benz 609D		Reeve Burgess Beaver	B20F	1988	Ex Edinburgh Transport, 1994		
M291	D906MVU	Mercedes-Benz 609D		Mercedes	B27F	1987	Ex ?, 19		

M292-M298 Mercedes-Benz L608D   Alexander   B18F*   1986*   Ex North Western 1992; *298 is B20F

M292	D222SKD	M293	D223SKD	M294	D224SKD	M296	D226SKD	M298	D218SKD

M299	D209SKD	Mercedes-Benz L608D		Reeve Burgess	B20F	1986	Ex North Western, 1992		
M301	F301RUT	Mercedes-Benz 709D		Robin Hood	B26F	1989			
M302	F302RUT	Mercedes-Benz 709D		Robin Hood	B26F	1989			

M303-M322 Mercedes-Benz 709D   Alexander Sprint   B25F   1994

M303	L303AUT	M307	L307AUT	M311	L311AUT	M315	L315AUT	M319	L319AUT
M304	L304AUT	M308	L308AUT	M312	L312AUT	M316	L316AUT	M320	L320AUT
M305	L305AUT	M309	L309AUT	M313	L313AUT	M317	L317AUT	M321	L321AUT
M306	L306AUT	M310	L310AUT	M314	L314AUT	M318	L318AUT	M322	L322AUT

M323	L323AUT	Mercedes-Benz 709D	Leicester Carriage	B25F	1994	
M324	L324AUT	Mercedes-Benz 709D	Leicester Carriage	B25F	1994	
M325	L325AUT	Mercedes-Benz 709D	Leicester Carriage	B25F	1994	
M326	N331OFP	Mercedes-Benz 709D	Leicester Carriage	B25F	1995	Ex Leicester Carriage demonstrator, 1996
M329	L227HRF	Mercedes-Benz 709D	Dormobile Routemaker	B29F	1993	Ex Stevensons, 1994
M330	L228HRF	Mercedes-Benz 709D	Dormobile Routemaker	B29F	1993	Ex Stevensons, 1994
M331	L231HRF	Mercedes-Benz 709D	Dormobile Routemaker	B27F	1993	Ex Stevensons, 1994
M333	L233HRF	Mercedes-Benz 709D	Dormobile Routemaker	B27F	1993	Ex Stevensons, 1994
M335	G65SNN	Mercedes-Benz 709D	Carlyle	B29F	1990	Ex Stevensons, 1994
M336	J151WEH	Mercedes-Benz 709D	Dormobile Routemaker	B29F	1992	Ex Stevensons, 1994
M337	K148BRF	Mercedes-Benz 709D	Dormobile Routemaker	B27F	1992	Ex Stevensons, 1994
M338	K158HRF	Mercedes-Benz 709D	Dormobile Routemaker	B27F	1993	Ex Stevensons, 1994
M339	G301RJA	Mercedes-Benz 709D	Reeve Burgess Beaver	B25F	1990	Ex Stevensons, 1994
M341	K131XRE	Mercedes-Benz 709D	Dormobile Routemaker	B??F	19??	Ex Stevensons, 1994
M342	G142GOL	Mercedes-Benz 709D	Carlyle	B29F	1990	Ex Stevensons, 1994
M343	G143GOL	Mercedes-Benz 709D	Carlyle	B29F	1990	Ex Stevensons, 1994

A number of Mercedes-Benz 709D midibuses new to Stevensons were transferred to Midland Fox in 1994 and carry a variety of different body styles, M341, K131XRE having been manufactured by the now defunct Dormobile company to their Routemaker pattern. *David Stanier*

M344-M358		Mercedes-Benz 709D		Alexander Sprint	B27F	1995			
M344	N344OBC	M347	N347OBC	M350	N350OBC	M353	N353OBC	M356	N356OBC
M345	N345OBC	M348	N348OBC	M351	N351OBC	M354	N354OBC	M357	N357OBC
M346	N346OBC	M349	N349OBC	M352	N352OBC	M355	N355OBC	M358	N358OBC

M402	F272OPX	Mercedes-Benz 811D	Robin Hood	B27F	1988	
M411	D111OWG	Renault-Dodge S56	Reeve Burgess	B25F	1986	Ex Stevensons, 1992
M413	E413EPE	Renault-Dodge S56	Northern Counties	B27F	1987	Ex Stagecoach South, 1992
M415	E415EPE	Renault-Dodge S56	Northern Counties	B27F	1987	Ex Stagecoach South, 1992
M417	E417EPE	Renault-Dodge S56	Northern Counties	B27F	1987	Ex Stagecoach South, 1992
M419	E419EPE	Renault-Dodge S56	Northern Counties	B27F	1988	Ex Stagecoach South, 1992

M460-M468		Renault-Dodge S56		Reeve Burgess	DP25F*	1986/7	Ex South Yorkshire's Transport, 1992
							M463 ex Deeward, 1993; *M461-3 B25F
M460	D130OWG	M462	D124OWG	M464	D134OWG	M465	D135OWG	M468	D138OWG
M461	D118OWG	M463	D162RAK						

Previous Registrations:

109CRC	A103HNC		JIL2163	GHB790N	
111XKT	A102HNC		JIL2164	XNG760S	
662NKR	OWA23X		JIL2165	JOX516P	
796UHT	NMV612W		JJF772L	HRP310L, 1273LJ	
81SVO	HHW471X		LJI5631	B568NJF	
A936MRW	429UFM, A919LJC, DJI1333		LJI5632	A104HNC, XPA110, A929KFP	
B310CRP	YCF826		LJI8154	A310XNV	
FAZ2784	?		LJI8157	B310LUT	
FBC191T	YNY590T, 5551PP		LVS422V	ELN928T, DJI6219	
FIL3451	F803TMD		NAC128V	LVF422V, DJI5578	
FIL3452	B104LJU		NEL1F	E707ERY	
GKV633T	ELN928T, DJI6219		RIB3686	ANA110Y	
JIL2156	GHB677N		RJU387Y	VUT1X, VRC214Y	
JIL2157	NPD142L		TNR787R	NOE611R, 796UHT	
JIL2158	PUK649R		TVC402W	PWK5W, DJI8467	
JIL2159	PUK643R		URH657	BRY1Y	
JIL2160	JOX482P		XPA110	F804TMD	
JIL2161	HWC87N		YCF826	JNK550N	
JIL2162	SEO208N				

Livery: Yellow and red; buscuit and orange (Fairtax 2933, M460-2/4/8); blue (Urban Fox 2160/1/3/66-75, 9045 & County Fox 2176-9); National Express 213/4/36/7.

Midland Fox minibuses are known as Fox Cubs. The large fleet of Ford Transits assembled soon after de-regulation have now been replaced by larger minibuses. M226, F26XVP is an Iveco Daily 49.10 with Carlyle Dailybus 25-seat bodywork.
Phillip Stephenson

MOXON

C W Moxon Ltd, Maltby Road Garage, Oldcotes, Worksop, Nottinghamshire, S81 8JN

Reg	Chassis	Body	Config	Year	Notes
FRR194J	Leyland Leopard PSU3B/4R	Plaxton Elite	C51F	1971	
5711MT	AEC Reliance 6U3ZR	Plaxton Supreme III (1978)	C53F	1973	Ex Mallam, South Shields, 1979
JGA183N	Leyland Atlantean AN68/1R	Alexander AL	H45/31F	1975	Ex Dunn Line, Nottingham, 1993
HIL3476	Bristol VRT/SL2/6G	MCW	H43/33F	1976	Ex Roger Hill, Congleton, 1992
LUX536P	Bedford YLQ	Duple Dominant	C28DL	1976	Ex Hughes, Ashford, 1984
HIL3075	Bristol VRT/SL2/6G	MCW	H43/33F	1976	Ex Roger Hill, Congleton, 1992
RDT89R	AEC Reliance 6U2R	Plaxton Supreme III	C51F	1977	Ex Hague, Sheffield, 1993
RWB801R	AEC Reliance 6U2R	Plaxton Supreme III	C51F	1977	Ex Hague, Sheffield, 1993
TTL541R	Bedford YMT	Plaxton Supreme III	C53F	1977	Ex Appleby, Conisholme, 1991
DNG233T	Bristol VRT/SL3/6LXB	Eastern Coach Works	H43/31F	1979	Ex MK CityBus, Milton Keynes, 1996
B85DTH	Bedford YNT	Plaxton Paramount 3200 II	C53F	1985	Ex Mullen, Cramlington, 1995
GIL4271	DAF SB2305DHS585	Van Hool Alizeé	C55F	1988	Ex Lowland, 1996
166YHK	DAF MB230LT615	Van Hool Alizeé	C49FT	1989	Ex London Coaches, 1994
FIL7997	DAF MB230LT615	Van Hool Alizeé	C51FT	1989	Ex London Coaches, 1994
JIL7889	DAF SB2305DHS585	Van Hool Alizeé	C53F	1989	Ex London Coaches, 1994
7715KV	DAF MB230LB615	Caetano Algarve	C53F	1989	Ex Traject, Halifax, 1991
F860YJX	DAF SB2305DHTD585	Duple 340	C51FT	1989	
F212LTV	Renault Master	Holdsworth	M12	1989	Ex Rhodes, Bestwood, 1996
J813KHD	DAF SB3000DKV601	Van Hool Alizeé	C51FT	1992	Ex Wood, Barnsley, 1996

Previous Registrations:

166YHK	F251RJX	FIL7997	F252RJX	HIL3476	GOG662N
5711MT	WCU816L	GIL4271	E606LVH	JIL7889	F257RJX
7715KV	F231RJX	HIL3075	JOV699P		

Named vehicles: DNG233T, *Baz*; JGA183N, *Bill*; HIL3075, *Daniel*; HIL3476, *Lynsey Michelle*.

Livery: Cream and red

Moxon's Tours operate three double-deck buses, primarily on school contract work. Two are former West Midlands Bristol VRs with Park Royal bodywork which were obtained second-hand from Hill of Congleton. HIL3476 is seen leaving a school in Worksop. Unusually it carries an index plate originating in Eire. *Paul Hill*

NOTTINGHAM CITY TRANSPORT

Nottingham City Transport Ltd, Lower Parliament Street, Nottingham, NG1 1GG

Depots : Piccadilly, Bulwell ; Leake Road, Gotham ; Lower Parliament Street, Nottingham ; Mansfield Road, Sherwood and Turney Street, Trent Bridge.

3	LRB213W	Leyland National 2 NL116L11/1R			B50F	1981	Ex Trent, 1992	
4	LRB214W	Leyland National 2 NL116L11/1R			B50F	1981	Ex Trent, 1992	
7	LRB207W	Leyland National 2 NL116L11/1R			B50F	1980	Ex Trent, 1990	
8	LRB208W	Leyland National 2 NL116L11/1R			B50F	1980	Ex Trent, 1990	
14	BVP814V	Leyland National 2 NL116L11/1R			B49F	1980	Ex Midland Red North, 1989	
19	ETT319Y	Leyland National 2 NL116HLXB/1R (Leyland)			B50F	1983	Ex Athelstan, Malmesbury, 1989	
24	EON824V	Leyland National 2 NL116L11/1R			B49F	1980	Ex Midland Red North, 1989	
33-39		Renault-Dodge S56		Alexander AM	DP23F	1987	Ex Northampton, 1991-93	
33	E103JNH	34	E104JNH	35	E105JNH	37	E107JNH	39	E109JNH
55	OTO555M	Leyland Atlantean AN68/1R		East Lancs Sprint(1994)	B45F	1974		
101-110		Mercedes-Benz 811D		Plaxton Beaver	B30F	1995		
101	N101WRC	103	N103WRC	105	N105WRC	107	N107WRC	109	N109WRC
102	N102WRC	104	N104WRC	106	N106WRC	108	N108WRC	110	N110WRC
111-120		Renault-Dodge S56		Reeve Burgess Beaver	B25F	1989		
111	F111JTO	113	F113JTO	115	F115JTO	117	F117JTO	119	F119JTO
112	F112JTO	114	F114JTO	116	F116JTO	118	F118JTO	120	F120JTO
121-135		Renault-Dodge S56		Reeve Burgess	B25F*	1987	*133-5 are DP25F	
121	D121URC	126	D126URC	130w	D130URC	132w	D132URC	134w	D134URC
123w	D123URC	127w	D127URC	131w	D131URC	133w	D133URC	135w	D135URC
124	D124URC	129w	D129URC						

Nottingham City Transport, as well as buying the type new, has acquired a number of Leyland National 2 vehicles from other operators. Several have now been withdrawn but former Trent example, now numbered 8, LRB208W continues in service.
David Stanier

136	D446GLS	Renault-Dodge S56		Alexander AM	B25F	1987	Ex Alexander demonstrator, 1987	
138	E138ATV	Renault-Dodge S56		Reeve Burgess Beaver	B25F	1987		
139	E139ATV	Renault-Dodge S56		Reeve Burgess Beaver	B25F	1987		
140	E140BNU	Renault-Dodge S56		Alexander AM	B25F	1987		
141	E577ANE	Renault-Dodge S56		Northern Counties	B25F	1988	Ex N Counties demonstrator, 1988	

142-146
Renault-Dodge S56 — Northern Counties — B25F — 1988

142	E142ERA	143	E143ERA	144	F144GVO	145	F145GVO	146	F146GVO

147	F147LNN	Renault-Dodge S56		Reeve Burgess Beaver	B25F	1989		
148	F148LNN	Renault-Dodge S56		Reeve Burgess Beaver	B25F	1989		
149	F149LNN	Renault-Dodge S56		Reeve Burgess Beaver	B25F	1989		
150	E70XKW	Mercedes-Benz 709D		Reeve Burgess Beaver	B25F	1988	Ex Reeve Burgess demonstrator, 1988	
151	F151GVO	Mercedes-Benz 709D		Reeve Burgess Beaver	B25F	1988		
152	F152GVO	Mercedes-Benz 709D		Reeve Burgess Beaver	B25F	1988		
153	F153GVO	Mercedes-Benz 709D		Reeve Burgess Beaver	B25F	1988		

154-164
Renault-Dodge S56 — Reeve Burgess Beaver — B25F — 1989-90

154	G154NRC	157	G157NRC	159	G159NRC	161	G161PVO	163	G163PVO
155	G155NRC	158	G158NRC	160	G160PTO	162	G162PVO	164	G164PVO
156	G156NRC								

165	G165RRA	Mercedes-Benz 709D	Reeve Burgess Beaver	B25F	1990		
166	G166RRA	Mercedes-Benz 709D	Reeve Burgess Beaver	B29F	1990		
167	H167ANU	Renault-Dodge S56	Reeve Burgess Beaver	B25F	1991		

168-176
Mercedes-Benz 709D — Plaxton Beaver — B29F — 1991

168	J168CTO	170	J170CNU	172	J172CNU	174	J174CNU	176	J176CNU
169	J169CTO	171	J171CNU	173	J173CNU	175	J175CNU		

177-184
Mercedes-Benz 811D — Carlyle — B31F — 1990-91 177/8 ex Carlyle demonstrators, 1991

177	H727LOL	179	J179CRB	181	J181CRB	183	J183CTO	184	J184CTO
178	H732LOL	180	J180CRB	182	J182CTO				

185-193
Mercedes-Benz 811D — Dormobile Routemaker — B31F — 1993

185	K185HTV	187	K187HTV	189	L189MAU	191	L191MAU	193	L193OVO
186	K186HTV	188	K188HTV	190	L190MAU	192	L192MAU		

194	L194OVO	Mercedes-Benz 811D	Plaxton Beaver	B31F	1994	
195	L195OVO	Mercedes-Benz 811D	Plaxton Beaver	B31F	1994	
196	M196SRR	Mercedes-Benz 811D	Alexander AM	B31F	1995	
197	M197SRR	Mercedes-Benz 811D	Alexander AM	B31F	1995	
198	M198TNU	Mercedes-Benz 811D	Alexander AM	B31F	1995	

201-219
Optare Metrorider MR15 — Optare — B30F — 1994-95

201	L201ONU	205	L205ONU	209	L209ONU	213	M213STO	217	N217VVO
202	L202ONU	206	L206ONU	210	L210ONU	214	M214STO	218	N218VVO
203	L203ONU	207	L207ONU	211	L211ONU	215	M215TNU	219	N219VVO
204	L204ONU	208	L208ONU	212	M212STO	216	M216TNU		

220-224
Optare Metrorider MR15 — Optare — B31F — 1996

220	N220BAL	221	N221BAL	222	N322BAL	223	N223BAL	224	N224BAL

Nottigham City Transport has a policy of dual-sourcing vehicle purchases and, for midibuses over recent years, both Mercedes-Benz and Optare products have been bought. One of the 1995 batch of Optare MetroRiders is 213, M213STO. *Tony Wilson*

301-307
Volvo Citybus B10M-50   East Lancashire   H51/35D   1985

301	B301KVO	303	B303KVO	305	B305KVO	306	B306KVO	307	B307KVO
302	B302KVO	304	B304KVO						

308-314
Volvo Citybus B10M-50   Northern Counties   H49/35D   1985-86

308	C308NRC	310	C310NRC	312	C312NRC	313	C313NRC	314	C314NRC
309	C309NRC	311	C311NRC						

315-329
Volvo Citybus B10M-50   East Lancashire   H47/38D   1988

315	E315BVO	318	E318BVO	321	E321BVO	324	E324BVO	327	E327BVO
316	E316BVO	319	E319BVO	322	E322BVO	325	E325BVO	328	E328BVO
317	E317BVO	320	E320BVO	323	E323BVO	326	E326BVO	329	E329BVO

330	E825OMS	Volvo Citybus B10M-50	Alexander RV	H47/37F	1987	Ex Volvo demonstrator, 1988
331	G331NRC	Volvo Citybus B10M-50	Alexander RV	H47/35F	1989	
332	G332NRC	Volvo Citybus B10M-50	Alexander RV	H47/35F	1989	
333	G333NRC	Volvo Citybus B10M-50	Alexander RV	H47/35F	1989	
334	G334NTV	Volvo Citybus B10M-50	Alexander RV	CH47/35F	1989	
335	G335PAL	Volvo Citybus B10M-50	Alexander RV	H47/37F	1987	Ex Volvo demonstrator, 1989

349-353
Scania N113DRB   East Lancashire   H49/35F   1994

349	L349MRR	350	L350MRR	351	L351MRR	352	L352MRR	353	L353MRR

354-358
Scania N112DRB   Alexander RH   H47/31F   1988   Ex Kentish Bus, 1992

354	E701GCU	355	F702JCN	356	F703JCN	357	F704JCN	358	F705JCN

359	E307EVW	Scania N112DRB	Alexander RH	H47/31F	1988	Ex Harris Bus, West Thurrock, 1991
360	G879TVS	Scania N113DRB	Alexander RH	H47/33F	1990	Ex Scania demonstrator, 1991
361	E200WHS	Scania N112DRB	East Lancashire	H47/31F	1987	Ex Brown, Dreghorn, (A1) 1990

The East Midland Bus Handbook

The Leyland Lion was developed from the Tiger in order to compete in the same market as the Volvo B10M double-deck Citybus. Very few Lions were built and with thirteen, Nottingham City Transport is the largest operator of this type. 392, D392TAU carries Northern Counties bodywork and is one of three built in 1986. *Tony Wilson*

362-379		Scania N113DRB		Alexander RH		H47/33F	1989-90		
362	G362SRB	366	G366SRB	370	G370RTO	374	G374NRC	377	G377NRC
363	G363SRB	367	G367SRB	371	G371RTO	375	G375NRC	378	G378NRC
364	G364SRB	368	G368RTO	372	G372RTO	376	G376NRC	379	G379NRC
365	G365SRB	369	G369RTO	373	G373RTO				
380	F380JTV		Scania N113DRB		Alexander RH		H47/33F	1989	Ex Scania demonstrator, 1989
381	E381ERB		Scania N112DRB		Alexander RH		H47/33F	1988	Ex Scania demonstrator, 1989

382-391			Leyland-DAB Lion LDTL11/1R		East Lancashire		DPH43/37F* 1988-89	*387-391 are H47/41F
								*383 is DPH43/33F, 384 is DPH43/35F
382	F382GVO	384	F384GVO	386	F386GVO	388	F388GVO	390	F390GVO
383	F383GVO	385	F385GVO	387	F387GVO	389	F389GVO	391	F391GVO

392	D392TAU	Leyland Lion LDTL11/1R	Northern Counties	H47/38D	1986	
393	D393TAU	Leyland Lion LDTL11/1R	Northern Counties	H47/37D	1986	
394	D394TAU	Leyland Lion LDTL11/1R	Northern Counties	H47/38D	1986	
395	EMJ560Y	Scania BR112DH	East Lancashire	H46/32F	1982	Ex Scania demonstrator, 1984
398	A398CRA	Volvo Citybus BD10-XB5	East Lancashire	H49/37D	1983	
399	A399CRA	Volvo Citybus BD10-XB7	East Lancashire	H49/37D	1983	
400	NRR400W	Scania BR112DH	East Lancashire	H46/32F	1980	Ex Scania demonstrator, 1981
401	N401ARA	Dennis Arrow DDA3116	Northern Counties Palatine II	DPH44/36F	1995	
402	N402ARA	Dennis Arrow DDA3116	Northern Counties Palatine II	DPH44/36F	1996	
403	N403ARA	Dennis Arrow DDA3116	Northern Counties Palatine II	H47/37F	1996	
404	N404ARA	Dennis Arrow DDA3116	Northern Counties Palatine III	H47/07F	1990	

Opposite: Contrasting styles of single-deck bus bodies are shown in the colour pictures for Nottingham City Transport. The upper picture shows 525, N525XRR, one of the Wright Access models built on the Scania L113 low-floor chassis, while the lower picture shows 769, N769WRC, a Volvo B10M with Alexander PS-type bodywork. Though the latter model is not considered to be a low floor variant, the wide and easy access is still held in high regard by passengers.

Chilwell via Q.M.C. 38
Nottingham City Transport
Nottingham City
N525 XRR

Carlton via City 28
Nottingham City Transport
Subway
VOLVO
N769 WRC

411-425
Leyland Atlantean AN68C/1R Northern Counties H47/31D* 1981 *414/5/9-21/3/4 are H47/33D

411	MVO411W	414	MVO414W	417	MVO417W	420	MVO420W	423	MVO423W
412	MVO412W	415	MVO415W	418	MVO418W	421	MVO421W	424	MVO424W
413	MVO413W	416	MVO416W	419	MVO419W	422	MVO422W	425	MVO425W

426-445
Leyland Atlantean AN68C/1R Northern Counties H47/31D* 1981 *437-45, are H47/33D, 433 is H47/32D

426	RNU426X	430	RNU430X	434	RNU434X	438	RTV438X	442	RTV442X
427	RNU427X	431	RNU431X	435	RNU435X	439	RTV439X	443	RTV443X
428	RNU428X	432	RNU432X	436	RTV436X	440	RTV440X	444	RTV444X
429	RNU429X	433	RNU433X	437	RTV437X	441	RTV441X	445	RTV445X

446-465
Leyland Atlantean AN68C/1R East Lancashire H47/31D* 1981-82 *456/7/59-65 is H47/33D

446	ORA446W	450	ORA450W	454	ORA454W	458	SNU458X	462	SNU462X
447	ORA447W	451	ORA451W	455	ORA455W	459	SNU459X	463	SNU463X
448	ORA448W	452	ORA452W	456	SNU456W	460	SNU460X	464	SNU464X
449	ORA449W	453	ORA453W	457	SNU457W	461	SNU461X	465	SNU465X

471-480
Leyland Atlantean AN68C/1R Roe H46/34F* 1981

471	NNN471W	473	NNN473W	475	NNN475W	477	NNN477W	479	NNN479W
472	NNN472W	474	NNN474W	476	NNN476W	478	NNN478W	480	NNN480W

481	K481GNN	Leyland Olympian ON2R56C19Z5	East Lancashire	H49/35F	1992
482	K482GNN	Leyland Olympian ON2R56C19Z5	East Lancashire	H49/35F	1992
483	L483LNN	Volvo Olympian YN2RV18Z5	East Lancashire	H49/35F	1993
484	L484LNN	Volvo Olympian YN2RV18Z5	East Lancashire	H49/35F	1993

485-489
Volvo Olympian YN2RV18Z5 East Lancashire H49/35F 1994

485	L485NTO	486	L486NTO	487	L487NTO	488	L488NTO	489	L489NTO

| 490 | P490xxx | Volvo Olympian YN2RV18Z5 | East Lancashire | H49/35F | 1996 |
| 491 | P491xxx | Volvo Olympian YN2RV18Z5 | East Lancashire | H49/35F | 1996 |

501-513
Volvo B6-9.9M Alexander Dash B40F 1994-95

501	L501OAL	504	L504OAL	507	L507OAL	510	L510OAL	512	M512TRA
502	L502OAL	505	L505OAL	508	L508OAL	511	M511TRA	513	M513TRA
503	L503OAL	506	L506OAL	509	L509OAL				

| 520 | M113SLS | Scania L113CRL | Wright Access | B46F | 1995 | Ex Scania Demonstrator, 1995 |

521-525
Scania L113CRL Wright Access B47F 1995-96

521	M521UTV	522	M522UTV	523	N523XRR	524	N524XRR	525	N525XRR

600	M664KHP	Volvo B10B-58	Alexander Strider	B51F	1995	Ex Volvo Demonstrator, 1995
601	M601TTV	Volvo B10B-58	Alexander Strider	B51F	1995	
602	M602TTV	Volvo B10B-58	Alexander Strider	B51F	1995	
603	M603TTV	Volvo B10B-58	Alexander Strider	B51F	1995	
604	M604TTV	Volvo B10B-58	Alexander Strider	B51F	1995	

605-610
Volvo B10B-58 Plaxton Verde B51F 1995

605	M605UTV	607	N607UTV	608	N608UTV	609	N609UTV	610	TN610XRC
606	M606UTV								

611-615
Volvo B10B-58 Alexander Strider B51F 1995-96

611	N611XVO	612	N612YRA	613	N613YRA	614	N614YRA	615	N615YRA

| 666 | ARC666T | Leyland Atlantean AN68A/1R | Northern Counties | H47/31D | 1978 |

676-681
Leyland Atlantean AN68A/1R Northern Counties H47/31D 1979

676	BAU676T	680	BRC680T	681	BRC681T

The Volvo B6 was placed into service with the Nottingham fleet in 1994-95. This large midibus has not been purchased in large numbers, 513, M513TRA being one of a batch of only three obtained in 1995. These vehicles all carry Alexander Dash bodywork. *David Stanier*

682-696   Leyland Atlantean AN68A/1R   Northern Counties   H47/31D   1980

682	JRC682V	685	LRR685W	688	LRR688W	691	LRR691W	694	MNU694W
683	LRR683W	686	LRR686W	689	LRR689W	692	MNU692W	695	MNU695W
684	LRR684W	687	LRR687W	690	LRR690W	693	MNU693W	696	MNU696W

698	F128KTV	Leyland Olympian ONCL10/2RZ	Northern Counties	H49/34F	1989	Ex South Notts, 1991	
699	G129NRC	Leyland Olympian ONCL10/2RZ	Northern Counties	H49/34F	1989	Ex South Notts, 1991	

701-711   Leyland National 2 NL116L11/1R   B50F   1980

701	GTO701V	704	GTO704V	706	GTO706V	708	GTO708V	710	GTO710V
702	GTO702V	705	GTO705V	707	GTO707V	709	GTO709V	711	GTO711V
703	GTO703V								

713-724   Leyland National 2 NL116TL11A/1R   B50F   1985

713	B713LAL	716	B716LAL	719	B719LAL	721	C721MRC	723	C723MRC
714	B714LAL	717	B717LAL	720	C720MRC	722	C722MRC	724	C724MRC
715	B715LAL	718	B718LAL						

725-739   Leyland Lynx LX112L10ZR1   Leyland Lynx   B49F*   1988   *725/7/32 are B51F, 729 is B48F

725	E725BVO	728	E728BVO	731	E731BVO	734	E734BVO	737	E737BVO
726	E726BVO	729	E729BVO	732	E732BVO	735	E735BVO	738	E738BVO
727	E727BVO	730	E730BVO	733	E733BVO	736	E736BVO	739	E739BVO

740-744   Leyland Lynx LX112L10ZR1R   Leyland Lynx   B49F   1989

740	F740HRC	741	F741HRC	742	F742HRC	743	F743HRC	744	F744HRC

745-749   Leyland Lynx LX2R11C15Z4R   Leyland Lynx   B50F   1989-90

745	G745PNN	746	G746PNN	747	G747PNN	748	G748PNN	749	G749PNN

750	H47NDU	Leyland Lynx LX2R11V18Z4R	Leyland Lynx 2	B50F	1991	Ex Volvo Euro Show bus, 1991	

For many years the Nottingham double deck fleet was built to a distinctive body style. Elsewhere in this publication, photographs of former Nottingham vehicles will be recognised with this style even when supplied by different body builders. Now representative of a reducing number of such vehicles still in service in Nottingham is 671, ATV671T a Northern Counties-bodied Atlantean.
Tony Wilson

751-758		Scania N113CRB		Alexander PS		B51F	1990		
751	G751SRB	753	G753SRB	755	G755SRB	757	G757SRB	758	G758SRB
752	G752SRB	754	G754SRB	756	G756SRB				
759	J759DAU	Leyland Lynx LX2R11V18Z4S		Leyland Lynx 2		B50F	1991		
760	J760DAU	Leyland Lynx LX2R11V18Z4S		Leyland Lynx 2		B50F	1991		
761	K761JTV	Scania N113CRB		Plaxton Verde		B50F	1993	Ex Plaxton demonstrator, 1993	
762	L829HEF	Volvo B10B-58		Alexander Strider		B51F	1994	Ex Volvo demonstrator, 1994	
763	M763SVO	Scania L113CRL		Northern Counties Paladin		B51F	1994		
764	M919MRW	Volvo B10B-58		Alexander Strider		B51F	1995	Ex Volvo demonstrator, 1996	
765	N480DKH	Volvo B10B-58		Plaxton Verde		B51F	1995	Ex Plaxton demonstrator, 1996	
766	N779DRH	Volvo B10B-58		Plaxton Verde		B51F	1995	Ex Plaxton demonstrator, 1996	
767-771		Volvo B10M-55		Alexander PS		B48F	1995		
767	N767WRC	768	N768WRC	769	N769WRC	770	N770WRC	771	N771WRC
772	A111EPA	Leyland Tiger TRCTL11/2R		Plaxton Paramount 3200 E		C53F	1983	Ex London Country NE, 1989	
776	A138EPA	Leyland Tiger TRCTL11/2R		Plaxton Paramount 3200 E		C53F	1984	Ex London Country NE, 1989	
777	ATO57Y	Leyland Tiger TRCTL11/2R		Plaxton Paramount 3200 E		C49F	1983	Ex Silcox, Pembroke Dock, 1985	
778	NDE748Y	Leyland Tiger TRCTL11/2R		Plaxton Paramount 3200 E		C49F	1983	Ex Silcox, Pembroke Dock, 1985	
784w	B784JAU	Leyland Tiger TRCTL11/3R		Duple Caribbean 2		C53F	1985		
785	75RTO	Leyland Royal Tiger RTC		Leyland Doyen		C53F	1988		
786	83RTO	Leyland Royal Tiger RTC		Leyland Doyen		C53F	1988		

787	77RTO	Volvo B10M-61		Plaxton Paramount 3500 II	C53F	1985	Ex South Notts, 1991
791	F791JTV	Leyland Tiger TRCTL11/3ARZ		Duple 320	C53F	1989	
792	F792JTV	Leyland Tiger TRCTL11/3ARZ		Duple 320	C53F	1989	
793	65RTO	Leyland Tiger TRCTL11/3RZ		Plaxton Paramount 3200 III	C53F	1988	
795w	ATO58Y	Leyland Tiger TRCTL11/3R		Duple Dominant IV	C49F	1982	
796	J796CNU	Leyland Tiger TRCL10/3ARZA		Plaxton Paramount 3200 III	C57F	1991	
797	M784RVY	Bova FLC12-280		Bova Futura Club	C53F	1995	Ex Bova demonstrator, 1996

Previous Registrations:

65RTO	E793BTV		83RTO	E786BTV	ATO58Y	75RTO, WAU795Y
75RTO	E785BTV		ATO57Y	77RTO, NDE749Y		
77RTO	UTV222S, B871XWR, 4831WA, B161XWR, EBW40A					

Liveries: Green and cream; South Notts (blue and cream): 4, 55, 150-6/65/6/8-76, 481-4, 698/9, 701-10/67/72/6-8/84-7, 791-3/5/6. Note: 33-5 & 121/4/6 are on long term hire to Barton as fleet numbers 33-5, 21/4/6.

NOTTINGHAMSHIRE COMMUNITY BUSES

Nottinghamshire County Council, Planning and Transport, Trent Bridge House, Fox Road, West Bridgford, Nottingham, NG2 6BJ

D167TRR	Mercedes-Benz 307D		Devon Conversions	M12	1987	
H998VRR	Mercedes-Benz 811D		Phoenix	C16F	1991	
P	Mercedes-Benz 609D		UVG CityStar	B16F	On order	

Liveries: White, Countryman (D167TRR and new P-reg) ; Orange, Soar Valley (H998VRR).

There are two community buses in Nottinghamshire, each driven by volunteer drivers and sponsored by the County Council. The Countryman provides services for the villages to the north west of Newark and is about to get a new vehicle. The Soar Valley minibus operates a number of routes centred upon Normanton upon Soar and the current vehicle is H998VRB, a Phoenix-bodied Mercedes-Benz 811D.
Steve Sanderson

P C COACHES

P C and J Smith, 110 Rasen Lane, Lincoln, LN1 3KD

Depot : Crofton Road, Allenby Road Industrial Estate, Lincoln

	Reg	Chassis	Body	Config	Year	History
	NOC396R	Leyland Fleetline FE30ALR	MCW	H43/33F	1976	Ex MTL, Heysham, 1995
	NOC454R	Leyland Fleetline FE30AGR	MCW	H43/33F	1977	Ex MTL, Heysham, 1995
	NOC526R	Leyland Fleetline FE30AGR	MCW	H43/33F	1977	Ex MTL, Heysham, 1995
	NFW501P	Bedford YMT	Plaxton Supreme III Express	C51F	1976	Ex Moxon, Oldcotes, 1992
	WUM127S	Leyland Fleetline FE30AGR	Roe	H43/33F	1978	Ex Yorkshire Rider, 1995
	KBV144S	Bedford YMT	Duple Dominant II	C53F	1978	Ex Arnold Shaw, 1995
	TFU751T	Bedford YMT	Duple Dominant II	C53F	1979	Ex Claret Coaches, Hibaldstow, 1991
	JTM105V	Bedford YMT	Plaxton Supreme IV	C53F	1979	Ex KM, Lundwood, 1991
	FUJ949V	Bedford YMT	Plaxton Supreme IV	C53F	1979	Ex Wing, Sleaford, 1991
	CDN711V	Bedford YMT	Plaxton Supreme IV	C53F	1980	Ex Kingston-upon-Hull, 1994
	CBB467V	Bedford YMT	Duple Dominant II	C53F	1980	Ex Kingsley, Hendon, 1995
	GRF703V	Bristol VRT/SL3/501	Eastern Coach Works	H43/31F	1980	Ex PMT, 1994
	PIB9214	Bedford YNT	Duple Dominant IV	C53F	1982	Ex Butler, Kirkby-in-Ashfield, 1990
	MIB9246	DAF SB2300DHTD585	Plaxton Paramount 3200	C53F	1984	Ex Dore, Leafield, 1992
	A448EVO	Mercedes-Benz L608D	Devon Conversions	C19F	1984	Ex Mertrux, Leicester, 1986
	B563PCC	Bedford YMP	Plaxton Paramount 3200	C35F	1984	Ex Roberts, Colwyn Bay, 1995
	D102SPP	Bedford YNT	Plaxton Paramount 3200 III	C53F	1987	Ex Cedar, Bedford, 1996
	E590BDB	Mercedes-Benz L307D	Mellor	M12	1988	Ex Taylor, Childwall, 1992
	F533EWJ	Mercedes-Benz 609D	Whittaker	C25F	1989	
	TIB4573	Scania K113CRB	Van Hool Alizée	C48FT	1990	Ex Happy Days, Woodseaves, 1994
	H799RWJ	Scania K93CRB	Duple 320	C51FT	1990	Ex Ashley Adams, Whitby, 1993
	H830RWJ	Scania K113CRB	Plaxton Paramount 3500 III	C53F	1990	
	H152DVM	Scania K113CRB	Van Hool Alizée	C49FT	1991	Ex Shearings, 1994
	J1PCC	Mercedes-Benz 811D	Reeve Burgess Beaver	C33F	1991	
	K813VNF	Ford Transit VE6	Ford	M14	1992	Ex S J Carlton, Hellaby, 1996
	L8PCC	Scania K113CRB	Irizar Century 12.35	C48FT	1994	
w	M6PCC	Ford Transit VE6	Mellor	M14	1994	
	M7PCC	Ford Transit VE6	Mellor	M14	1994	
	M8PCC	Mercedes-Benz 609D	Autobus Classique	C23FL	1994	
	M99PCC	Scania K113CRB	Irizar Century 12.35	C48FT	1995	
	N10PCC	Scania K113CRB	Irizar Century 12.35	C49FT	1995	
	N11PCC	Scania K113CRB	Irizar Century 12.35	C49FT	1996	
	N12PCC	Scania K113CRB	Irizar Century 12.35	C49FT	1996	

Previous Registrations:

B563PCC	B722RNG, A7WTR	MIB9246	A875PJX, 1576CD	TIB4573	G779CFA
KBV144S	FFR531S, 1302TJ	PIB9214	UNN755X		

Livery : White, orange and maroon ; blue (Travelsphere) - TIB4573

The local bus service between Lincoln and Saxilby is operated by PC Coaches. Small vehicles are used because of restrictions in one of the villages served. The regular performer on this route is J1PCC, a Mercedes-Benz 811D which is fitted with a Reeve Burgess Beaver body. The livery on this midicoach extends onto the glass. *Tony Wilson*

The P C Coaches fleet contains a number of executive coaches which are used extensively on UK and continental tour work. L8PCC is one of five Spanish-assembled Irizar Century coaches in the fleet, all integrally constructed on Scania K113CRB underframes. *Bill Potter*

PAM'S COACHES

Mrs G L Gray, 35 Blaby Road, Enderby, Leicestershire, LE9 5AP

Depot: Desford Road, Kirby Muxloe

HPG316N	Bedford YRT	Plaxton Supreme III	C53F	1975	Ex Ross, Cotgrave, 1987
WFP360X	Leyland Tiger TRCTL11/3R	Plaxton Supreme V	C53F	1982	Ex Rothwell, Heywood, 1988
DNK571Y	Leyland Tiger TRCTL11/3R	Plaxton Viewmaster IV	C49FT	1982	Ex Enterprise, Chatteris, 1991
A442HNF	Ford Transit	Mellor	B16F	1983	Ex G J Travel, Ottershaw, 1995
SIJ385	Volvo B10M-61	Berkhof Esprite 340	C53F	1984	Ex Cullinan, London E11, 1992
JIL4006	Mercedes-Benz 709D	Reeve Burgess Beaver	B25F	1988	Ex Kentish Bus, 1991
N11PAM	Mercedes-Benz 709D	Mellor	B25F	1995	

Previous Registrations:
JIL4006 F127TRU   SIJ385   A584RVW

Livery: Maroon, grey and pink

PATHFINDER

Pathfinder (Newark) Ltd, Brunel Drive, Newark, Nottinghamshire, NG24 2EG

1	L967VGE	Mercedes-Benz 709D	Dormobile Routemaker	B29F	1993
2	M665JFP	Mercedes-Benz 709D	Alexander AM	B29F	1994
3	N744LUS	Mercedes-Benz 811D	WS Wessex II	B33F	1995
4	L971VGE	Mercedes-Benz 709D	Dormobile Routemaker	B29F	1993
5	L964VGE	Mercedes-Benz 811D	Dormobile Routemaker	B33F	1993
6	M42DLN	Mercedes-Benz 709D	WS Wessex II	B29F	1995
7	N743LUS	Mercedes-Benz 709D	WS Wessex II	B29F	1995
8	L848WDS	Mercedes-Benz 709D	Dormobile Routemaker	B29F	1994
9	L138XDS	Mercedes-Benz 709D	Dormobile Routemaker	DP29F	1994
10	M424GUS	Mercedes-Benz 709D	WS Wessex II	B29F	1995
11	M983CYS	Mercedes-Benz 811D	WS Wessex II	B33F	1994
12	L256VSU	Mercedes-Benz 811D	Dormobile Routemaker	B33F	1993
14	N983XCT	Peugeot Boxer	TBP Freeway II	B25F	1996
15	M996CYS	Mercedes-Benz 811D	WS Wessex II	B33F	1994
16	L257VSU	Mercedes-Benz 709D	Dormobile Routemaker	B29F	1993
17	L965VGE	Mercedes-Benz 709D	Dormobile Routemaker	B29F	1993
18	J602KGB	Mercedes-Benz 709D	Dormobile Routemaker	B29F	1992
20	M882DDS	Mercedes-Benz 709D	WS Wessex II	B29F	1994
21	L258VSU	Mercedes-Benz 709D	Dormobile Routemarker	B29F	1993
22	M879DDS	Mercedes-Benz 709D	WS Wessex II	B29F	1994
23	N991XCT	Peugeot Boxer	TBP Freeway II	B25F	1996
24	N984XCT	Peugeot Boxer	TBP Freeway II	B25F	1996
25	N985XCT	Peugeot Boxer	TBP Freeway II	B25F	1996
26	N992XCT	Peugeot Boxer	TBP Freeway II	B25F	1996
	L988AEA	Iveco Turbo Daily 59-12	Marshall C31	B29F	1993
	L865BEA	Iveco Turbo Daily 59-12	Marshall C31	B29F	1993
667	M667JFP	Mercedes-Benz 709D	Alexander AM	B29F	1995
668	M453LJF	Mercedes-Benz 709D	Alexander AM	B29F	1995

Previous Registrations:
L988AEA L773YHA

Livery: White; **Note**: 667 and 668 are on long term hire to Barton as fleet numbers 667 & 668.

Pam's Coaches operate service 140 from Leicester to Rugby on behalf of Leicestershire County Council. N11PAM is a Mellor-bodied Mercedes-Benz 709D which was bought new for the service in 1995. It is seen in the centre of Leicester. *Tony Wilson*

The fleet of midibuses operated by Pathfinder are all less than 4 years old. The Shuttle concept has been expanded to incorporate Barton and Travel Wright who both use vehicles in Pathfinder Shuttle livery. Pathfinder were involved in the development of the tri-axle TBP Freeway II low floor midibus depicted on the rear cover of this publication. It is envisaged that this type will replace the Mercedes-Benz 709D midibuses such as 12, L256VSU. *Steve Sanderson*

PAUL JAMES

K S & PJ O'Brien, A Houlker & K Markham, 9 Church Lane,
Ratcliffe-on-the-Wreake, Leicestershire, LE7 8JF

Depot : Ratcliffe Farm, Fosseway.

AYA199	Leyland Leopard PSU3B/4R	Duple Dominant	C53F	1974	Ex Bancroft & Powers, Coalville, 1990
LWC444V	Bedford YMT	Plaxton Supreme IV Express	C53F	1979	Ex Bancroft & Powers, Coalville, 1990
PTV601X	Bedford YNT	Plaxton Supreme IV Express	C53F	1981	Ex Barton, 1987
VFA70X	Leyland Leopard PSU3F/4R	Willowbrook 003	C49F	1982	Ex Reliance, Sutton-in-the-Forest, 1989
PJI7929	Bedford YNT	Plaxton Paramount 3200	C49F	1982	
PJI7930	Bova FLD12.250	Bova Futura	C49F	1984	Ex Harnard, Brinsworth, 1988
PJI7931	Bova EL28/581	Bova Europa	C53F	1984	Ex Tom Jackson, Chorley, 1989
B63AOP	Ford Transit 190	Carlyle	B16F	1985	Ex Routledge, Cockermouth, 1993
PJI7754	Kässbohrer Setra S215HR	Kässbohrer Rational	C53F	1986	Ex Anglian, Loddon, 1992
C113AFX	Bedford YNV	Plaxton Paramount 3200	C49F	1986	Ex Kevin Radley, Broughton, 1996
E639NEL	Dennis Javelin 12SDA1907	Plaxton Paramount 3200 III	C53F	1988	Ex Kingston Coaches, Winterslow, 1991
J8PJC	Dennis Javelin 12SDA1929	Caetano Algarve	C49FT	1992	Ex Smithson, Spixworth, 1995

Previous Registrations:

AYA199	PKO121M	PJI7929	SMK146Y	PJI7931	A829RHG
J8PJC	J915OAY	PJI7930	A145BET	PJI7754	C385XLL, 5579MW

Livery: Cream and red

Opposite: Paul S Winson Ltd operated this Jonckheere Jubilee P50. It is mounted on a Volvo B10M chassis. As well as running an extensive holiday tour programme, the company also runs a former Nottingham Atlantean on Centrelink bus services. *Colin Lloyd*

Paul James Coaches operate a number of tendered services on behalf of Leicestershire County Council. Additionally, coaching and contract work is undertaken. Seen in London is PJI7931 a Dutch-built Bova Europa. *Colin Lloyd*

PAUL S WINSON

Paul S Winson Ltd, Station Avenue, Derby Road, Loughborough, Leicestershire, LE11 0DZ

20w	2968PW	Volvo B10M-61	Jonckheere Jubilee P50	C51FT	1984	Ex Fairtax, Melton Mowbray, 1987
24	C21PSW	Volvo B10M-61	Plaxton Paramount 3200 II	C57F	1985	Ex Wings, Sleaford, 1990
25	G25YRY	Bova FHD12.290	Bova Futura	C55F	1990	
26	HOD76	Bedford OB	Duple Vista	C27F	1949	Ex preservation, 1993
27	FJU973	Leyland Leopard PSU3C/4R	Plaxton Supreme III Express	C49F	1976	Ex Castleways, Winchcombe, 1990
28	H2PSW	DAF SB2305DHTD585	Plaxton Paramount 3200 III	C53F	1991	
32	F896SMU	Volvo B10M-60	Plaxton Paramount 3500 III	C53F	1990	Ex Horseshoe, Tottenham, 1991
33	H3PSW	Mercedes-Benz 609D	Made-to-Measure	C24F	1990	Ex Burton, Finchley, 1992
35	HIL5677	Scania K112CRB	Van Hool Alizée	C51FT	1988	Ex Merlyns, Skewen, 1992
36	UHJ495V	Volvo B58-61	Plaxton Supreme IV	C57F	1980	Ex Smith, Barton le Clay, 1992
39	F424RTL	DAF MB230LB615	Plaxton Paramount 3500 III	C53F	1989	Ex Wing, Sleaford, 1993
40	J40PSW	DAF SB2305DHS585	Caetano Algarve II	C53F	1992	Ex Brittain's, Northampton, 1994
41	YNR778	Leyland Atlantean AN68A/1R	East Lancashire	H47/31D	1976	Ex Nottingham, 1994
42	J10PSW	DAF SB3000DKV601	Caetano Algarve II	C51FT	1991	Ex Brittain's, Northampton, 1995
43	N3PSW	DAF DE33WSSB3000	Van Hool Alizée	C53F	1995	
44	L4PSW	Mercedes-Benz 709D	Dormobile	C16FL	1993	Ex Turner, Huyton, 1995
45	MNM31V	Leyland Leopard PSU3E/4R	Plaxton Supreme	C53F	1980	Ex Andy James, Tetbury, 1996
46	BTV656T	Leyland Atlantean AN68A/1R	Northern Counties	H47/31D	1978	Ex Nottingham, 1996
47	M300ARJ	Mercedes-Benz 709D	Autobus Classique 2	C25F	1994	
48	PJI	Leyland National 11351/1R		DP48F	1975	Ex ?, 1996
49	PJI	Leyland National 11351/1R		DP48F	1975	Ex ?, 1996
50	P50PSW	Bova FHD12.290	Bova Futura	C53F	1996	

Previous Registrations:

2968PW	B23MAY, NEL1F, B963PJF	H3PSW	H423DVM	L4PSW	L924UGA	
C21PSW	C799RJU, YNR778	HIL5677	E803XKY	PJI....	?	
F424RTL	F229RJX, VTL627	HOD76	From new	PJI....	?	
FJU973	MDF112P	J10PSW	J30KFP	UHJ495V	NRO230V, 999BWC	
H2PSW	H28GFP	J40PSW	J508LRY	YNR778	MNU626P	

Livery: White, blue and red (Red, orange & cream "Centrelink" YNR778)

RELIANCE

W J Simmons (Coaches) Ltd, 47 High Street, Great Gonerby,
Grantham, Lincolnshire, NG31 8JR

JAL573N	Leyland Leopard PSU3B/4R	Duple Dominant	B64F	1975	
YIA9006	Leyland Leopard PSU3D/4R	Duple Dominant (1986)	B55F	1976	Ex National Travel (West), 1986
KBT343S	Volvo B58-56	East Lancashire (1993)	CH40/26F	1978	Ex Skills, Nottingham, 1994
YTO996T	Leyland Leopard PSU3E/4R	Duple Dominant	B53F	1978	
DRC216T	Leyland Leopard PSU3E/4R	Plaxton Supreme IV Express	C53F	1979	
FRR143V	Volvo B58-56	Plaxton Supreme IV Express	C53F	1979	
LNU558W	Bedford YMT	Plaxton Supreme IV	C53F	1980	
NPA218W	Leyland Leopard PSU3E/4R	Plaxton Supreme IV Express	C49F	1981	Ex London Country, 1986
PNW306W	Leyland Leopard PSU3F/4R	Plaxton Supreme IV	C49F	1981	Ex Wallace Arnold, 1986
B641JVO	Bova FHD12.280	Bova Futura	C49FT	1985	
B405DGH	Mercedes-Benz L608D	Robin Hood	C21F	1985	
D748XAU	MCW MetroRider MF150/12	MCW	B23F	1987	
D749XAU	MCW MetroRider MF150/12	MCW	B23F	1987	
F367MUT	Dennis Javelin 8.5SDL1903	Plaxton Paramount 3200 III	C35F	1988	
F691PAY	Dennis Javelin 12SDA1907	Duple 320	C57F	1988	
F883SMU	Leyland Lynx LX112LXCTZR1S	Leyland	B51F	1989	
H790RWJ	Scania K113CRB	Van Hool Alizée	C55F	1990	
H845UUA	Optare MetroRider	Optare	B29F	1991	
J861KFP	Toyota Coaster HDB30R	Caetano Optimo	C21F	1991	Ex Wheadon's Greyhound, Cardiff, 1996
L547EHD	EOS E180Z	EOS 90	C47FT	1994	Ex Landtourers, Farnham, 1995
M821RCP	Dennis Dart 9.8SDL3040	Plaxton Pointer	B40F	1994	
N290DWY	MAN 11.190	Optare Vecta	B40F	1995	Ex Optare Demonstrator, 1996

Previous Registrations:
YIA9006　　PWD841R　　　　　　　　KBT343S　　WUF155, BGG166S

Livery:　Red and ivory (buses) ; white, blue and black (coaches).

The bus service between Grantham and Nottingham is primarily operated by Reliance of Great Gonerby. Seen in the centre of Nottingham is M821RCP, a Dennis Dart acquired in 1994. This Plaxton Pointer-bodied vehicle has recently been joined in the Reliance fleet by a former demonstrator Optare Vecta. *Tony Wilson*

ROADCAR

Lincolnshire Road Car Co Ltd, PO Box 15, St Mark Street, Lincoln, LN5 7BB
Lincoln City Transport Ltd, PO Box 15, St Mark Street, Lincoln, LN5 7BB

Part of the Yorkshire Traction group

Depots : Ropery Road, Gainsborough ; Huntingtower Road, Grantham ; Garden Street, Grimsby ; Gt Northern Terrace, Lincoln ; Orme Lane, Louth ; Lombard Street, Newark ; John Street, Scunthorpe ; Grosvenor Road, Skegness and Main Street, Walcott.

DD1	KAL578	Daimler CVD6	Massey(1962)	H33/28RD	1948	Ex Gash, Newark, 1989	
15 w	F515CDT	Mercedes-Benz L608D	Whittaker	B19F	1988	Ex Yorkshire Traction, 1989	
16 w	F516CDT	Mercedes-Benz L608D	Whittaker	B19F	1988	Ex Yorkshire Traction, 1989	
27	E287OMG	Mercedes-Benz 709D	Reeve Burgess Beaver	B25F	1988	Ex Barnsley & District, 1991	
28	E285OMG	Mercedes-Benz 609D	Reeve Burgess	DP23F	1988	Ex Tom Jowitt, Barnsley, 1990	
30	E730VWJ	Mercedes-Benz 609D	Whittaker Europa	DP24F	1987	Ex Tom Jowitt, Barnsley, 1990	
55	D105OWG	Renault-Dodge S56	Reeve Burgess	B25F	1986	Ex Barnsley & District, 1996	
56	D456BEO	Renault-Dodge S56	East Lancashire	B25F	1986	Ex Preston Bus, 1995	
58	D458BEO	Renault-Dodge S56	East Lancashire	DP22F	1986	Ex Preston Bus, 1994	
59	D459BEO	Renault-Dodge S56	East Lancashire	DP22F	1986	Ex Preston Bus, 1995	
62	D312RVR	Renault-Dodge S56	Northern Counties	B22F	1987	Ex Barnsley & District, 1995	
65	D765YCW	Renault-Dodge S56	Northern Counties	B22F	1987	Ex Preston Bus, 1995	
66	D36NFU	Renault-Dodge S56	Alexander AM	B25F	1987	Ex Chester, 1994	
68	D38NFU	Renault-Dodge S56	Alexander AM	B25F	1987	Ex Chester, 1994	
69	D39NFU	Renault-Dodge S56	Alexander AM	B25F	1987	Ex Chester, 1994	
70	D158RAK	Renault-Dodge S56	Reeve Burgess	B25F	1987	Ex Yorkshire Buses, 1995	
71-81		Renault-Dodge S56	Reeve Burgess	B25F	1986-87 Ex Lincoln City, 1993		
71	D101OWG	74	D104OWG	76	D116OWG	78	D125OWG	80	D120OWG
72	D113OWG	75	D115OWG	77	D123OWG	79	D119OWG	81	D121OWG
73	D103OWG						
82	D127OWG	Renault-Dodge S56	Reeve Burgess	DP25F	1987	Ex Lincoln City, 1993	
83	D180UWF	Renault-Dodge S56	Reeve Burgess	B25F	1987	Ex Barnsley & District, 1996	
84	D184UWF	Renault-Dodge S56	Reeve Burgess	B25F	1987	Ex Barnsley & District, 1996	
85	E35RBO	Renault-Dodge S56	Reeve Burgess	B25F	1987	Ex Windsorian, 1994	
86	E65RBO	Renault-Dodge S56	Reeve Burgess	B25F	1987	Ex Windsorian, 1994	
87	G327MUA	Renault-Dodge S56	Reeve Burgess Beaver	B23F	1990	Ex Harrogate Independent, 1993	

RoadCar have pursued a policy of introducing minibuses fitted with automatic gearboxes. As a result, the Mercedes-Benz L608D vehicles have been replaced with Renault-Dodge S56 types from a number of sources. 100, E480JVN is an Alexander-bodied example new to United but purchased from West Riding.
Mark Bailey

88	E318NSX	Renault-Dodge S56		Alexander AM		B25F	1988	Ex Fife Scottish, 1994	
89	E319NSX	Renault-Dodge S56		Alexander AM		B25F	1988	Ex Fife Scottish, 1994	
91	D701THF	Renault-Dodge S56		Alexander AM		B23F	1987	Ex Barnsley & District, 1996	
92	D692SEM	Renault-Dodge S56		Alexander AM		B23F	1987	Ex Barnsley & District, 1996	
93	D822RYS	Renault-Dodge S56		Alexander AM		B25F	1987	Ex Barnsley & District, 1996	
95	E705UEM	Renault-Dodge S56		Alexander AM		B23F	1987	Ex Barnsley & District, 1996	

96-106

Renault-Dodge S56   Alexander AM   B25F*   1987   Ex Yorkshire Buses, 1995**
* 97 is B23F ; **98,100/1/3 ex West Riding   99,105 Ex S Yorkshire R T.

96	E69KAJ	99	E482JVN	101	E510HHN	103	E512HHN	105	E505HHN
97	E72KAJ	100	E480JVN	102	E502HHN	104	E504HHN	106	E506HHN
98	E498HHN								

107	D307MHS	Renault-Dodge S56	Alexander AM	B21F	1986	Ex Strathtay, 1995	
108	D308MHS	Renault-Dodge S56	Alexander AM	B21F	1986	Ex Strathtay, 1995	
109	D309MHS	Renault-Dodge S56	Alexander AM	B21F	1986	Ex Strathtay, 1995	
110	D310MHS	Renault-Dodge S56	Alexander AM	B21F	1986	Ex Strathtay, 1995	

121-136

MCW MetroRider MF150/22   MCW   B23F   1987   Ex Yorkshire Traction, 1992-6

121	D521SKY	127	D527SKY	130	D530SKY	132	D532SKY	136	D536SKY
123	D523SKY	129	D529SKY	131	D531SKY				

139	E539VKY	MCW MetroRider MF150/33	MCW	B23F	1987	Ex Yorkshire Traction, 1995
201	EDT201V	Leyland National 2 NL116L11/1R		B52F	1980	Ex Yorkshire Traction, 1995
204	EDT204V	Leyland National 2 NL116L11/1R		B52F	1980	Ex Yorkshire Traction, 1995
214	EDT214V	Leyland National 2 NL116L11/1R		B52F	1980	Ex Yorkshire Traction, 1995
290	RFS590V	Leyland National 2 NL116L11/1R(6HLXB)		B52F	1980	Ex Yorkshire Buses, 1993
292	PNW605W	Leyland National 2 NL116L11/1R		B52F	1982	Ex Keighley & District, 1995
293	UWY73X	Leyland National 2 NL116AL11/1R		B52F	1982	Ex Harrogate & District, 1994
295	UWY65X	Leyland National 2 NL116AL11/1R		B52F	1981	Ex Harrogate & District, 1994
296	UWY76X	Leyland National 2 NL116AL11/1R		B52F	1982	Ex Keighley & District, 1995
297	UWY70X	Leyland National 2 NL116AL11/1R		B52F	1982	Ex Harrogate & District, 1995
299	YSX929W	Leyland National 2 NL106L11/1R		B44F	1980	Ex Fife Scottish, 1996
300	YSX930W	Leyland National 2 NL106L11/1R		B44F	1980	Ex Fife Scottish, 1996

301-308

Dennis Dart 9.8SDL3035*   Wright HandyBus   B40F   1992-93 *301-3 are 9.8SDL3017

301	K301NJL	303	K303NJL	305	L305VFE	307	L307VFE	308	L308VFE
302	K302NJL	304	L304VFE	306	L306VFE				

321-328

Volvo B6-9.5M   East Lancashire EL2000   B44F   1995

321	N321JTL	323	N323JTL	325	N325JTL	327	N327JTL	328	N328JTL
322	N322JTL	324	N324JTL	326	N326JTL				

351-358

Optare MetroRider MR15   Optare   B31F   1994

351	M351BFE	353	M353BFE	355	M355BFE	357	M357BFE	358	M358BFE
352	M352BFE	354	M354BFE	356	M356BFE				

368	J134HME	Renault S75	Plaxton Beaver	B31F	1991	Ex Strathtay, 1996
369	H129AML	Renault S75	Reeve Burgess Beaver	B31F	1990	Ex Strathtay, 1996
370	G895WML	Renault S75	Reeve Burgess Beaver	DP29F	1990	Ex Strathtay, 1996
371	H191YMA	Renault S75	Wright TS303 Citybus	B31F	1990	Ex The Wright Company, Wrexham, 1994
372	H127AML	Renault S75	Reeve Burgess Beaver	B31F	1990	Ex London Buses, 1995
373	G894WML	Renault S75	Reeve Burgess Beaver	DP29F	1990	Ex Strathtay, 1996
374	G294MWU	Renault S75	Reeve Burgess Beaver	DP31F	1990	Ex Harrogate & District, 1994
375	G295MWU	Renault S75	Reeve Burgess Beaver	DP31F	1990	Ex Harrogate & District, 1994
376	G448LKW	Renault S75	Reeve Burgess Beaver	B31F	1989	Ex Harrogate & District, 1993
377	H737THL	Renault S75	Whittaker-Europa	B29F	1990	Ex Renault demonstrator, 1991
378	K378RFE	Renault S75	Wright TS303 Citybus	B31F	1992	
379	K379RFE	Renault S75	Wright TS303 Citybus	B31F	1992	
380	K380RFE	Renault S75	Wright TS303 Citybus	B31F	1992	

381-393

Renault S75   Reeve Burgess Beaver   B31F   1990   Ex London Buses, 1994-95

381	G881WML	384	G884WML	387	G887WML	390	G890WML	392	H126AML
382	G882WML	385	G885WML	388	G888WML	391	G891WML	393	H128AML
383	G883WML	386	G886WML	389	G889WML				

A batch of eight 31-seat Optare MetroRiders was purchased by RoadCar in 1994. All are allocated to the Scunthorpe depot for town service duties. No.354, M354BFE is seen arriving in Scunthorpe from Ashby. *Tony Wilson*

The Yorkshire Traction Group operate the entire London Buses RB class. Sixteen are now in the RoadCar fleet with a further pair running with Lincoln City Transport. Once London RB20 is 390, G890WML. This vehicle carries a Reeve Burgess Beaver body on the Renault S75 chassis which is favoured for 29/31 seat buses in the RoadCar fleet. *Tony Wilson*

365
BRIGG
RoadCar
HUMBERLINK
457
PIW 4457

8
BROXHOLME GARDENS
RoadCar
It's end to end stuff.
1378
LRB 578W

The first coach purchased new by RoadCar since 1986 was 401, N401LTL. This Bova Futura Club arrived in late 1995 and is fitted with the express coach Cummins/Allison transmission pack. The livery on RoadCar coaches has been changed to the style applied to this Bova with all coaches now carrying the white, lime green and yellow scheme. *Richard Belton*

394	J394LJL	Mercedes-Benz 811D	Optare StarRider E	B31F	1991	
395	J395LJL	Mercedes-Benz 811D	Optare StarRider E	B31F	1991	
396	J396LJL	Mercedes-Benz 811D	Optare StarRider E	B31F	1991	
397	H397SYG	Mercedes-Benz 811D	Optare StarRider	B31F	1990	Ex Optare demonstrator, 1991
400	D606SGA	Bedford PJK	Wright	DP25FL	1987	Ex Mobilinc, North Hykeham, 1996
401	N401LTL	Bova FLC 12.280	Bova Futura Club	C53F	1995	
411	WOI3001	Leyland Tiger TRCTL11/3R	Plaxton Supreme IV	C51F	1980	Ex Lincoln City, 1993
412	WOI3002	Leyland Tiger TRCTL11/3R	Duple Dominant IV	C53F	1983	Ex Lincoln City, 1993
415	EAH891Y	Leyland Tiger TRCTL11/3R	Plaxton Paramount 3200E	C53F	1983	Ex United, 1996
416	ESK965	Leyland Tiger TRCTL11/3R	Plaxton Paramount 3200	C53F	1983	Ex Yorkshire Traction, 1990
417	MSV927	Leyland Tiger TRCTL11/3R	Van Hool Alizeé	C51F	1981	Ex Gash, Newark, 1989
418	HIL8418	Leyland Tiger TRCTL11/3R	Plaxton Paramount 3200	C53F	1983	Ex Yorkshire Traction, 1991
419	HIL8419	Leyland Tiger TRCTL11/3R	Plaxton Paramount 3200	C46FT	1983	Ex Yorkshire Traction, 1992
420	HIL8420	Leyland Tiger TRCTL11/3R	Plaxton Paramount 3200	C53F	1983	Ex Yorkshire Traction, 1992
421	KIB6620	Leyland Tiger TRCTL11/3R	Plaxton Paramount 3200	C53F	1983	Ex Yorkshire Traction, 1992
422	MSV922	Leyland Tiger TRCTL11/3RH	Plaxton Paramount 3500 II	C46FT	1985	Ex Yorkshire Traction, 1992
423	AKG265A	Leyland Tiger TRCTL11/3R	Duple Laser	C51F	1984	Ex Rhondda, 1995
424	AKG282A	Leyland Tiger TRCTL11/3R	Duple Laser	C51F	1984	Ex Rhondda, 1995
425	A185AHB	Leyland Tiger TRCTL11/3R	Duple Laser	C51F	1984	Ex Rhondda, 1995
426	A186AHB	Leyland Tiger TRCTL11/3R	Duple Laser	C51F	1984	Ex Rhondda, 1995
427	KIB6527	Leyland Tiger TRCTL11/3R	Duple 340 (1987)	C51F	1982	Ex Strathtay, 1993
439	UJI2439	Leyland Tiger TRCTL11/3RZ	Plaxton Paramount 3200 II	C48FT	1986	Ex Yorkshire Traction, 1995
440	IIL6440	Leyland Tiger TRCTL11/3RZ	Plaxton Paramount 3200 II	C50FT	1986	Ex Yorkshire Traction, 1995
441	XPM41	Leyland Tiger TRCTL11/3RZ	Plaxton Paramount 3200 III	C53F	1988	Ex Shearings, 1992
442	XPM42	Leyland Tiger TRCTL11/3RZ	Plaxton Paramount 3200 III	C53F	1988	Ex Shearings, 1992

Opposite, top: One of three Leyland Tiger re-bodied in 1995 for the Humberlink service between Scunthorpe and Hull over the Humber Bridge. The chassis of 457, PIW4457 was purchased from Troika Travel of South Norwood where it was fitted with a Goldliner body and was once part of the Strathtay Scottish fleet, also part of the Yorkshire Traction group.
Opposite, bottom: Part of the policy of replacing Bristol VRs, RoadCar have acquired a substantial number of second-hand Leyland Atlanteans. An entire batch from Trent are now in the fleet one of which came via Sheffield Omnibus. Seen passing Lincoln Cathedral is 1378, LRB578W.

451	929GTA	Leyland Tiger TRCTL11/3R	East Lancs EL2000(1992)	DP57F	1983	Ex Strathtay, 1992	
452	TWO84	Leyland Tiger TRCTL11/3R	East Lancs EL2000(1992)	DP57F	1984	Ex Rhondda, 1992	
453	WVL515	Leyland Tiger TRCTL11/3R	East Lancs EL2000(1992)	DP57F	1984	Ex Rhondda, 1992	
454	MSV926	Leyland Tiger TRCTL11/3R	East Lancs EL2000(1993)	DP57F	1981	Ex SMT, 1993	
455	DAZ5455	Leyland Tiger TRCTL11/3R	East Lancs EL2000(1994)	B72F	1983	Ex SMT, 1994	
456	PIW4456	Leyland Tiger TRCTL11/3R	East Lancs EL2000(1995)	DP57F	1983	Ex Northern Bus, Anston, 1994	
457	PIW4457	Leyland Tiger TRCTL11/3R	East Lancs EL2000(1995)	DP57F	1982	Ex Troika Travel,South Norwood, 1994	
458	AKG213A	Leyland Tiger TRCTL11/3R	East Lancs EL2000(1995)	DP57F	1984	Ex Rhondda, 1994	
463	TDC853X	Leyland Tiger TRCTL11/3R	East Lancs EL2000(1996)	DP53F	1982	Ex Midland, 1995	
466	EWY26Y	Leyland Tiger TRCTL11/2R	Alexander TE	DP49F	1983	Ex Tees & District, 1996	
474	KIB6474	Scania K92CRB	Plaxton Paramount 3200 III	C55F	1988	Ex Yorkshire Traction, 1996	
476	F256CEW	Scania K93CRB	Plaxton Derwent II	B57F	1989	Ex Fowler, Holbeach Drove, 1996	
477	F257CEW	Scania K93CRB	Plaxton Derwent II	B57F	1989	Ex Fowler, Holbeach Drove, 1996	
478	F258CEW	Scania K93CRB	Plaxton Derwent II	B57F	1989	Ex Fowler, Holbeach Drove, 1996	
601	B501FFW	Leyland Olympian ONLXB/1R	Eastern Coach Works	DPH42/30F	1985		
602	B502FFW	Leyland Olympian ONLXB/1R	Eastern Coach Works	DPH42/30F	1985		
603	B503FFW	Leyland Olympian ONLXB/1R	Eastern Coach Works	DPH42/30F	1985		
642	DFW42X	Leyland Olympian ONLXB/2R	East Lancashire	H49/35F	1982	Ex Lincoln City, 1993	
643	KTL43Y	Leyland Olympian ONLXB/2R	East Lancashire	H49/35F	1982	Ex Lincoln City, 1993	
644	KTL44Y	Leyland Olympian ONLXB/2R	East Lancashire	H49/35F	1982	Ex Lincoln City, 1993	
645	KTL45Y	Leyland Olympian ONLXB/2R	East Lancashire	H49/35F	1982	Ex Lincoln City, 1993	
646	C46KBE	Leyland Olympian ONLXCT/2R	East Lancashire	DPH47/29F	1985	Ex Lincoln City, 1993	
647	C47KBE	Leyland Olympian ONLXCT/2R	East Lancashire	DPH47/29F	1985	Ex Lincoln City, 1993	
648	C48KBE	Leyland Olympian ONLXCT/2R	East Lancashire	DPH47/29F	1985	Ex Lincoln City, 1993	
649	A208DTO	Leyland Olympian ONLXB/1R	East Lancashire	H45/27F	1984	Ex Lincoln City, 1993	

681-686

		Volvo Olympian YN2RV18Z4		East Lancashire		H51/37F	1996	
681	P681SVL	683	P683SVL	684	P684SVL	685	P685SVL	686	P686SVL
682	P682SVL							

701	KCK201W	Leyland Atlantean AN68C/2R	East Lancashire	H50/36F	1981	Ex Barnsley & District, 1996	
702	KCK202W	Leyland Atlantean AN68C/2R	East Lancashire	H50/36F	1981	Ex Barnsley & District, 1996	
703	KCK203W	Leyland Atlantean AN68C/2R	East Lancashire	H50/36F	1981	Ex Barnsley & District, 1996	
704	KCK204W	Leyland Atlantean AN68C/2R	East Lancashire	H50/36F	1981	Ex Sheffield Omnibus, 1996	
707	URN207V	Leyland Atlantean AN68A/2R	East Lancashire	H45/33F	1979	Ex Barnsley & District, 1995	
708	URN208V	Leyland Atlantean AN68A/2R	East Lancashire	H45/33F	1979	Ex Barnsley & District, 1996	
709	URN209V	Leyland Atlantean AN68A/2R	East Lancashire	H45/33F	1979	Ex Barnsley & District, 1996	
710	DHG210W	Leyland Atlantean AN68B/2R	East Lancashire	H45/33F	1980	Ex Sheffield Omnibus, 1996	
711	DHG211W	Leyland Atlantean AN68B/2R	East Lancashire	H45/33F	1980	Ex Sheffield Omnibus, 1996	
732	YJK932V	Leyland Atlantean AN68A/2R	East Lancashire	H47/35F	1979	Ex Barnsley & District, 1996	
734	YJK934V	Leyland Atlantean AN68A/2R	East Lancashire	H47/35F	1979	Ex Eastbourne, 1996	
735	YJK935V	Leyland Atlantean AN68A/2R	East Lancashire	H47/35F	1979	Ex Eastbourne, 1996	
740	VCX340X	Leyland Atlantean AN68D/2R	Northern Counties	H47/36F	1982	Ex Sheffield Omnibus, 1996	
746	UHG146V	Leyland Atlantean AN68A/2R	Alexander AL	H49/36F	1980	Ex Preston Bus, 1995	

1301-1306

		Leyland Atlantean AN68A/1R		Northern Counties		H43/32F	1976	Ex Greater Manchester, 1988	
								*1304/6 are O43/32F	
1301	LJA609P	1302	LJA608P	1304	LJA642P	1305	LJA612P	1306	LJA622P

1309	UBV85L	Leyland Atlantean AN68/1R	East Lancashire	O45/31F	1972	Ex Lancaster, 1989	
1311	ETO911V	Leyland Atlantean AN68A/1R	Roe	H43/34F	1979	Ex Gash, Newark, 1989	
1314	UBV84L	Leyland Atlantean AN68/1R	East Lancashire	O45/31F	1972	Ex Lancaster, 1993	
1316	BNE751N	Leyland Atlantean AN68/1R	Northern Counties	H43/32F	1974	Ex Gash, Newark, 1989	
1317	UBV87L	Leyland Atlantean AN68/1R	East Lancashire	O45/31F	1972	Ex Lancaster, 1993	
1318	DBV198W	Leyland Atlantean AN68B/1R	East Lancashire	O45/33F	1980	Ex Hyndburn, 1992	
1319	MRT7P	Leyland Atlantean AN68/1R	Roe	H43/32F	1976	Ex Ipswich, 1994	
1320	HDX906N	Leyland Atlantean AN68/1R	Roe	H43/29F	1975	Ex Ipswich, 1994	

1321-1329

		Leyland Atlantean AN68A/1R		Roe	H43/32F*	1976-77	Ex Ipswich, 1994-95		
							*1322/4/7 are H43/29F, 1321 is H43/26F		
1321	RDX11R	1323	RDX13R	1325	RDX15R	1327	RDX17R	1329	SDX26R
1322	RDX12R	1324	RDX14R	1326	RDX16R	1328	SDX28R		

1334	LEO734Y	Leyland Atlantean AN68D/1R	Northern Counties	H43/32F	1983	Ex Sheffield Omnibus, 1996	
1335	LEO735Y	Leyland Atlantean AN68D/1R	Northern Counties	H43/32F	1983	Ex Ribble, 1995	

Three Scania K92CRB buses joined the RoadCar fleet from Fowler's of Holbeach Drove in early 1996. These 57-seat Plaxton Derwent-bodied vehicles are all allocated to Newark. No.476, F256CEW is seen leaving the town on the tendered service 87 which terminates in Lincoln having served many villages to the south of the A46. *Tony Wilson*

1367-1373

		Leyland Atlantean AN68A/1R		Eastern Coach Works		H43/31F	1979-80 Ex Sheffield Omnibus, 1995/6		
1367	TRN467V	1369	TRN479V	1371	TRN471V	1372	TRN472V	1373	TRN473V
1368	TRN468V								

1374-1383

		Leyland Atlantean AN68C/1R		Eastern Coach Works		H43/31F	1981	Ex Trent, 1995*	
								*1382 Ex Sheffield Omnibus, 1995	
1374	LRB584W	1378	LRB578W	1380	LRB580W	1382	LRB582W	1383	LRB583W
1377	LRB577W	1379	LRB579W	1381	LRB581W				

1384	TRN484V	Leyland Atlantean AN68A/1R	Eastern Coach Works	H43/31F	1980	Ex Ribble ,1995	
1385	TRN485V	Leyland Atlantean AN68A/1R	Eastern Coach Works	H43/31F	1980	Ex Ribble ,1995	
1389	TRN469V	Leyland Atlantean AN68A/1R	Eastern Coach Works	H43/31F	1979	Ex Ribble ,1995	
1395	OEM785S	Leyland Atlantean AN68/1R	M.C.W	H43/32F	1978	Ex Nottingham Omnibus,1995	
1415w	KIB6708	Leyland Leopard PSU3E/4R(DAF)	Duple Dominant	C49F	1977	Ex Yorkshire Traction, 1993	
1418	PFE39P	Leyland Leopard PSU5A/4R(DAF)	Duple Dominant	C53F	1976	Ex Gash, Newark, 1989	
1419	JFW915T	Leyland Leopard PSU3E/4R	Alexander AT	DP49F	1979	Ex Strathtay, 1991	
1421	ULS321T	Leyland Leopard PSU3E/4R	Alexander AYS	DP49F	1979	Ex Strathtay, 1993	
1422	ULS335T	Leyland Leopard PSU3E/4R	Alexander AYS(1981)	B53F	1979	Ex Strathtay, 1995	

1431-1442

		Leyland Leopard PSU3D/4R*		Alexander AYS		B53F	1977	Ex Strathtay, 1991-93	
								*1431-32 are type PSU3E/4R	
1431	XSG71R	1433	YSF73S	1436	YSF81S	1440	YSF80S	1442	YSF82S
1432	XSG72R	1434	YSF74S	1439	YSF89S				

1443	TSJ73S	Leyland Leopard PSU3D/4R	Alexander AY	B53F	1977	Ex Clydeside, 1995	
1444	TSJ58S	Leyland Leopard PSU3D/4R	Alexander AY	B53F	1978	Ex Clydeside, 1995	
1446	TSJ46S	Leyland Leopard PSU3D/4R	Alexander AY	B53F	1978	Ex Clydeside, 1995	
1447	GSO87V	Leyland Leopard PSU3E/4R	Alexander AYS	B53F	1980	Ex Strathtay, 1994	
1449	WFS149W	Leyland Leopard PSU3E/4R	Alexander AYS	B53F	1980	Ex Fife Scottish, 1996	
1450w	XTL466X	Leyland Leopard PSU3F/4R	Willowbrook 003	C53F	1981		
1451	XTL467X	Leyland Leopard PSU3F/4R	Willowbrook 003	DP53F	1981		
1452	XTL468X	Leyland Leopard PSU3F/4R	Willowbrook 003	C53F	1981		
1453	XTL469X	Leyland Leopard PSU3F/4R	Willowbrook 003	DP53F	1981		

Fleet No	Reg	Chassis	Body	Seating	Year	Notes
1455	AVL744X	Leyland Leopard PSU3G/4RT	Eastern Coach Works B51	DP53F	1982	
1456	AVL745X	Leyland Leopard PSU3G/4RT	Eastern Coach Works B51	DP53F	1982	
1458	AVL747X	Leyland Leopard PSU3G/4RT	Eastern Coach Works B51	DP53F	1982	
1464	GLS277N	Leyland Leopard PSU3/3R	Alexander AYS	B53F	1974	Ex Vanguard, Bedworth, 1989
1476	NPA223W	Leyland Leopard PSU3E/4R	Plaxton Supreme IV Express	C53F	1981	Ex Gash, Newark, 1989
1477	NPA224W	Leyland Leopard PSU3E/4R	Plaxton Supreme IV Express	C53F	1981	Ex Gash, Newark, 1989
1478	FTL992X	Leyland Leopard PSU3/4R	Duple Dominant IV	C49F	1981	Ex Yorkshire Traction, 1990
1479	FTL993X	Leyland Leopard PSU3/4R	Duple Dominant IV	C49F	1981	Ex Yorkshire Traction, 1990
1482w	DAK260V	Leyland Leopard PSU3E/4R	Plaxton Supreme IV Express	C49F	1979	Ex Yorkshire Traction, 1991
1483	NWB163X	Leyland Leopard PSU3/4R	Duple Dominant IV Express	C49F	1981	Ex Yorkshire Traction, 1994
1832	EFE32T	Bristol VRT/SL3/6LXB	East Lancashire	H45/32F	1979	Ex Lincoln City, 1993
1835	NFW35V	Bristol VRT/LL3/6LXB	East Lancashire	H50/36F	1980	Ex Lincoln City, 1993
1839w	UFW39W	Bristol VRT/LL3/6LXB	East Lancashire	H50/36F	1981	Ex Lincoln City, 1993
1840	UFW40W	Bristol VRT/LL3/6LXB	East Lancashire	H50/36F	1981	Ex Lincoln City, 1993
1841	UFW41W	Bristol VRT/SL3/6LXB	East Lancashire	H50/36F	1981	Ex Lincoln City, 1993
1904	XAK904T	Bristol VRT/SL3/501(Gardner)	Eastern Coach Works	H43/31F	1978	Ex Yorkshire Traction, 1978

1941-1970		Bristol VRT/SL3/6LXB		Eastern Coach Works	H43/31F	1979-81		
1941	KTL24V	1951	LVL806V	1956	PFE540V	1960	PFE544V	1969w SVL179W
1944	KTL27V	1952	LVL807V	1957	PFE541V	1967w	SVL177W	1970w SVL180W
1949	LVL804V	1954	LVL809V	1958	PFE542V	1968w	SVL178W	

Fleet No	Reg	Chassis	Body	Seating	Year	Notes
1971	HWJ924W	Bristol VRT/SL3/6LXB	Eastern Coach Works	H43/31F	1980	Ex Yorkshire Traction, 1988
1972	HWJ922W	Bristol VRT/SL3/6LXB	Eastern Coach Works	H43/31F	1980	Ex Yorkshire Traction, 1991
1973	HWJ923W	Bristol VRT/SL3/6LXB	Eastern Coach Works	DPH39/31F	1980	Ex Yorkshire Traction, 1991
1975	HWJ925W	Bristol VRT/SL3/6LXB	Eastern Coach Works	DPH39/31F	1980	Ex Yorkshire Traction, 1991
1990	MWG940X	Bristol VRT/SL3/6LXB	Eastern Coach Works	DPH41/31F	1981	Ex Yorkshire Traction, 1991
2310	SPC270R	Leyland National 10351A/1R		B41F	1977	Ex South Riding, 1995
2312	THX212S	Leyland National 10351A/2R		B44F	1978	Ex Stanley Gath, Dewsbury, 1992
2313	TRN803V	Leyland National 10351B/1R		B44F	1979	Ex Cumberland, 1993
2315	CHH215T	Leyland National 10351B/1R		B44F	1979	Ex Cumberland, 1993
2316	CHH212T	Leyland National 10351B/1R		B44F	1979	Ex Cumberland, 1993
2317	AHH207T	Leyland National 10351B/1R		B44F	1979	Ex Cumberland, 1993
2494	NVL165	Bristol SC4LK	Eastern Coach Works	B35F	1961	Ex Majestic, Barnsley, 1989
2802	MBZ7142	Leyland National 11351/1R		B49F	1976	Ex South Riding, 1995
2818	LTL388P	Leyland National 11351/1R		B52F	1975	
2829	NTV729M	Leyland National 1151/2R/0101		DP32DL	1973	Ex Mobilinc, North Hykeham, 1995
2830	RVL143R	Leyland National 11351A/1R		B48F	1976	
2831	UHG756R	Leyland National 11351A/1R		B49F	1977	Ex Cumberland, 1993
2832	UHG752R	Leyland National 11351A/1R		B49F	1977	Ex Cumberland, 1993

The Bristol VRT is rapidly disappearing from the RoadCar fleet, being replaced by secondhand Leyland Atlanteans and new Volvo Olympians. Only ten VRs are expected to still be in the fleet by the end of 1996. Photographed while passing Lincoln cathedral is 1967, SVL177W one of ten Eastern Coach Works bodied examples new to RoadCar in 1981.
Steve Sanderson

2836-2846

Leyland National 11351A/1R — B52F* — 1976-77 Ex Yorkshire Traction, 1989-91
*2840-2/46 are B48F

2836	RKW603R	2839	RKW606R	2841	RKW610R	2843w	RKW607R	2845	SWE439S
2838	OWF425R	2840	RKW608R	2842	SWE436S	2844	SWE442S	2846	SWE434S

2848	NWO455R	Leyland National 11351A/1R/SC		B49F	1977	Ex Barnard, Kirton-in-Lindsey, 1992
2849	UFG53S	Leyland National 11351A/2R		B52F	1977	Ex Barnard, Kirton-in-Lindsey, 1992
2850	EPT881S	Leyland National 11351A/1R		B48F	1978	Ex Barnard, Kirton-in-Lindsey, 1992
2851	VUA151R	Leyland National 11351A/1R		B49F	1977	Ex Barnard, Kirton-in-Lindsey, 1992
2852	VUA152R	Leyland National 11351A/1R		B48F	1977	Ex Barnard, Kirton-in-Lindsey, 1992
2853	XAK453T	Leyland National 11351A/1R		B52F	1978	Ex Yorkshire Traction, 1991
2860	RAU600R	Leyland National 11351A/1R		B49F	1976	Ex South Riding, 1995

2865-2879

Leyland National 11351A/1R — B49F* — 1978-79 Ex Yorkshire Traction, 1991
*2865/77/8 are B52F

2865	YWG465T	2870	YWG470T	2877	DET477V	2878	DET478V	2879	DET479V
2866	YWG466T	2872	DET472V						

Previous Registrations:

KAL578	From new
929GTA	A508HVT
A185AHB	A228VWO, AKG231A
A186AHB	A233VWO, AKG293A
AKG213A	A226VWO
AKG265A	A230VWO
AKG282A	A232VWO
DAZ5455	RCY121Y, MKH48A, SWN820Y
ESK965	UWJ53Y, 928GTA
FTL992X	NAK5X, 3880HE
FTL993X	NAK6X, 2316HE
HIL8418	A57WDT, VHE890, 3141HE, MSV922
HIL8419	A56WDT, YTC856
HIL8420	VET54Y, 1619HE
IIL6440	C419VDO, 1737HE
JFW915T	CRS66T ,565BNX
KIB6474	E51WWF, HE8054, E797AHL
KIB6527	VSS5X, WLT921, MSL185X
KIB6620	VET55Y, 2408HE, MSV922
KIB6708	PWB251R, HE8899, RKY774R
MBZ7142	MEL552P
MSV922	B63EWE, 1533HE, KIB6474
MSV926	BSG550W
MSV927	FRN816W, MSV927, BFW233W
NVL165	RFE482, OWJ339A
PFE39P	MWG496P, MSV922
PIW4456	BDF204Y
PIW4457	VSS6X, WLT759, KSP329X, IIL6440
TWO84	A254VWO
UJI2439	C418VDO, YTC49, MSV922
WOI3001	FRN801W
WOI3002	PYE838Y
WVL515	A258VWO, AAX399A
XPM41	E679UNE
XPM42	E693UNE

Livery: Green, yellow and white ; White, red and blue (EconomyLink): 2313/6, 2860/6.
Operations: Lincoln City: 201/4/14/90/2/6/7, 325/6, 381/2, 642-5, 1335/85/9, 2317.
Mobilinc: 400, 2829; Roadcar, remainder.

The Lincoln City Transport fleet currently contains only nineteen vehicles and shares premises with Roadcar in Lincoln. The new garage is on the site of the former railway maintainence depot. All four 84-seat Olympians bought by Lincoln City in 1982 remain in the fleet. 642, DFW42X, which carries an East Lancashire body, is seen in Lincoln High Street when operating route 66 to the Birchwood Estate.
Steve Sanderson

SKILLS

Skill's Motor Coaches Ltd, 1 St Peter's Street, Radford, Nottingham, NG7 3EL

6	6EBH	Bedford SB3		Duple Embassy	C37F	1958	Ex Soul, Olney, 1992	
21	N21ARC	DAF DE33WSSB30000		Plaxton Premiére 350	C49FT	1996		

31-38		Volvo B10M-62		Plaxton Premiére 350	C49FT*	1995	*36/7 are C53F	
31	M31TRR	33	M133TRR	35	M35TRR	37	M37TRR	38	M38TRR
32	M32TRR	34	M34TRR	36	M36TRR				

39-44		Volvo B10M-62		Plaxton Premiére 350	C49FT	1996		
39	N39ARC	42	N1SMC	43	N43ARC	44	N144ARC	45	N45ARC
40	N140ARC								

41	RXI5441	Volvo B58-61	Jonckheere Bermuda (1983)	C57F	1982	
46	F46LCH	Volvo B10M-60	Plaxton Paramount 3200 III	C53F	1989	
47	L47ORC	Volvo B10M-60	Jonckheere Deauville 45	C49FT	1994	
48	L48ORC	Volvo B10M-60	Jonckheere Deauville 45	C49FT	1994	
49	L49ORC	Volvo B10M-60	Jonckheere Deauville 45	C49FT	1994	
50	G50ONN	Volvo B10M-60	Plaxton Paramount 3200 III	C53F	1989	
51	G51ONN	Volvo B10M-60	Plaxton Paramount 3200 III	C53F	1989	
52	J693LGA	Volvo B10M-60	Van Hool Alizée	C49FT	1992	Ex Park's, 1996
53	G553RRR	Volvo B10M-60	Plaxton Paramount 3200 III	C53DL	1990	

54-58		Volvo B10M-61		Van Hool Alizée	C53F	1989	Ex Shearings, 1996	
54	YXI7380	55	YXI7381	56	YXI9256	57	YXI5503	58	YXI9258

59	TJI4859	Volvo B10M-61	Van Hool Alizée	C53F	1988	Ex Park's, 1995
60	TJI4860	Volvo B10M-61	Van Hool Alizée	C53F	1988	Ex Park's, 1995
61	L61LRC	Mercedes-Benz 208D	Devon Conversions	M12	1993	
62		Mercedes-Benz			On order	
63	L63ORC	Mercedes-Benz 609D	Onyx	C21FL	1994	
64	M64RRA	Mercedes-Benz 609D	Onyx	C21F	1994	
65	L65ORB	Mercedes-Benz 711D	Marshall C19	C29F	1994	
66	YXI7906	Volvo B10M-61	Van Hool Alizée	C53F	1989	Ex Shearings, 1996
67	YXI5860	Volvo B10M-61	Van Hool Alizée	C53F	1989	Ex Shearings, 1996
68	YXI8421	Volvo B10M-61	Van Hool Alizée	C53F	1989	Ex Shearings, 1996
69	YXI9243	Volvo B10M-61	Van Hool Alizée	C53F	1989	Ex Shearings, 1996
70	K770JRA	Toyota Coaster HDB30R	Caetano Optimo II	C21F	1993	
74	IIL7074	Leyland Tiger TRCTL11/3ARZ	Duple 340	C53F	1989	Ex Shearings, 1993
76	IIL7076	Leyland Tiger TRCL10/3ARZM	Plaxton Paramount 3200 III	C53F	1989	Ex Shearings, 1993
79	L79VMW	Mercedes Benz 208D	Devon Conversions	M12	1993	Ex Churchfields, 1995
82	J82CRR	Hestair Duple SDA1517	Duple 425	C53FT	1991	
85	F812TMD	Volvo B10M-60	Van Hool Alizée	C52F	1989	Ex Ralph's, Langley, 1996
86	J669LGA	Volvo B10M-60	Van Hool Alizée	C49DT	1992	Ex Park's, 1996
87	J688LGA	Volvo B10M-60	Van Hool Alizée	C49DT	1992	Ex Park's, 1996
88	NIB2796	Volvo B10M-61	Plaxton Paramount 3500 II	C53F	1986	Ex Horton's, Ripley, 1994
89	NIB8762	Volvo B10M-61	Plaxton Paramount 3500 II	C53F	1986	Ex Horton's, Ripley, 1994

Previous Registrations:

6EBH	From new		NIB8762	C103DWR	YXI7381	F743ENE
IIL7074	F786GNA		TJI4859	E630UNE, LSK812, E955CGA	YXI7906	F744ENE
IIL7076	F712ENE		TJI4860	E636UNE, LSK825, E957CGA	YXI8421	F745ENE
J669LGA	J459HDS, LSK499		RXI5441	TRB24X	YXI9243	F748ENE
J688LGA	J458HDS, LSK498		YXI5503	F739ENE	YXI9256	F750ENE
J693LGA	J464HDS, LSK504		YXI5860	F740ENE	YXI9258	F751ENE
NIB2796	C106DWR		YXI7380	F742ENE		

Livery: Green, blue, black, and yellow ; white and red (Eurolines) - 31, 31, 47; white (National Express) - 52

Skills of Nottingham have recently changed their livery. This new style incorporates many colours and is rapidly being applied to the fleet. One of the first coaches to receive the new scheme was 33, M133TRR, a Plaxton Premiére-bodied Volvo B10M seen leaving Ferrybridge services.
Steve Sanderson

Displaying the older Skills livery is 50, G50ONN, one of only two Plaxton Paramount-bodied Volvo B10M coaches built in 1989 to remain in the fleet. It was captured by our photographer in London when it was working on behalf of Wallace Arnold. *Colin Lloyd*

Scutt operates both double-deck vehicles and coaches; the coaches carry the Raynors Travel fleetname - a reference to the proprietors son. This depot view shows JVY676S, a Bedford YMT that was purchased by Scutt from York Pullman in 1991. *Steve Sanderson*

Sweyne are based at Swinefleet near Goole and provide the bus service between Goole and Scunthorpe. The coach fleet contains this narrow Leyland Leopard which was built to negotiate the narrow lanes of Devon for Wallace Arnold. CSU935 was re-bodied with a Plaxton Paramount 3200 body in 1987 because there were no suitable narrow width chassis available at the time. One of only four of the type, the other three remain with Wallace Arnold. *Richard Belton*

SCUTT

H A Scutt, 57 High Street, Owston Ferry, North Lincolnshire, DN9 1RH

JVY676S	Bedford YMT	Plaxton Supreme III	C53F	1978	Ex York Pullman, 1991
CWU151T	Leyland Fleetline FE30AGR	Roe	H44/33F	1978	Ex Rider Group, 1995
HSD87V	Leyland Fleetline FE30AGR	Alexander AL	H44/31F	1980	Ex Clydeside, 1995
WFU470V	Leyland Fleetline FE30AGR	Roe	H45/29D	1980	Ex Grimsby Cleethorpes, 1996
JSV365	Leyland Tiger TRCTL11/3R	Plaxton Supreme V	C53F	1982	Ex Armchair, Brentford, 1991
BUA711X	Leyland Tiger TRCTL11/3R	Plaxton Viewmaster IV	C51F	1982	Ex Wray, Harrogate, 1993
A530LPP	Leyland Tiger TRCTL11/3R	Plaxton Paramount 3200	C57F	1983	Ex WHM, Hutton, 1991

Previous Registrations:
JSV365 XPP296X   BUA711X   TRN91X, HSV126

Livery: Red and white

SKINNER

T A & T J Skinner, Main Street, Saltby, Melton Mowbray, Leicestershire, LE14 4QW

TKW335S	Bedford YLQ	Plaxton Supreme III	C45F	1978	Ex Angel Motors, Edmonton, 1984
XJF888S	Bedford YMT	Plaxton Supreme III	C53F	1978	Ex Land Hirst, Leicester, 1983
AKK176T	Bedford YMT	Duple Dominant	B61F	1978	Ex Boro'line, Maidstone, 1990
VJU261X	Bedford YNT	Plaxton Supreme III Express	C53F	1982	Ex Wainfleet, Nuneaton, 1986
A141BTV	Bedford YNT	Plaxton Paramount 3200	C53F	1983	Ex Leah, Huthwaite, 1988
A837EAY	Bedford YNT	Plaxton Paramount 3200	C53F	1983	Ex Lester, Long Whatton, 1985
E752HJF	Dennis Javelin 12SDA1907	Duple 320	C57F	1988	Ex Lewis, Pailton, 1990
E131PLJ	Dennis Javelin 12SDA1907	Plaxton Paramount 3200 III	C53F	1988	Ex Winterbourne Pioneer, 1993
G324BHN	Dennis Javelin 12SDA1916	Plaxton Paramount 3200 III	C53F	1989	Ex Winn Bros, Brompton, 1995
G48HDW	Dennis Javelin 12SDA1907	Duple 320	C57F	1990	Ex Bebb, Llanwit Fardre, 1992

Livery: Blue and white

SWEYNE

JE, JJ & M Holt, Longshores, Reedness Road, Swinefleet, North Lincolnshire, DN14 8EL

Depot: Shrubland Farm, Swinefleet.

	TUB13M	Leyland Leopard PSU3B/4R	Plaxton Elite III	C53F	1974	Ex Tower, Liversege, 1981
	KHE448P	Leyland Leopard PSU3C/4R	Plaxton Elite III	C53F	1975	Ex Shennan, Drongan, 1981
	CSU935	Leyland Leopard PSU4E/2R	Plaxton P'mount 3200 (1987)	C45F	1977	Ex Wallace Arnold, 1990
	HSC104T	Leyland National 11351A/1R (DAF)		B49F	1978	Ex Fife Scottish, 1992
w	LUP895T	Leyland National 11351A/1R (DAF)		DP48F	1979	Ex Tees & District, 1992
	LUA278N	Leyland Leopard PSU3F/4R	Plaxton Supreme IV	C46F	1980	Ex King, Kirkcowan, 1987
	104JEH	DAF MB200DKTL600	Plaxton Supreme IV	C50F	1981	Ex Harris Coaches, West Thurrock, 1990
	OUH738N	DAF MB200DKTL600	Plaxton Supreme V	C51F	1982	Ex City Centre, Cardiff, 1994
	TIB2875	Bova EL28/581	Duple Calypso	C53F	1984	Ex Woods, Wigston 1995
	RND212X	DAF MB200DKTL600	Plaxton Supreme V	C51F	1982	Ex Eavesway, North Ashton, 1993
	D167WRC	DAF SB2300DHS585	Plaxton Paramount 3200 III	C53F	1987	Ex Slack, Tansley, 1993
	J77OLT	DAF SB2305DHS585	Van Hool Alizée	C53FT	1991	

Previous Registrations:
104JEH	UHK202W	OUH738N	TND404X, RJI1977	TIB2875	B554KRY
CSU935	SWW125R	RND212X	TND402X, FSU343		

Livery: -Turquoise, grey and white

SLEAFORDIAN

Sleaford Taxi Co Ltd, 49 Westgate, Sleaford, Lincolnshire, NG34 7PU

UJL270	Volvo B10M-61	Plaxton Paramount 3500 III	C55F	1987	Ex Park's, 1988
YCT463	Volvo B10M-61	Plaxton Paramount 3200 III	C55F	1987	
E23EFW	Ford Transit VE6	Deansgate	M14	1988	
KTL982	Volvo B10M-61	Plaxton Paramount 3200 III	C55F	1988	Ex Fleet Coaches, 1994
KVL261	Volvo B10M-60	Plaxton Paramount 3500 III	C53F	1989	Ex Dodsworth, Boroughbridge, 1994
VCT418	Volvo B10M-60	Plaxton Paramount 3200 III	C53F	1989	Ex Fleet Coaches, 1996
NTL939	Volvo B10M-60	Plaxton Première 320	C53F	1993	Ex Supreme, Coventry, 1996
M953CJN	Ford Transit VE6	Ford	M14	1993	Ex private owner, 1996

Previous Registrations:

KTL982	F233DWF	NTL939	K887BRW	VCT418	F473WFX
KVL261	F429DUG	UJL270	D815SGB	YCT463	D501YFW

Livery: White and Yellow

On Mondays to Saturdays, Sleafordian operate a service five times a day to Billingborough, a village to the east of Sleaford. Often touring coaches can be found on this route, and shown here is VCT418, a Volvo B10M that carries a Plaxton Paramount 3200 body. *Steve Sanderson*

TRS

TRS Coach Services, Scudamore Road, Leicester, Leicestershire LE

Depots: Scudamore Road, Leicester ; Merrylees Ind Est, Merrylees, Desford.

Reg	Chassis	Body	Seat	Year	History
TUT888R	Bedford VAL70	Plaxton Elite	C53F	1970	Ex Sandhurst, Leicester, 1986
OTO576M	Leyland Atlantean AN68/1R	East Lancashire	H47/30D	1974	Ex Holloway, Scunthorpe, 1994
TRT96R	Leyland Atlantean AN68/1R	Roe	H43/29D	1974	Ex Eastbourne, 1990
HOR307N	Leyland Atlantean AN68/1R	Alexander	H45/30D	1975	Ex Shire Coaches, St Albans, 1994
THX289S	Leyland Fleetline FE30ALR	MCW	H44/24D	1977	Ex Bryan A Garratt, Leicester, 1996
OEM776S	Leyland Atlantean AN68/1R	MCW	H43/32F	1978	Ex Sheffield Omnibus, 1994
OEM794S	Leyland Atlantean AN68/1R	MCW	H43/32F	1978	Ex Sheffield Omnibus, 1994
THX643S	Leyland Fleetline FE30ALR	Park Royal	H46/24F	1978	Ex Bryan A Garratt, Leicester, 1996
RJI2709	Leyland Leopard PSU3E/4R	Duple Dominant II	C47F	1978	Ex Bryan A Garratt, Leicester, 1996
JIL8326	Ford A0609	Moseley Faro	C25F	1978	Ex Glan Harris, Morriston, 1994
BKA911X	Ford A0609	Moseley Faro	C25F	1982	Ex Timewell, Maghull, 1995
UTC872	Aüwaerter Neoplan N122/3	Aüwaerter Skyliner	CH57/20CT	1983	Ex Caelloi, Pwllheli, 1992
2320DD	Van Hool T818	Van Hool Astron	CH49/11FT	1983	Ex Globe, North Common, 1988
TRS332	Aüwaerter Neoplan N112/3	Aüwaerter Skyliner	CH57/20DT	1984	Ex Park's, 1994
NIW2312	Leyland Royal Tiger B50	Van Hool Alizeé	C49FT	1984	Ex London Cityrama, Battersea, 1992
A866DCN	Leyland Royal Tiger B54	Roe Doyen	C46F	1984	Ex Annison, Ilkeston, 1996
ROI5013	MCW Metroliner DR130/10	MCW	CH53/17CT	1985	Ex Bond, Willington, 1994
GIL6239	MCW Metroliner DR130/8	MCW	CH53/16DT	1985	Ex Alpha, Hull, 1992
TRS574	Bedford YNV	Plaxton Paramount 3200	C57F	1986	Ex Mayne, Buckie, 1987
JIL8324	Bedford YNV	Duple 320	C57F	1986	Ex BRC, Tockington, 1990
JIL8325	Bedford YNV	Duple 320	C55F	1987	Ex Bywater, Rochdale, 1990
TRS835	Hestair Duple 425 SDAK1512	Duple 425	C53FT	1987	Ex Myall, Birmingham, 1989
LIL6287	Dennis Javelin 12SDA1907	Plaxton Paramount 3200	C57F	1989	Ex Clarkes Coaches, Pailton, 1994
G105AVX	Dennis Javelin 12SDA1907	Duple 320	C53FT	1990	Ex Colchester, 1994
G37HDW	Freight Rover Sherpa	Carlyle Citybus 2	B20F	1990	Ex Shamrock, Pontypridd, 1996
J241MFP	Dennis Javelin 12SDA1934	Plaxton Paramount 3200 III	C55F	1992	Ex Clarkes Coaches, Pailton, 1994
J242MFP	Dennis Javelin 12SDA1921	Plaxton Paramount 3200 III	C53F	1992	Ex Clarkes Coaches, Pailton, 1994
TXI2437	Volkswagen Transporter LT37D	Volkswagen	M12	19??	Ex Private owner, 1992
N1TRS	Ford Transit VE6	Ford	M16	1996	

Previous Registrations:

A866DCN	A721ANL, CU7661	RJI2709	KRN99T
GIL6236	B54DVK, KSU464, B847DCU	ROI5103	C158UHN
JIL8324	C346UNR	TRS332	A350UFE, SKY784, LSK634
JIL8325	E902EAY	TRS574	C888GSE, TRS332, C502WRY
JIL8326	KWP2T	TRS835	E907EAY
LIL6287	F627SAY	TXI2437	??
NIW2312	B77AMH	UTC872	BDF875Y

Livery: White, red and blue

TRS Coaches use two MCW Metroliner double-deck coaches for their coach services. Photographed here on rally duty it can normally be found on private hire. Three other double-deck coaches are also owned.
Andy Chown

TRAVEL WRIGHT

T D & M Wright, Lincoln Road Garage, Newark, Nottinghamshire, NG24 2DR

	Reg	Chassis	Body	Type	Year	Notes
	SNN747R	Bedford YLQ	Plaxton Supreme III	C41F	1977	
	ANJ306T	Leyland Leopard PSU3E/4RT	Plaxton Supreme III Express	C53F	1979	Ex Brighton & Hove, 1986
	CAL845T	Bedford YMT	Plaxton Supreme IV	C53F	1979	
	HAL242V	Bedford YMT	Duple Dominant II	C53F	1980	
	SGR791V	Bristol VRT/SL3/6LXB	Eastern Coach Works	H42/31F	1980	Ex Northumbria, 1993
	JRB416V	Volvo B58-56	Duple Dominant II	C53F	1980	
	NAU292W	Volvo B58-61	Duple Dominant II	C57F	1981	
	ORR904W	Bedford YNT	Plaxton Supreme IV	C53F	1981	
	LAK985W	Bristol VRT/SL3/6LXB	Eastern Coach Works	H43/31F	1981	Ex RoadCar, 1995
	TNN696X	Volvo B10M-61	Plaxton Supreme V	C51F	1981	
	YTO861Y	Volvo B10M-61	Plaxton Paramount 3200	C53F	1983	
	7179TW	Van Hool T815H	Van Hool Alicron	C53FT	1985	
	C35VJF	Bova FLD12.250	Bova Futura	C57F	1986	
	E434YHL	Mercedes-Benz 709D	Reeve Burgess Beaver	B25F	1988	Ex Smith, Alcester, 1991
	E761JAY	Dennis Javelin 12SDA1912	Duple 320	C57F	1988	
	PJI3042	Volvo B10M-46	Caetano Algarve	C41F	1988	Ex Greenway Cs, Nottingham, 1992
	PJI3043	Scania K113CRB	Van Hool Alizée	C51FT	1988	Ex Smith, Marple, 1992
	F692PAY	Dennis Javelin 8.5SDL1903	Plaxton Paramount 3200 III	C35F	1989	
	G865VAY	Mercedes-Benz 609D	Reeve Burgess Beaver	C23F	1989	
	G430YAY	Dennis Javelin 12SDA1916	Plaxton Paramount 3200	C53FT	1990	
	H160DJU	Dennis Javelin 12SDA1907	Plaxton Paramount 3200 III	C57F	1990	
SL1	H34DGD	Mercedes-Benz 811D	Dormobile Routemaker	B33F	1991	Ex Pathfinder, Newark, 1993
SL2	J914HGD	Mercedes-Benz 814D	Dormobile Routemaker	DP33F	1991	Ex Pathfinder, Newark, 1994
	K118KUA	Mercedes-Benz 609D	Autobus Classique	DP23F	1993	
	LIL9842	Van Hool T815	Van Hool Alizée	C49F	1993	Ex White & Urquhart, Newmarket, 1996
	L29CAY	Dennis Javelin 12SDA2136	Caetano Algarve II	C53F	1994	
	N240NNR	MAN 11-190	Caetano Algarve II	C35F	1995	
	N795PDS	Mercedes-Benz 814D	Marshall	B29F	1996	

Previous Registrations:

7179TW	B925OFP	PJI3042	E998KJF
LIL9842	K546GSS	PJI3043	F99CWG

Named vehicles; H160DJU, *Paula Jane* ,LIL9842, *Shannon Jade*

Livery: Biscuit, red and brown (SL1 & SL2 white "ShuttleCo")

One of the oldest vehicles in the Travel Wright fleet is CAL845T, a Bedford YMT with Plaxton Supreme bodywork. It is seen entering Newark bus station from Harby on service 67. This route has been operated by Travel Wright for many years on tender to Nottinghamshire county council.
Tony Wilson

TRENT

Barton Buses Ltd, Mansfield Road, Heanor, Derbyshire, DE75 7BG
Trent Motor Traction Co Ltd, Mansfield Road, Heanor, Derbyshire, DE75 7BG

Depots : Bradwell; Bridge Street, Buxton; Meadow Road, Derby; Portland Street, Hucknall; Station Road, Langley Mill; Bath Street, Ilkeston; Sutton Junction, Sutton in Ashfield; Manvers Street, Nottingham. **Outstations** : Ashbourne, Belper, Bingham, Calverton, Castle Donington, Grantham, Harby, Hatton, Leicester, Matlock, Melton Mowbray, Stamford and Uppingham.

1-8			Volvo B10M-60		Plaxton Expressliner 2		C49FT	1993		
1	L801MRA	3	L803MRA	5	L805MRA	7	L807MRA	8	L808MRA
2	L802MRA	4	L804MRA	6	L806MRA				

45w	C685WNX	Freight Rover Sherpa	Carlyle	B16F	1985	Ex Saxton, Langley Mill 1995
46w	D129WCC	Freight Rover Sherpa	Carlyle	B18F	1987	Ex Saxton, Langley Mill 1995
47w	D47TKA	Freight Rover Sherpa	Dormobile	B16F	1987	Ex Saxton, Langley Mill 1995
48	C548TJF	Ford Transit 190	Rootes	B16F	1989	Ex Erewash Valley, 1990

51-55			Volvo B10M-60		Alexander Q		DP51F	1994		
51	M51PRA	52	M52PRA	53	M53PRA	54	M54PRA	55	M455TCH

101-128			Volvo B10B-58		Northern Counties Paladin		B49F	1993-94		
101	L101LRA	107	L107LRA	113	L113LRA	119	L119LRA	124	L124LRA
102	L102LRA	108	L108LRA	114	L114LRA	120	L120LRA	125	L125LRA
103	L103LRA	109	L109LRA	115	L115LRA	121	L121LRA	126	L126LRA
104	L104LRA	110	L110LRA	116	L116LRA	122	L122LRA	127	L127LRA
105	L105LRA	111	L911LRA	117	L117LRA	123	L123LRA	128	L128LRA
106	L106LRA	112	L112LRA	118	L118LRA				

129-138			Volvo B10B-58		Northern Counties Paladin		B49F	1994		
129	M129PRA	131	M131PRA	133	M133PRA	135	M135PRA	137	M137PRA
130	M130PRA	132	M132PRA	134	M134PRA	136	M136PRA	138	M138PRA

The service from Nottingham and Derby through The Peak District National Park to Manchester is marketed by Trent as Trans Peak. The vehicles dedicated to this route were upgraded in 1994 with the purchase of five Alexander Q-bodied Volvo B10M's. These unusual bodies were constructed at Alexander's Belfast factory. No.51, M51PRA is seen in Bakewell bound for Nottingham.
Tony Wilson

R54 Derby
Rainbow
Rainbow
M133 PRA

R5 Derby
NATTRASS GILES
0115 958 8599
KallKwik
Rainbow
OPTARE
Rainbow
N368 VRC

Trent has, until recently, not been involved in the operation of smaller sized buses. The first midibuses to be bought arrived in 1995 when four Mercedes-Benz 811D 31-seaters were delivered followed by 26 similar sized Optare MetroRiders. No.204, N204VRC is one of the initial batch. A further ten similar buses were received in August 1996 with another five due. *Tony Wilson*

151	P151CTV	Optare Excel	Optare	B45F	on order 1996		
152	P152CTV	Optare Excel	Optare	B45F	on order 1996		
153	P153CTV	Optare Excel	Optare	B45F	on order 1996		

201-241

Optare Metrorider MR15   Optare   B31F   1995-96

201	M201URC	210	N210VRC	218	N218VRC	226	N226VRC	234	P234CTV
202	M202URC	211	N211VRC	219	N219VRC	227	N227CTV	235	P235CTV
203	N203VRC	212	N212VRC	220	N220VRC	228	P228CTV	236	P236CTV
204	N204VRC	213	N213VRC	221	N221VRC	229	P229CTV	237	P237CTV
205	N205VRC	214	N214VRC	222	N322WCH	230	P230CTV	238	P238CTV
206	N206VRC	215	N215VRC	223	N223VRC	231	P231CTV	239	P239CTV
207	N207VRC	216	N216VRC	224	N224VRC	232	P232CTV	240	P240CTV
208	N208VRC	217	N217VRC	225	N225VRC	233	P233CTV	241	P241CTV
209	N209VRC								

271	M271URC	Mercedes-Benz 811D	Wright Nim-bus	B31F	1995	
272	M272URC	Mercedes-Benz 811D	Wright Nim-bus	B31F	1995	
273	M273URC	Mercedes-Benz 811D	Wright Nim-bus	B31F	1995	
274	M274URC	Mercedes-Benz 811D	Wright Nim-bus	B31F	1995	
300	G600NRC	DAF SB220LC550	Optare Delta	B49F	1990	Ex DAF demonstrator, 1992

301-325

DAF SB220LC550   Optare Delta   B49F   1991-92

301	J201BVO	306	J306BVO	311	J311BVO	316	J316BVO	321	J321BVO
302	J302BVO	307	J307BVO	312	J312BVO	317	J317BVO	322	J322BVO
303	J303BVO	308	J308BVO	313	J313BVO	318	J318BVO	323	J323BVO
304	J304BVO	309	J309BVO	314	J314BVO	319	J319BVO	324	J324BVO
305	J305BVO	310	J310BVO	315	J315BVO	320	J320BVO	325	J325BVO

Opposite: Trent introduced Rainbow routes as part of a major market-research led project to increase passenger journeys. A number of routes have been re-launched under the Rainbow Routes banner which guarantees cleanliness and punctuality, backed by a customers charter. Modern vehiclesare the norm on these services, represented here by Northern Counties-bodied Volvo 133, M133PRA, and Optare-bodied DAF SB220 368, N368VRC.

326-353

				DAF SB220LC550		Optare Delta		B48F	1992-93		
326	K326FAL	332	K332FAL	338	K338FAL	344	K344FAL	349	K349FAL
327	K327FAL	333	K633FAU	339	K339FAL	345	K645FAU	350	K350FAL
328	K328FAL	334	K334FAL	340	K640FAU	346	K346FAL	351	K651FAU
329	K329FAL	335	K335FAL	341	K341FAL	347	K347FAL	352	K352FAL
330	K330FAL	336	K336FAL	342	K342FAL	348	K348FAL	353	K353FAL
331	K331FAL	337	K337FAL	343	K343FAL				

354	M354PRA		Dennis Lance 11SDA3115		Optare Sigma	B46F	1994
355	M355PRA		Dennis Lance 11SDA3115		Optare Sigma	B46F	1994

356-370

				Dennis Lance 11SDA3113		Optare Sigma		B46F	1995		
356	N356VRC	359	N359VRC	362	N362VRC	365	N365VRC	368	N368VRC
357	N357VRC	360	N360VRC	363	N363VRC	366	N366VRC	369	N369VRC
358	N358VRC	361	N361VRC	364	N364VRC	367	N367VRC	370	N370VRC

417	OHW492R	Leyland National 11351A/1R	B52F	1977	Ex MTL Manchester, 1995
418	FBV525S	Leyland National 11351A/1R	B49F	1978	Ex MTL Manchester, 1995
419	KCG627L	Leyland National 1151/1R/0402	B49F	1973	Ex Alder Valley, 1985
420	PJT268R	Leyland National 11351A/1R	B49F	1976	Ex Solent Blue Line, 1993

421-427

				Leyland National 11351/1R			B49F	1974-75	
421	GNU568N	423	GNU570N	424w	GNU571N	425w	GNU572N	426	GNU573N

428	TWN740N	Leyland National 11351/1R	B52F	1974	Ex South Wales, 1989
429	KVO429P	Leyland National 11351/2R	B50F	1975	
430	JHW103P	Leyland National 11351/1R	B52F	1975	Ex Cheltenham & Gloucester 1995
431	KVO431P	Leyland National 11351/2R	B50F	1975	
432	KVO432P	Leyland National 11351/2R	B52F	1975	
433	KVO433P	Leyland National 11351A/2R	B50F	1976	
434	NRB434P	Leyland National 11351A/2R	B50F	1976	
435	NRB435P	Leyland National 11351A/2R	B50F	1976	
436	JTH772R	Leyland National 11351/1R	B52F	1976	Ex South Wales, 1989
437	EGB92T	Leyland National 11351A/1R	B52F	1979	Ex Paul S Winson, Loughborough, 1991

438-450

				Leyland National 11351A/2R		*	B50F	1976	
438	PRR438R	442	PRR442R	445	PRR445R	447	PRR447R	449	PRR449R
439	PRR439R	443	PRR443R	446	PRR446R	448	PRR448R	450	PRR450R
441	PRR441R	444	PRR444R						

451-460

				Leyland National 11351A/1R			B49F	1976	
451	PRR451R	453	PRR453R	455	PRR455R	457	PRR457R	459	PRR459R
452	PRR452R	454	PRR454R	456	PRR456R	458	PRR458R	460	PRR460R

461-472

				Leyland National 11351A/2R			B50F*	1977	*463/7/8 are B52F
461	RTO461R	464	RTO464R	466	RTO466R	468	URB468S	471	URB471S
462	RTO462R	465	RTO465R	467	URB467S	469	URB469S	472	URB472S
463	RTO463R								

473	VCH473S	Leyland National 11351A/1R	B49F	1977
474	VCH474S	Leyland National 11351A/1R	B49F	1977
475w	VCH475S	Leyland National 11351A/1R	B49F	1977
476	VCH476S	Leyland National 11351A/1R	B49F	1977

477-503

				Leyland National 11351A/2R		B50F*	1977-78	*501-4 have DAF engines
								*478/81/3/5/7/9/93/9-503 are B52F ; 486 is B48F
477	VCH477S	484	XAL484S	489	XAL489S	494	XAL494S	499	XAL499S
478	VCH478S	485	XAL485S	490	XAL490S	495	XAL495S	500	XAL500S
479	VCH479S	486	XAL486S	491	XAL491S	496	XAL496S	501	YRR501T
481	XAL481S	487	XAL487S	492	XAL492S	497	XAL497S	502	YRR502T
482	XAL482S	488	XAL488S	493	XAL493S	498	XAL498S	503	YRR503T
483	XAL483S								

The dominant single-deck bus in the Trent and Barton fleets is still the Leyland National. A number of secondhand examples had been added to the fleet to combat competition from the now ceased Delta though these are now displacing Leopards from the Barton fleet. The majority of the early Leyland Nationals have been extensively refurbished including 501, YRR501T new to Trent in 1978 and now fitted with a DAF engine. *David Stanier*

504-535   Leyland National 11351A/1R*   B52F   1978-80 *525-35 have Volvo engines

504	ACH504T	511	ACH511T	518	FRA518V	524	FRA524V	530	FRA530V
505	ACH505T	512	ACH515T	519	FRA519V	525	FRA525V	531	FRA531V
506	ACH506T	513	ACH513T	520	FRA520V	526	FRA526V	532	FRA532V
507	ACH507T	514	ACH514T	521	FRA521V	527	FRA527V	533	FRA533V
508	ACH508T	515	FRA515V	522	FRA522V	528	FRA528V	534	FRA534V
509	ACH509T	516	FRA516V	523	FRA523V	529	FRA529V	535	FRA535V
510	ACH510T	517	FRA517V						

536-540   Leyland National 11351A/1R   B49F   1978   Ex West Riding, 1989

536	CWX656T	537w	CWX658T	538	CWX659T	539	CWX660T	540	CWX661T

541	JBR684T	Leyland National 11351A/1R (DAF)		B49F	1978	Ex Tees & District, 1992
542	LUP894T	Leyland National 11351A/1R (DAF)		B49F	1979	Ex Tees & District, 1992
543	EPT879S	Leyland National 11351A/1R (DAF)		B49F	1978	Ex Tees & District, 1992
544	VKE565S	Leyland National 11351A/1R (DAF)		B49F	1977	Ex Stagecoach South 1992
545	UFX849S	Leyland National 11351A/1R (DAF)		B49F	1977	Ex Solent Blue Line, 1993
546	UFX852S	Leyland National 11351A/1R		B49F	1977	Ex Solent Blue Line, 1994
547	VFX985S	Leyland National 11351A/1R (DAF)		B49F	1978	Ex Solent Blue Line, 1994
548	WPR150S	Leyland National 11351A/1R (DAF)		B49F	1978	Ex Solent Blue Line, 1994
550	SKG919S	Leyland National 11351A/1R		B49F	1977	Ex Peoples Provincial, 1995
551	FPR65V	Leyland National 11351A/1R (DAF)		B49F	1980	Ex Solent Blue Line, 1995

552-567   Leyland National 11351A/1R   B52F   1976-9   Ex Cheltenham & Gloucester 1995
*552/3 have DAF engines

552	PHW987S	556	VEU232T	559	UHW101T	562	NOE584R	565	SAE751S
553	TAE638S	557	VEU230T	560	NFB602R	563	NOE585R	566	SAE755S
554	VEU228T	558	TTC532T	561	NOE555R	564	PHW986S	567	TAE643S
555	VEU229T								

568	DAR120T	Leyland National 11351A/1R		B49F	1979	Ex Thamesway, 1996
569	JHJ139V	Leyland National 11351A/1R		B49F	1979	Ex Thamesway, 1996
570	JHJ146V	Leyland National 11351A/1R		B49F	1979	Ex Thamesway, 1996
571	ONN571P	Leyland Atlantean AN68/1R	Willowbrook (1977)	H43/31F	1976	

The East Midland Bus Handbook

600-623
Volvo Citybus B10M-50   Alexander RV   H47/37F   1988-90

600	F600GVO	605	F605GVO	610	F610GVO	615	G615OTV	620	G620OTV
601	F601GVO	606	F606GVO	611	F611GVO	616	G616OTV	621	G621OTV
602	F602GVO	607	F607GVO	612	G612OTV	617	G617OTV	622	G622OTV
603	F603GVO	608	F608GVO	613	G613OTV	618	G618OTV	623	G623OTV
604	F604GVO	609	F609GVO	614	G614OTV	619	G619OTV		

700-711
Leyland Olympian ONLXB/1R   Eastern Coach Works   H45/32F*   1983-84 *707-711 are H45/30F

700	XAU700Y	703	XAU703Y	706	XCH706Y	708	A708DAU	710	A710DAU
701	XAU701Y	704	XAU704Y	707	A707DAU	709	A709DAU	711	A711DAU
702	XAU702Y	705	XAU705Y						

712-723
Leyland Olympian ONLXB/1RV   Eastern Coach Works   H45/30F   1985

712	B712HVO	715	B715HVO	718	C718LTO	720	C720NNN	722	C722NNN
713	B713HVO	716	C716LTO	719	C719LTO	721	C721NNN	723	C723NNN
714	B714HVO	717	C717LTO						

801-815
MAN 11.190   Optare Vecta   B40F   1994

801	M801PRA	804	M804PRA	807	M807PRA	810	M810PRA	813	M813PRA
802	M802PRA	805	M805PRA	808	M808PRA	811	M811PRA	814	M814PRA
803	M803PRA	806	M806PRA	809	M809PRA	812	M812PRA	815	M815PRA

901-916
Dennis Dart SLF   Plaxton Pointer   B39F   on order 1996

901	P901CTO	905	P905CTO	908	P908CTO	911	P911CTO	914	P914CTO
902	P902CTO	906	P906CTO	909	P909CTO	912	P912CTO	915	P915CTO
903	P903CTO	907	P907CTO	910	P910CTO	913	P913CTO	916	P916CTO
904	P904CTO								

1487	RRC487R	Leyland Leopard PSU3C/4R	Plaxton Supreme III Express C51F	1976
1532	ERC357T	Leyland Leopard PSU3E/4R	Plaxton Supreme IV C47F	1979

1583-1592
Leyland Leopard PSU3F/4R   Plaxton Supreme IV Express C51F*   1981   *1584/6/8 are C53F

1583w	PTV583X	1586w	PTV586X	1588	PTV588X	1591	PTV591X	1592	PTV592X
1585w	PTV585X	1587	PTV587X	1589	PTV589X				

1604-1612
Leyland Leopard PSU3G/4R   Plaxton Supreme V Express C53F   1982   *1605/8 are C51F

1605	VRC605Y	1608	VRC608Y	1610w	VRC610Y	1611w	VRC611Y	1612w	VRC612Y
1606	VRC606Y	1609	VRC609Y						

1623-1627
DAF MB200DKFL600   Plaxton Paramount 3200   C51F*   1985   *1623/7 are Paramount 3200 E

1623	B623JRC	1626	B626JRC	1627	B627JRC		

1623	B623JRC	DAF MB200DKFL600	Plaxton Paramount 3200 E	C51F	1985
1626	B626JRC	DAF MB200DKFL600	Plaxton Paramount 3200 E	C51F	1985
1627	B627JRC	DAF MB200DKFL600	Plaxton Paramount 3200 E	C51F	1985

1634-1640
DAF MB230DKFL600   Plaxton Paramount 3200 III C53F*   1987   *1640-2 are C49F

1634	D634WNU	1637	D637WNU	1639	D639WNU	1641	D641WNU	1643	D643WNU
1635	D635WNU	1638	D638WNU	1640	D640WNU	1642w	D642WNU	1644	D644WNU
1636	D636WNU								

Previous Registrations:
ERC357T   CVO3T, YRC182   G600NRC   G910XFC

Livery: Red and cream : Park and Ride (Blue), 326/7/8; National Express, 1-8)

Operations: Barton: 124-8, 185, 250/72/4, 301-11/26-8, 441-6/8/51-79/81-99, 505-24/58/60/1, 667/8, 721-3, 1532 1612/23/31 6/8/0.
Trent: Remainder.

Note: Leicester City 185 and 250 are currently on long term hire as 185 and 250.
Nottingham City 121/4/6 & 33-5 are currently on long term hire as 21/4/6/33-5.
Pathfinder 667/8 are on long term hire as 667/8.

The modern Trent double-deck fleet consists of Volvo Citybuses and Leyland Olympians. Three of the latter type, which all have bodies constructed at the now closed Lowestoft factory of Eastern Coach Works, are in the Barton livery, including 723, C723NNN. It is seen in Nottingham when carrying out park and ride duties.
Tony Wilson

The non-stop express service from Nottingham to Derby runs every 30 minutes and is now marketed by Trent as The Red Arrow. The current vehicles employed on this route are former Barton Plaxton Paramount-bodied DAFs as shown by 1641, D641WNU which is seen arriving in Derby.
Tony Wilson

The large number of Plaxton-bodied Leyland Leopards acquired with the Barton business is rapidly dwindling and with many new buses expected in the next year it is unlikely that any will be in service in 1997. One of the few survivors is 1611, VRC611Y seen here on a Saturday summer season express service in Llandudno.
Ralph Stevens

125

TRENT MOTORS

B Williams & K Robinson, 43 Station Road, Scunthorpe,
North Lincolnshire, DN15 6QE

SGR545R	Leyland National 11351A/1R		B49F	1976	Ex Barnard, Kirton-in-Lindsey, 1990
OWJ167X	Leyland Leopard PSU3G/4R	Eastern Coach Works B51	DP47F	1982	Ex AJC Coaches, Leeds, 1994
MFS579X	Leyland Leopard PSU5C/4R	Duple Dominant III	C48FT	1982	Ex Goldgrove, Erith, 1995
BXI7406	Leyland Royal Tiger B50	Roe Doyen	C51F	1983	Ex Jaronda Travel, Selby, 1991

Previous Registrations:
BXI7406   GWY551Y   MFS579X   PWB659X, MSP333

Livery: White and blue

UNITY

F & J Marriott, Beck Garage, Clayworth, Retford, Nottinghamshire, DN22 9AQ

PRW137M	Leyland Leopard PSU3B/4R	Plaxton Elite III	C51F	1974	Ex Red House, Coventry, 1979
TUA707R	Bedford YMT	Plaxton Supreme III Express	C53F	1976	Ex Shipley, Baildon, 1982
UFX628X	Bristol LHS6L	Plaxton Supreme V	C35F	1982	Ex Cross Gates Coaches, 1991
CAZ6836	Kässbohrer Setra S215HD	Kässbohrer Tornado	C53FT	1982	Ex Walter Martin, Sheffield, 1994
UXI6833	Scania K112CRS	Jonckheere Jubilee P599	C49FT	1984	Ex Lockley, Stafford, 1993
HIL7198	DAF MB200DKFL600	Plaxton Paramount 3500	C49FT	1984	Ex Seaview, Parkstone, 1995
D167LNA	Mercedes-Benz 609D	Made-to-Measure	C27F	1986	
D428JDB	Freight Rover Sherpa	Made-to-Measure	C16F	1986	
G110OFE	Bedford Midi	Bedford	M4	1990	Ex Private Owner, 1994

Previous Registrations:
CAZ6836   GGK724X, 806ECV, JFM541   XI6833   A58JLW
HIL7198   A106XTXU

Livery: Blue, grey and cream

VIRGIN BUS

C & J McDonald, 10 Churchill Close, Oadby, Leicester, LE2 4AJ

Depot : Knighton Junction Lane, Leicester.

GLJ674N	Leyland National 11351/1R/SC		DP48F	1974	Ex Annison, Ilkeston, 1996
GOG581N	Daimler Fleetline CRG6LX	Park Royal	H43/33F	1975	Ex British Shoe, Leicester, 1996
NOC406R	Leyland Fleetline FE30ALR	MCW	H43/33F	1976	Ex Smith, Mkt Harborough, 1995
OJD267R	Leyland Fleetline FE30ALR	MCW	H44/24D	1977	Ex Kinch, Barrow-on-Soar, 1995

Livery: Blue

Williams Coaches of Scunthorpe, who trade as Trent Motors, operate a service from Winterton to Scunthorpe. OWJ167X is a Leyland Leopard shown at the Scunthorpe terminus in Little John Street. The Eastern Coach Works body is the B51 type developed from the body fitted to Bristol RE in the 1970's. *Roy Marshall*

At de-regulation, Unity secured a number of tendered services though most routes have since been lost to other companies. The 695 school service to the village of Bole is, however, still operated and is often the duty for PRW137M. This Plaxton Elite-bodied Leopard is now 22 years old and has been in the Unity fleet for seventeen of those years. *Steve Sanderson*

Virgin Bus are a relatively new operator based in Leicester. For a while the company operated in competition with Leicester Citybus on route 54 with Virgin vehicles displaying route 54V. This depot view shows a pair of Fleetlines including GOG581N which was part of the British Shoe Shuttle fleet which ceased operating in the spring of 1996. *Steve Sanderson*

127

WING

M V & D E Wing, 77 Mareham Lane, Sleaford, Lincolnshire, NG34 7JZ

30	OIB9392	Bedford YRQ	Plaxton Elite Express II	C45F	1972	
64	HCT990	Volvo B10M-61	Van Hool Alizée	C46FT	1983	Ex Iberian, Kensington, 1984
70	LBH297P	Bedford YRT	Plaxton Supreme III	C53F	1976	Ex Travel Wide, Sparham, 1987
79	DNW951T	Ford A0609	Moseley Faro	C25F	1978	Ex Howells, Blackwood, 1990
91	C823CBU	Renault-Dodge S56	Northern Counties	B18F	1986	Ex Hayre, Wednesbury, 1995
93	SNM74R	Bedford YMT	Duple Dominant	C53F	1977	Ex Beardon, Colchester, 1996
94	MMJ474V	Bedford YLQ	Duple Dominant II	C45F	1980	Ex Barnard, Kirton-in-Lindsey, 1995
95	JTL37T	Bedford YMT	Plaxton Supreme III Express	C53F	1978	Ex Barnard, Kirton-in-Lindsey, 1995
	PAY9W	Bedford YNT	Plaxton Supreme IV	C53F	1981	Ex Sun Star, Skegness, 1996
	E200XWG	Renault-Dodge S56	Reeve Burgess Beaver	B25F	1988	Ex Mainline, 1996
	MIW2418	DAF MB230LB615	Van Hool Alizée	C51F	1989	Ex Clarkson, South Elmsall, 1996
	G165LWN	Volvo B10M-60	Plaxton Expressliner	C46FT	1990	Ex SWT, 1996
	G379REG	Volvo B10M-60	Plaxton Expressliner	C49F	1990	Ex Premier Travel Services, 1996

Previous Registrations:
HCT990   PCG521Y, HCT990, ODO842Y   MIW2418   F271RJX
JTL37T   ARB525T   OIB9392   VTL990K

Livery: Blue

Wings of Sleaford have changed their livery to an all-over dark blue with gold lettering. HCT990 now carries this scheme. It is a Volvo B10M purchased by Wings when only one year old in 1984. The Van Hool coachwork has changed little in design over the years, making this still a modern looking coach. *Steve Sanderson*

WIDE HORIZON

RT, EM & J Clarke, 48 Coventry Road, Burbage, Leicestershire LE10 2HD

Depot: Jacknell Road, Hinckley.

ECG666S	Bedford YMT	Duple Dominant II	C44F	1977	Ex Powner, Hinckley, 1994
457NWL	Leyland Leopard PSU3E/4R	Plaxton Supreme III	C53F	1978	Ex Tappins, Didcot, 1991
MGV613V	Bedford YMT	Plaxton Supreme IV	C53F	1980	Ex Monaham, Kentford, 1991
BBB542V	Bedford YMT	Plaxton Supreme IV	C53F	1980	Ex Verulam, St Albans, 1989
XYN670	Bedford YMT	Duple Dominant II	C53F	1980	Ex Howells, Dunstable, 1994
TMR66Y	DAF MB200DKTL600	Plaxton Paramount 3500	C53F	1983	Ex Lever, East Knoyle, 1992
VWG360Y	DAF MB200DKTL600	Plaxton Paramount 3500	C57F	1983	Ex Truronian, Truro, 1992
TJI4028	DAF SB2300DHS585	Jonckheere Jubilee	C49F	1984	Ex Winsley Garage, 1986
B57AMH	Bedford YNT	Duple Laser	C53F	1984	Ex McDonnel, Penkridge, 1994
TJI4027	DAF SB2305DHS585	Van Hool Alizeé	C55F	1987	Ex Sleight, Swinton, 1995
LAT256	DAF SB2300DHS585	Jonckheere Jubilee	C51FT	1987	Ex County, Brentwood, 1995
F427RRY	DAF SB2305DHS585	Caetano Algarve	C53F	1989	
F208EWN	DAF SB2300DHS585	Caetano Algarve	C53F	1987	Ex D Coaches, Morriston, 1994
L643AYS	Volvo B10M-60	Van Hool Alizeé	C53F	1994	Ex Park's, 1996
N196DYB	Bova FHD 12-340	Bova Futura	C49FT	1996	

Previous Registrations:

457NWL	WFH172S	TJI4027	D66CUY
LAT256	DJ94BNV	TJI4028	A258UHY
MGV613V	VNL817, GBW96V, XWL539, CJO322V	XYN670	KRE814V

Livery: Blue and white

Wide Horizon operate a service between Hinckley and Sapcote, a village to the east of the town. The route is a circular also covering Sharnford and Stoney Stanton. Depicted loading passengers in Hinckley is B57AMH, a Duple Laser-bodied Bedford YNT. *Steve Sanderson*

WOODS

Woods Coaches Ltd, Bedford Road, Wigston, Leicester, LE8 2XD

6477WF	Bedford YRQ	Duple Dominant	C45F	1976	Ex Cooper, Rothwell, 1983
RJI4240	Volvo B58-56	Duple Dominant II	C53F	1980	
2557NU	Volvo B58-61	Duple Dominant IV	C53F	1981	
4687NU	Volvo B58-61	Duple Dominant IV	C53F	1981	
JIW9464	Volvo B10M-61	Plaxton Paramount 3500	C49FT	1983	Ex Mandy, Hornsey, 1989
782EUL	Volvo B10M-61	Plaxton Paramount 3500	C49FT	1983	Ex Baker, Biddulph, 1989
564YYB	Volvo B10M-61	Plaxton Paramount 3500	C42FT	1983	Ex Watson, Staindrop, 1995
FIL6217	Volvo B10M-61	Duple Dominant IV	C53FT	1984	
NIB6433	Volvo B10M-61	Plaxton Paramount 3500 II	C50F	1986	Ex Wallace Arnold, 1990
SIB1998	Volvo B10M-46	Caetano Algarve	C39FT	1986	Ex Essex Cs, Bethnal Green, 1992
XIB3473	Volvo B9M	Plaxton Bustler	DP41F	1986	Ex ?, 1996
OIW1321	Volvo B10M-61	Plaxton Paramount 3500 II	C49FT	1986	Ex Appleby, Conisholme, 1993
D171LTA	Renault-Dodge S56	Reeve Burgess	B23F	1986	Ex Barnsley and District, 1996
GIL8879	Volvo B10M-61	Plaxton Paramount 3500 III	C53FT	1987	Ex Wing, Sleaford, 1995
E120BHS	Mercedes-Benz 709D	Alexander AM	B25F	1988	
6962WF	Mercedes-Benz 811D	Robin Hood	C25F	1988	Ex Smith, High Wycombe, 1994
F137KAO	Mercedes-Benz 609D	Reeve Burgess	B20F	1989	Ex North Western, 1994
6844WF	Mercedes-Benz 711D	Dormobile Routemaker	DP25F	1992	Ex Nuttall, Penwortham, 1994
N957SAY	Mercedes-Benz 709D	Reeve Burgess Beaver	B F	1996	

Previous Registrations:

2557NU	PBC459W	6962WF	F350JUS	RJI4240	KBC609V, 5566WF
4687NU	PBC460W	782EUL	8399RU	SIB1998	C625KDS
564YYB	RME973Y	FIL6217	A230GNR	NIB6433	C124DWR
6477WF	LUX524P	GIL8879	D101VRM	OIW1321	C92RFE, ASV895
6844WF	K660NGB	JIW9464	A243HMD	XIB3473	C853CML

Livery: Blue, yellow, orange and white.

Woods have expanded their involvement in Leicestershire tendered services recently and a number of minibuses have been acquired for this work. D171LTA was new to the Plymouth fleet but was purchased by Barnsley and District in 1995 with the Globe Coaches bus services. Woods obtained this Reeve Burgess-bodied Renault-Dodge S56 in a blue and orange livery which was applied in Barnsley prior to sale.
Steve Sanderson

Index to Vehicles

Reg	Operator	Reg	Operator	Reg	Operator	Reg	Operator	Reg	Operator
6EBH	Skills	4506UB	Cropley	A125EPA	Midland Fox	A737HFP	Albert Wilde		
20VWC	Lamcote	4687NU	Woods	A129DTO	City Rider	A820LEL	Brylaine		
38FGC	Lamcote	5447FH	Applebys	A130DTO	City Rider	A837EAY	Skinner		
65RTO	Nottingham	5517RH	Applebys	A131DTO	City Rider	A866DCN	T R S		
68BUT	Butler Brothers	5611FH	Hunt's	A131EPA	Fowler's Travel	ABA21T	Emmerson		
75RTO	Nottingham	5711MT	Moxon	A132DTO	City Rider	ABA25T	East Midland		
77RTO	Nottingham	6053RH	Hornsby	A132SMA	Midland Fox	ACH504T	Trent		
81SVO	Midland Fox	6077RE	Eagre	A133DTO	City Rider	ACH505T	Trent		
83BUT	Butler Brothers	6257RO	Applebys	A133SMA	Midland Fox	ACH506T	Trent		
83RTO	Nottingham	6477WF	Woods	A134SMA	Midland Fox	ACH507T	Trent		
104JEH	Sweyne	6510RE	Eagre	A135SMA	Midland Fox	ACH508T	Trent		
105NHY	Applebys	6844WF	Woods	A138EPA	Nottingham	ACH509T	Trent		
109CRC	Midland Fox	6962WF	Woods	A141BTV	Skinner	ACH510T	Trent		
111XKT	Midland Fox	7126RE	Eagre	A168OHJ	Lamcote	ACH511T	Trent		
166YHK	Moxon	7179TW	Travel Wright	A185AHB	RoadCar	ACH513T	Trent		
173LYB	Emmerson	7455RH	Hornsby	A186AHB	RoadCar	ACH514T	Trent		
179BUT	Butler Brothers	7683FH	Hunt's	A206LPP	Albert Wilde	ACH515T	Trent		
217MYB	Emmerson	7715KV	Moxon	A208DTO	RoadCar	ACM705X	Midland Fox		
232ENX	Lamcote	7822VW	Lamcote	A243YGF	East Midland	ACM706X	Midland Fox		
251CNX	Applebys	7980R	Eagre	A254LLL	Kettlewell's	ACM707X	Midland Fox		
276EPX	Maun Crusader	8227RH	Hornsby	A261OWL	A B C	ACM710X	Midland Fox		
326WAL	Lamcote	8302NF	Cropley	A278ROW	Midland Fox	ACM711X	Midland Fox		
329FBH	A&S, Leicester	8955RH	Hornsby	A280ROW	Midland Fox	ACT540L	The Delaine		
329FTU	A&S, Leicester	9882FH	Hunt's	A281FAL	Glovers	ACX783Y	Brylaine		
345BLA	Andrews	9962R	Eagre	A314XWG	East Midland	ADC176A	Albert Wilde		
361EKH	Applebys	A3BOB	Dunn-Line	A315XWG	East Midland	AFE595A	Eagre		
388XYC	Applebys	A4BOB	Dunn-Line	A316XWG	East Midland	AFE610A	Eagre		
457NWL	Wide Horizon	A5BOB	Dunn-Line	A317XWG	East Midland	AFE719A	Grayscroft		
470WYA	Maun Crusader	A10RHE	Eagre	A318XWG	East Midland	AFP440Y	Dee Ward		
476BTO	Andrews	A10WHF	Fowler's Travel	A319YWJ	East Midland	AHA451J	Confidence		
485DKH	Applebys	A14ABU	A&S, Leicester	A320YWJ	East Midland	AHH207T	RoadCar		
519SLG	Fowler's Travel	A14SMT	Leicester CityBus	A321YWJ	East Midland	AJV555W	Grayscroft		
520FUM	Applebys	A15DAF	Marshall	A322AKU	East Midland	AKG213A	RoadCar		
542GRT	Leicester CityBus	A16ABU	A&S, Leicester	A323AKU	East Midland	AKG265A	RoadCar		
564YYB	Woods	A17ABU	A&S, Leicester	A324AKU	East Midland	AKG282A	RoadCar		
577TVO	Lamcote	A19ABU	A&S, Leicester	A325AKU	East Midland	AKK176T	Skinner		
662NKR	Midland Fox	A19HOD	Hodson	A330VHB	MacPhearson	ALM59B	The Delaine		
670PUO	Kettlewell's	A20ABU	A&S, Leicester	A354BHL	East Midland	ANA224T	The Delaine		
706STT	Fowler's Travel	A20PSV	Cavalier	A398CRA	Nottingham	ANJ304T	Applebys		
782EUL	Woods	A24OVL	The Delaine	A399CRA	Nottingham	ANJ306T	Travel Wright		
795BFU	Applebys	A37SMA	Midland Fox	A442HNF	Pam's Coaches	ANJ313T	Applebys		
796UHT	Midland Fox	A38SMA	Midland Fox	A448EVO	P C Coaches	ARB527T	Johnson's		
805AFC	Bowers	A39XHE	East Midland	A501EJF	Midland Fox	ARC641T	Dunn-Line		
841TPU	Applebys	A41XHE	East Midland	A502EJF	Midland Fox	ARC643T	Dunn-Line		
869NHT	Applebys	A42XHE	East Midland	A503EJF	Midland Fox	ARC645T	Dunn-Line		
899DXV	Maun Crusader	A43XHE	East Midland	A504EJF	Midland Fox	ARC666T	Nottingham		
929GTA	RoadCar	A44XHE	East Midland	A505EJF	Midland Fox	ARC668T	Dunn-Line		
957XYB	Applebys	A53HRE	Hulley's	A506FSS	Glovers	ASP281T	Johnson Bros		
966GXP	Lamcote	A71FRY	Leicester CityBus	A507EJF	Midland Fox	ASV247	Dunn-Line		
971OHT	Hornsby	A71GEE	East Midland	A508EJF	Midland Fox	ATH108T	Grayscroft		
990ULG	Applebys	A72FRY	Leicester CityBus	A509EJF	Midland Fox	ATO57Y	Nottingham		
1642RH	Hornsby	A72GEE	East Midland	A510EJF	Midland Fox	ATO58Y	Nottingham		
1878R	Eagre	A73FRY	Leicester CityBus	A511EJF	Midland Fox	AUT31Y	Leicester CityBus		
2160RE	Eagre	A73GEE	East Midland	A512EJF	Midland Fox	AUT32Y	Leicester CityBus		
2191RO	Dunn-Line	A74FRY	Leicester CityBus	A522LCX	Albert Wilde	AUT33Y	Leicester CityBus		
2320DD	T R S	A74GEE	East Midland	A530LPP	Scutt	AUT34Y	Leicester CityBus		
2557NU	Woods	A75FRY	Leicester CityBus	A546HEF	A B C	AUT35Y	Leicester CityBus		
2732RH	Hornsby	A76FRY	Leicester CityBus	A575GJV	Emmerson	AUT70Y	Leicester CityBus		
2968PW	Paul Winson	A77FRY	Leicester CityBus	A680JCM	Brylaine	AVL744X	RoadCar		
3064RE	Eagre	A78FRY	Leicester CityBus	A707DAU	Trent	AVL745X	RoadCar		
3275FH	Hunt's	A81RGE	Cropley	A708DAU	Trent	AVL747X	RoadCar		
3613FH	Hunt's	A100AVO	Camms	A709DAU	Trent	AWE113T	Carnell		
3653RE	Eagre	A108EPA	Midland Fox	A710DAU	Trent	AYA199	Paul James		
3730RH	Hornsby	A111EPA	Nottingham	A711DAU	Trent	AYR315T	Kettlewell's		

AYR322T	East Midland	B526AHD	Carnell	BTB692T	Albert Wilde	C551TJF	Cavalier
B6WER	Bowers	B563PCC	P C Coaches	BTV648T	Dunn-Line	C559TUT	Cavalier
B8WER	Bowers	B569LSC	Leicester CityBus	BTV651T	Dunn-Line	C572TUT	Brylaine
B49DWE	East Midland	B623JRC	Trent	BTV653T	Dunn-Line	C603NPU	Brylaine
B52DWE	East Midland	B623JRC	Trent	BTV654T	Marshall	C62LHL	Brylaine
B53DWJ	East Midland	B625DWF	East Midland	BTV656T	Paul Winson	C632PAU	Midland Fox
B54DWJ	East Midland	B626DWF	East Midland	BUA705X	Blands of Cottesmore	C633PAU	Midland Fox
B57AMH	Wide Horizon	B626JRC	Trent	BUA711X	Scutt	C663MCN	A&S, Leicester
B63AOP	Paul James	B626JRC	Trent	BUT2B	Butler Brothers	C685WNX	Trent
B79MJF	Leicester CityBus	B627DWF	East Midland	BVP784V	Midland Fox	C716LTO	Trent
B80MJF	Leicester CityBus	B627JRC	Trent	BVP785V	Midland Fox	C717LTO	Trent
B81MJF	Leicester CityBus	B627JRC	Trent	BVP805V	Midland Fox	C718LTO	Trent
B82MJF	Leicester CityBus	B628DWF	East Midland	BVP814V	Nottingham	C719LTO	Trent
B83MJF	Leicester CityBus	B629DWF	East Midland	BXI7406	Trent Motors	C720MRC	Nottingham
B84MRY	Leicester CityBus	B630DWF	East Midland	C21PSW	Paul Winson	C720NNN	Trent
B85DTH	Moxon	B631DWF	East Midland	C30EUH	Midland Fox	C721MRC	Nottingham
B85MRY	Leicester CityBus	B632DWF	East Midland	C35FEC	Everett	C721NNN	Trent
B86MRY	Leicester CityBus	B633DWF	East Midland	C35VJF	Travel Wright	C722MRC	Nottingham
B101BYS	Dunn-Line	B641JVO	Reliance	C42HHJ	Midland Fox	C722NNN	Trent
B102BYS	Dunn-Line	B673EHL	Isle Coaches	C46KBE	RoadCar	C723MRC	Nottingham
B134GAU	City Rider	B675EWE	Marshall	C47KBE	RoadCar	C723NNN	Trent
B135GAU	City Rider	B705GFE	Kime's	C48KBE	RoadCar	C724NRC	Nottingham
B136GAU	City Rider	B712HVO	Trent	C58USS	MacPhearson	C823CBU	Wing
B137GAU	City Rider	B713HVO	Trent	C113AFX	Paul James	C925WFO	Kime's
B138GAU	City Rider	B713LAL	Nottingham	C127PPE	A B C	CAL845T	Travel Wright
B139GAU	City Rider	B714HVO	Trent	C136DWT	Carnell	CAX14V	Hylton & Dawson
B140GAU	City Rider	B714LAL	Nottingham	C144NRR	City Rider	CAZ6836	Unity
B141GAU	City Rider	B715HVO	Trent	C145NRR	City Rider	CBB467V	P C Coaches
B142GAU	City Rider	B715LAL	Nottingham	C146NRR	City Rider	CDH275T	Cropley
B143GAU	City Rider	B716LAL	Nottingham	C147NRR	City Rider	CDN711V	P C Coaches
B146ALG	Midland Fox	B717LAL	Nottingham	C148NRR	City Rider	CEC475S	Carnell
B150DHL	East Midland	B718LAL	Nottingham	C167JVL	Kettlewell's	CFE782S	Eagre
B151ALG	Midland Fox	B719LAL	Nottingham	C181KET	Kettlewell's	CHH212T	RoadCar
B151DHL	East Midland	B784JAU	Nottingham	C210VCT	Carnell	CHH215T	RoadCar
B152ALG	Isle Coaches	B833KRY	Johnson Bros	C286BBP	Midland Fox	CIB9152	Hodson
B152DHL	East Midland	B873YYX	Hulley's	C308NRC	Nottingham	CJL639V	Brylaine
B153DHL	East Midland	BAU674T	Kinch	C309NRC	Nottingham	CJN441C	Fowler's Travel
B154DHL	East Midland	BAU675T	Kinch	C310NRC	Nottingham	CKC627S	Hulley's
B155DHL	East Midland	BAU676T	Nottingham	C311LWG	Andrews	CKN332Y	Hylton & Dawson
B160WRN	Leicester CityBus	BAZ8577	Andrews	C311NRC	Nottingham	CKS386X	Midland Fox
B165WRN	Leicester CityBus	BAZ8578	Andrews	C312NRC	Nottingham	CKS389X	Midland Fox
B186BLG	Midland Fox	BBB542V	Wide Horizon	C313NRC	Nottingham	CKS390X	Midland Fox
B187BLG	Midland Fox	BBT513V	Dunn-Line	C314NRC	Nottingham	CKS391X	Midland Fox
B190BLG	Midland Fox	BBY430Y	Brylaine	C321UFP	Hylton & Dawson	CNG525K	Brylaine
B193DVL	Kime's	BES270V	Felix	C326HWJ	East Midland	CNH170X	Blands of Cottesmore
B217WEU	Butler Brothers	BFU909W	Kettlewell's	C327HWJ	East Midland	CSU935	Sweyne
B220WEU	Butler Brothers	BFW136M	East Midland	C328HWJ	East Midland	CUL81V	Kinch
B252KTO	Glovers	BGS287X	Butler Brothers	C329HWJ	East Midland	CUL119V	Kinch
B290TCT	Carnell	BGY595T	Carnell	C329PEW	Johnson's	CWG681V	Holloways
B301KVO	Nottingham	BHO441V	East Midland	C330HWJ	East Midland	CWG684V	Holloways
B302KVO	Nottingham	BJV103L	East Midland	C330SFL	Cavalier	CWG699V	Holloways
B303KVO	Nottingham	BJV787	Applebys	C331HWJ	East Midland	CWG746V	Holloways
B304KVO	Nottingham	BKA911X	T R S	C332HWJ	East Midland	CWU151T	Scutt
B305KVO	Nottingham	BKR945T	Maun Crusader	C332SFL	Cavalier	CWX656T	Trent
B306KVO	Nottingham	BLN591Y	Bestwicks	C333HWJ	East Midland	CWX658T	Trent
B307KVO	Nottingham	BLS423Y	Leicester CityBus	C334HWJ	East Midland	CWX659T	Trent
B405DGH	Reliance	BLS432Y	Leicester CityBus	C335HWJ	East Midland	CWX660T	Trent
B406VWX	Dee Ward	BLS443Y	Leicester CityBus	C336HWJ	East Midland	CWX661T	Trent
B428PJF	Cavalier	BNC952T	Eagre	C353SVV	Dunn-Line	D22SAO	Applebys
B429DDT	Kettlewell's	BNE751N	RoadCar	C395RRY	Avisdors	D32SAO	Applebys
B469WTC	Cavalier	BPR99Y	Midland Fox	C426MFE	The Delaine	D34UAO	East Midland
B493UNB	Kettlewell's	BPR103Y	Midland Fox	C446SJU	Johnson Bros	D36NFU	RoadCar
B496UNB	Johnson's	BPR108Y	Midland Fox	C475TAY	Midland Fox	D38NFU	RoadCar
B500SJL	Carnell	BRC677T	Kinch	C509TJF	Johnson Bros	D39NFU	RoadCar
B501FFW	RoadCar	BRC678T	Kinch	C517DYM	Midland Fox	D41TKA	Avisdors
B502FFW	RoadCar	BRC679T	Kinch	C538TJF	Lamcote	D44RWC	Midland Fox
B503FFW	RoadCar	BRC680T	Nottingham	C540TJF	Cavalier	D47TKA	Trent
B510BJO	Dee Ward	BRC681T	Nottingham	C543TJF	Dunn-Line	D52TLV	Dunn-Line
B513LFP	Midland Fox	BRO486T	Brylaine	C548TJF	Trent	D80UTF	Midland Fox
B514LFP	Midland Fox	BRR684T	Felix	C550TJF	Andrews	D81UTF	Midland Fox

D101OWG	RoadCar	D446GLS	Nottingham	DAR120T	Trent	E100AFW	The Delaine
D102SPP	P C Coaches	D451CNR	Hulley's	DAZ4300	Kime's	E103JNH	Nottingham
D103OWG	RoadCar	D456BEO	RoadCar	DAZ4301	Kime's	E104JNH	Nottingham
D104OWG	RoadCar	D458BEO	RoadCar	DAZ4302	Kime's	E105JNH	Nottingham
D105OWG	RoadCar	D459BEO	RoadCar	DAZ5455	RoadCar	E107JNH	Nottingham
D111OWG	Midland Fox	D498NYS	Dunn-Line	DBV198W	RoadCar	E109JNH	Nottingham
D113OWG	RoadCar	D500RWF	Isle Coaches	DET472V	RoadCar	E112YNM	Elsey
D115OWG	RoadCar	D503RCK	East Midland	DET477V	RoadCar	E120BHS	Woods
D116OWG	RoadCar	D504RCK	East Midland	DET478V	RoadCar	E131PLJ	Skinner
D118OWG	Midland Fox	D511RCK	East Midland	DET479V	RoadCar	E138ATV	Nottingham
D119OWG	RoadCar	D518RCK	East Midland	DFW42X	RoadCar	E139ATV	Nottingham
D120OWG	RoadCar	D519NDA	Cavalier	DHG210W	RoadCar	E140BNU	Nottingham
D121OWG	RoadCar	D519RCK	East Midland	DHG211W	RoadCar	E142ERA	Nottingham
D121URC	Nottingham	D520FYL	Midland Fox	DJL581V	Brylaine	E143ERA	Nottingham
D123OWG	RoadCar	D521SKY	RoadCar	DLJ112L	Brylaine	E149BTO	City Rider
D123URC	Nottingham	D521WNN	Dunn-Line	DLJ118L	Brylaine	E150BTO	City Rider
D124OWG	Midland Fox	D522RCK	East Midland	DNG233T	Moxon	E151BTO	City Rider
D124URC	Nottingham	D523SKY	RoadCar	DNK571Y	Pam's Coaches	E152BTO	City Rider
D125OWG	RoadCar	D527SKY	RoadCar	DNK585Y	Marshall	E153BTO	City Rider
D126URC	Nottingham	D529SKY	RoadCar	DNW951T	Wing	E181UWF	City Rider
D127OWG	RoadCar	D530SKY	RoadCar	DRC216T	Reliance	E183BNN	Midland Fox
D127URC	Nottingham	D531SKY	RoadCar	DSV710	Daisy	E184BNN	Midland Fox
D129URC	Nottingham	D532SKY	RoadCar	DSV721	Applebys	E186UWF	Bowers
D129WCC	Trent	D534HNW	Cavalier	DTL382X	Midland Fox	E188CNE	Midland Fox
D130OWG	Midland Fox	D536SKY	RoadCar	DTN958W	Felix	E188UWF	City Rider
D130URC	Nottingham	D538VRR	Kettlewell's	DVL940T	Hunt's	E200WHS	Nottingham
D131OWG	Grayscroft	D539RCK	East Midland	DWF22V	East Midland	E200XWG	Wing
D131URC	Nottingham	D546SRM	Cavalier	DWF23V	East Midland	E201HRY	Midland Fox
D132URC	Nottingham	D547RCK	East Midland	DWF24V	East Midland	E202HRY	Midland Fox
D133URC	Nottingham	D552HNW	Hail & Ride	DWF26V	East Midland	E203HRY	Midland Fox
D134OWG	Midland Fox	D561RCK	East Midland	DWU293T	Fowler's Travel	E204HRY	Midland Fox
D134URC	Nottingham	D571VBV	Hulley's	E21ECH	City Rider	E205HRY	Midland Fox
D135OWG	Midland Fox	D601RGJ	Fowler's Travel	E23ECH	City Rider	E206HRY	Midland Fox
D135URC	Nottingham	D604RGJ	Fowler's Travel	E23EFW	Sleafordian	E207HRY	Midland Fox
D138OWG	Midland Fox	D606SGA	RoadCar	E24ECH	City Rider	E208HRY	Midland Fox
D146RAK	City Rider	D634WNU	Trent	E25ECH	City Rider	E209HRY	Midland Fox
D152RAK	City Rider	D635WNU	Trent	E26ECH	City Rider	E210HRY	Midland Fox
D154HML	Fowler's Travel	D636WNU	Trent	E35RBO	RoadCar	E211ETN	Hodson
D154RAK	City Rider	D637WNU	Trent	E43MMT	Johnson Bros	E212HRY	Midland Fox
D156RAK	City Rider	D638WNU	Trent	E48MCK	Applebys	E213HRY	Midland Fox
D158RAK	RoadCar	D639WNU	Trent	E60WDT	East Midland	E214HRY	Midland Fox
D162RAK	Midland Fox	D640WNU	Trent	E61WDT	East Midland	E215HRY	Midland Fox
D163KDN	Avisdors	D641WNU	Trent	E65RBO	RoadCar	E216HRY	Midland Fox
D167LNA	Unity	D642WNU	Trent	E69KAJ	RoadCar	E217HRY	Midland Fox
D167TRR	Nottinghamshire CC	D643WNU	Trent	E70XKW	Nottingham	E218HRY	Midland Fox
D167WRC	Sweyne	D644WNU	Trent	E72KAJ	RoadCar	E250ACC	Midland Fox
D169VRA	Kettlewell's	D692SEM	RoadCar	E75LFR	Applebys	E250ADO	Haines
D171LTA	Woods	D701THF	RoadCar	E87HNR	Leicester CityBus	E254ACC	Midland Fox
D180UWF	RoadCar	D748XAU	Reliance	E88HNR	Leicester CityBus	E285OMG	RoadCar
D184UWF	RoadCar	D749XAU	Reliance	E89HNR	Leicester CityBus	E287OMG	RoadCar
D209SKD	Midland Fox	D756PTU	Hail & Ride	E90HNR	Leicester CityBus	E289MMM	Hulley's
D218SKD	Midland Fox	D758WRR	Hail & Ride	E90OUH	Hail & Ride	E307EVW	Nottingham
D222SKD	Midland Fox	D765YCW	RoadCar	E90YWB	East Midland	E315BVO	Nottingham
D223SKD	Midland Fox	D768YCW	Applebys	E91HNR	East Midland	E316BVO	Nottingham
D224SKD	Midland Fox	D769YCW	Applebys	E91YWB	East Midland	E317BVO	Nottingham
D226SKD	Midland Fox	D776WVO	Glovers	E92HNR	Leicester CityBus	E318BVO	Nottingham
D307MHS	RoadCar	D800KSE	Everett	E92YWB	East Midland	E318NSX	RoadCar
D308MHS	RoadCar	D811SGB	Carnell	E93HNR	Leicester CityBus	E319BVO	Nottingham
D309MHS	RoadCar	D817KWT	Avisdors	E93YWB	East Midland	E319NSX	RoadCar
D310MHS	RoadCar	D822RYS	RoadCar	E94HNR	Leicester CityBus	E320BVO	Nottingham
D312RVR	RoadCar	D823UBH	Fowler's Travel	E94YWB	East Midland	E321BVO	Nottingham
D321REF	Leicester CityBus	D850CNV	Dee Ward	E95HNR	Leicester CityBus	E322BVO	Nottingham
D323CLB	Hail & Ride	D850PWN	Hulley's	E95YWB	East Midland	E323BVO	Nottingham
D390PYS	Dunn-Line	D854KWR	Haines	E96HNR	Leicester CityBus	E324BVO	Nottingham
D391PYS	Dunn-Line	D861LWR	Hail & Ride	E96YWB	East Midland	E325BVO	Nottingham
D392TAU	Nottingham	D906MVU	Midland Fox	E97HNR	Leicester CityBus	E326BVO	Nottingham
D393TAU	Nottingham	D930ARE	Bowers	E97YWB	East Midland	E326LHN	City Rider
D394TAU	Nottingham	D956WJH	Johnson's	E98HNR	Leicester CityBus	E327BVO	Nottingham
D404EFA	Hail & Ride	DAK220L	Applebys	E98YWB	East Midland	E327LHN	City Rider
D428JDB	Unity	DAK360V	RoadCar	E99HNR	Leicester CityBus	E328BVO	Nottingham

E328LHN	City Rider	E825OMS	Nottingham	F24HGG	Hulley's	F263CEY	Midland Fox
E329BVO	Nottingham	E861URH	Kettlewell's	F24XVP	Midland Fox	F264CEY	Midland Fox
E329LHN	City Rider	E880DRA	East Midland	F25XVP	Midland Fox	F272OPX	Midland Fox
E330LHN	City Rider	E903DRG	Brylaine	F26XVP	Midland Fox	F274CEY	Midland Fox
E331LHN	City Rider	E911EAY	Johnson Bros	F27JRC	City Rider	F301RUT	Midland Fox
E332LHN	City Rider	E927PBE	East Midland	F27XVP	Midland Fox	F302RUT	Midland Fox
E333EVH	Elsey	E928PBE	East Midland	F28JRC	City Rider	F307EKP	Avisdors
E346EVH	MacPhearson	E929PBE	East Midland	F28XVP	Midland Fox	F334SPY	City Rider
E381ERB	Nottingham	E930PBE	East Midland	F29XVP	Midland Fox	F350WCS	A B C
E393HNR	Butler Brothers	E933UBO	City Rider	F37ENF	Leicester CityBus	F367MUT	Reliance
E399DNR	Carnell	E964SVU	Glovers	F38ENF	Leicester CityBus	F379UCP	Midland Fox
E404EPE	Hunt's	E985GFW	Applebys	F46LCH	Skills	F380JTV	Nottingham
E405BHK	Avisdors	EAH891Y	RoadCar	F50ENF	Leicester CityBus	F382GVO	Nottingham
E413EPE	Midland Fox	EAT170Y	Applebys	F62XRP	Hulley's	F383GVO	Nottingham
E415EPE	Midland Fox	EAZ4709	Cropley	F75TFU	East Midland	F384GVO	Nottingham
E417EPE	Midland Fox	EAZ5347	Cropley	F76TFU	East Midland	F385GVO	Nottingham
E419EPE	Midland Fox	ECG666S	Wide Horizon	F77TFU	East Midland	F386GVO	Nottingham
E433PFU	Enterprise & SD	EDT201V	RoadCar	F78TDE	A B C	F387GVO	Nottingham
E434YHL	Travel Wright	EDT204V	RoadCar	F78TFU	East Midland	F388GVO	Nottingham
E443JSG	Leicester CityBus	EDT214V	RoadCar	F92WFA	Holloways	F389GVO	Nottingham
E444JSG	Leicester CityBus	EFE32T	RoadCar	F109YVP	Express Motors	F390GVO	Nottingham
E459WJK	Applebys	EFN178L	Kinch	F111JTO	Nottingham	F391GVO	Nottingham
E477GBV	Andrews	EFU613Y	Emmerson	F112JTO	Nottingham	F406DUG	Midland Fox
E480JVN	RoadCar	EFU935Y	East Midland	F113JTO	Nottingham	F407DUG	Midland Fox
E481DAU	East Midland	EGB50T	Leicester CityBus	F114JTO	Nottingham	F424RTL	Paul Winson
E482JVN	RoadCar	EGB68T	Applebys	F115JTO	Nottingham	F427RRY	Wide Horizon
E498HHN	RoadCar	EGB92T	Trent	F116JTO	Nottingham	F515CDT	RoadCar
E502HHN	RoadCar	EJV31Y	East Midland	F117JTO	Nottingham	F516CDT	RoadCar
E504HHN	RoadCar	EJV32Y	East Midland	F118JTO	Nottingham	F519TOV	Midland Fox
E505HHN	RoadCar	EJV33Y	East Midland	F119JTO	Nottingham	F520TOV	Midland Fox
E506HHN	RoadCar	EJV34Y	East Midland	F120JTO	Nottingham	F533EWJ	P C Coaches
E510HHN	RoadCar	EKW614V	East Midland	F128KTV	Nottingham	F597HYC	Holloways
E512HHN	RoadCar	EKW615V	East Midland	F137KAO	Woods	F600GVO	Trent
E539VKY	RoadCar	EKW616V	East Midland	F143MBC	Leicester CityBus	F601GVO	Trent
E562MAC	Butler Brothers	EKY21V	East Midland	F144GVO	Nottingham	F602GVO	Trent
E577ANE	Nottingham	EKY22V	East Midland	F145GVO	Nottingham	F603GVO	Trent
E590BDB	P C Coaches	EKY23V	East Midland	F146GVO	Nottingham	F603VEW	The Delaine
E639NEL	Paul James	EKY24V	East Midland	F146MBC	Leicester CityBus	F604GVO	Trent
E650KYW	Bowers	EKY25V	East Midland	F147LNN	Nottingham	F605GVO	Trent
E691UNE	Hulley's	EKY26V	East Midland	F148LNN	Nottingham	F606GVO	Trent
E692UNE	Holloways	EKY27V	East Midland	F149LNN	Nottingham	F607GVO	Trent
E701GCU	Nottingham	EKY28V	East Midland	F149MBC	Leicester CityBus	F608GVO	Trent
E701XKR	Midland Fox	EKY29V	East Midland	F150MBC	Leicester CityBus	F609GVO	Trent
E702XKR	Midland Fox	EMJ560Y	Nottingham	F151GVO	Nottingham	F610GVO	Trent
E705UEM	RoadCar	ENF514Y	Albert Wilde	F151MBC	Leicester CityBus	F611GVO	Trent
E721BVO	East Midland	ENF572Y	Carnell	F152GVO	Nottingham	F691PAY	Reliance
E725BVO	Nottingham	ENF574Y	Carnell	F152MBC	Leicester CityBus	F692PAY	Travel Wright
E726BVO	Nottingham	ENP666W	Brylaine	F153DET	Midland Fox	F697HNU	Felix
E726HBF	Cavalier	EON824V	Nottingham	F153GVO	Nottingham	F702JCN	Nottingham
E727BVO	Nottingham	EPT879S	Trent	F154DET	Midland Fox	F703JCN	Nottingham
E728BVO	Nottingham	EPT881S	RoadCar	F155DET	Midland Fox	F704JCN	Nottingham
E729BVO	Nottingham	ERC357T	Trent	F156DET	Midland Fox	F705JCN	Nottingham
E730BVO	Nottingham	ESK965	RoadCar	F157DET	Midland Fox	F718PFP	Leicester CityBus
E730VWJ	RoadCar	ETL508T	Applebys	F158DET	Midland Fox	F720PFP	Leicester CityBus
E731BVO	Nottingham	ETO911V	RoadCar	F180CGN	A B C	F721PFP	Leicester CityBus
E732BVO	Nottingham	ETT319Y	Nottingham	F201HSO	Holloways	F723PFP	Leicester CityBus
E733BVO	Nottingham	ETU531X	Bowers	F208EWN	Wide Horizon	F724PFP	Leicester CityBus
E734BVO	Nottingham	EUA366	Andrews	F212LTV	Moxon	F725PFP	Leicester CityBus
E735BVO	Nottingham	EUG125Y	Lamcote	F218AKG	Hail & Ride	F726PFP	Leicester CityBus
E736BVO	Nottingham	EWE203V	East Midland	F232RNR	Butler Brothers	F740HRC	Nottingham
E737BVO	Nottingham	EWE206V	East Midland	F238MVS	Johnson Bros	F741HRC	Nottingham
E738BVO	Nottingham	EWF474V	Midland Fox	F242SJU	Midland Fox	F742HRC	Nottingham
E738VWJ	Avisdors	EWF484V	Midland Fox	F249RJX	MacPhearson	F743HRC	Nottingham
C709DVO	Nottingham	EWF488V	Midland Fox	F256CEW	RoadCar	F744HRC	Nottingham
E747JAY	MacPhearson	EWF491V	Midland Fox	F257CEW	RoadCar	F757SPU	Eagre
E752HJF	Skinner	EWY26Y	RoadCar	F258CEW	RoadCar	F774GNA	Holloways
E753HJF	Hulley's	F21XVP	Midland Fox	F259CEW	Fowler's Travel	F791JTV	Nottingham
E760JAY	Hylton & Dawson	F22TBC	Blands of Cottesmore	F260CEY	Midland Fox	F792JTV	Nottingham
E761JAY	Travel Wright	F22XVP	Midland Fox	F261CEY	Midland Fox	F812TMD	Skills
E824MDO	Applebys	F23XVP	Midland Fox	F262CEY	Midland Fox	F860YJX	Moxon

RoadCar have taken several former Lancaster double-deck buses into the fleet as part of the VRT replacement programme. Most have come from sister operations in Yorkshire after the Yorkshire Traction group took over Sheffield Omnibus in 1995. All nine carry East Lancashire bodywork and represented here by 707, URN207V. *Steve Sanderson*

F883SMU	Reliance	FMO841V	Haines	FTO544V	Applebys	G84OTU	Midland Fox
F896SMU	Paul Winson	FP5992	Blands of Cottesmore	FUJ949V	P C Coaches	G85OTU	Midland Fox
F970GJK	Applebys	FPR65V	Trent	FUT179V	Leicester CityBus	G86OTU	Midland Fox
FAX2784	Midland Fox	FRA515V	Trent	FUT182V	Leicester CityBus	G87OTU	Midland Fox
FBV271W	Express Motors	FRA516V	Trent	FUT184V	Leicester CityBus	G105AVX	T R S
FBV525S	Trent	FRA517V	Trent	FUT185V	Leicester CityBus	G110OFE	Unity
FCT703V	Kime's	FRA518V	Trent	FUT187V	Leicester CityBus	G129NRC	Nottingham
FDC414V	Hornsby	FRA519V	Trent	FUT240V	Leicester CityBus	G142GOL	Midland Fox
FDC419V	Kinch	FRA520V	Trent	FUT241V	Leicester CityBus	G143GOL	Midland Fox
FDC420V	Kinch	FRA521L	Fowler's Travel	FUT245V	Leicester CityBus	G154NRC	Nottingham
FDO802	Lamcote	FRA521V	Trent	FUT250V	Leicester CityBus	G155NRC	Nottingham
FDV142Y	Brylaine	FRA522V	Trent	FVL353X	Bestwicks	G156NRC	Nottingham
FDZ4731	Carnell	FRA523V	Trent	FVR256V	The Delaine	G157NRC	Nottingham
FFE477T	Applebys	FRA524V	Trent	FWA472V	Isle Coaches	G158NRC	Nottingham
FFK312	Leicester CityBus	FRA525V	Trent	FWA475V	Isle Coaches	G159NRC	Nottingham
FFW263T	Applebys	FRA526V	Trent	FXI7116	Lamcote	G160PTO	Nottingham
FGE435X	Eagre	FRA527V	Trent	G25YRY	Paul Winson	G161PVO	Nottingham
FGE438X	Camms	FRA528V	Trent	G37HDW	T R S	G162PVO	Nottingham
FGE440X	Maun Crusader	FRA529V	Trent	G39HKY	Johnson Bros	G163PVO	Nottingham
FHA609Y	Felix	FRA530V	Trent	G48HDW	Skinner	G164PVO	Nottingham
FIL3451	Midland Fox	FRA531V	Trent	G50ONN	Skills	G165LWN	Wing
FIL3452	Midland Fox	FRA532V	Trent	G51ONN	Skills	G165RRA	Nottingham
FIL4032	Haines	FRA533V	Trent	G53RND	Leicester CityBus	G166RRA	Nottingham
FIL6617	Woods	FRA534V	Trent	G54RND	Leicester CityBus	G208YDL	Daisy
FIL7615	Dunn-Line	FRA535V	Trent	G55RND	Leicester CityBus	G218EOA	Haines
FIL7997	Moxon	FRH615T	Applebys	G56RND	Leicester CityBus	G228FJX	Marshall
FIW567	Dunn-Line	FRR143V	Reliance	G64SNN	City Rider	G230EOA	Midland Fox
FJF193	Leicester CityBus	FRR194J	Moxon	G65SNN	Midland Fox	G231EOA	Midland Fox
FJU973	Paul Winson	FSD89V	Isle Coaches	G79VFW	East Midland	G232EOA	Midland Fox
FJV931	Applebys	FTL817T	Applebys	G80VFW	East Midland	G232GOJ	Haines
FKM303V	Maun Crusader	FTL992X	RoadCar	G81VFW	East Midland	G233EOA	Midland Fox
FKM304V	Maun Crusader	FTL993X	RoadCar	G83OTU	Midland Fox	G234EOA	Midland Fox

The East Midland Bus Handbook

Reg	Operator	Reg	Operator	Reg	Operator	Reg	Operator
G235EOA	Midland Fox	G521WJF	Midland Fox	G886WML	RoadCar	GTO711V	Nottingham
G236EOA	Midland Fox	G522WJF	Midland Fox	G887WML	RoadCar	GTX755W	Carnell
G237EOA	Midland Fox	G523WJF	Midland Fox	G888WML	RoadCar	GVO717N	Confidence
G238EOA	Midland Fox	G524WJF	Midland Fox	G889WML	RoadCar	GWE617V	East Midland
G238GCC	Midland Fox	G525WJF	Midland Fox	G890WML	RoadCar	GWE618V	East Midland
G239EOA	Midland Fox	G545PRH	Applebys	G891WML	RoadCar	GWE619V	East Midland
G239GCC	Midland Fox	G553RRR	Skills	G894WML	RoadCar	H2PSW	Paul Winson
G240EOA	Midland Fox	G600NRC	Trent	G895WML	RoadCar	H3PSW	Paul Winson
G244GCC	Midland Fox	G601XMD	Fowler's Travel	G945JPW	Hulley's	H3YRR	Marshall
G245GCC	Midland Fox	G612OTV	Trent	G961SND	A B C	H4JBT	Johnson Bros
G247GCC	Midland Fox	G613OTV	Trent	G979APJ	Emmerson	H34DGD	Travel Wright
G249GCC	Midland Fox	G614OTV	Trent	G997KJX	Elsey	H47NDU	Nottingham
G250GCC	Midland Fox	G615OTV	Trent	G998KJX	Elsey	H126AML	RoadCar
G252LWF	Leicester CityBus	G616OTV	Trent	GBH511T	Brylaine	H127AML	RoadCar
G253LWF	Leicester CityBus	G617OTV	Trent	GDB179N	The Delaine	H128AML	RoadCar
G254LWF	Leicester CityBus	G618OTV	Trent	GDB180N	The Delaine	H129AML	RoadCar
G255LWF	Leicester CityBus	G619OTV	Trent	GDB181N	The Delaine	H152DVM	P C Coaches
G256LWF	Leicester CityBus	G620OTV	Trent	GDO27V	Brylaine	H160DJU	Travel Wright
G257LWF	Leicester CityBus	G621OTV	Trent	GFE343T	Applebys	H167ANU	Nottingham
G258LWF	Leicester CityBus	G622OTV	Trent	GFO754C	Hail & Ride	H191YMA	RoadCar
G274HDW	Hail & Ride	G623OTV	Trent	GHR302W	Camms	H231FFE	Holloways
G276VML	Hornsby	G698PRH	Applebys	GHV67N	Kettlewell's	H245MOE	Midland Fox
G294MWU	RoadCar	G698PRR	Felix	GIJ9093	Isle Coaches	H246MOE	Midland Fox
G295MWU	RoadCar	G699OCH	Glovers	GIL4271	Moxon	H247MOE	Midland Fox
G301RJA	Midland Fox	G699PRR	Felix	GIL6239	T R S	H257THL	East Midland
G316XEE	Hornsby	G700OCH	Glovers	GIL8879	Woods	H284HLM	Hodson
G324BHN	Skinner	G704EOX	Haines	GLJ674N	Virgin Bus	H344SWA	East Midland
G327MUA	RoadCar	G704HPW	Kettlewell's	GLS277N	RoadCar	H345SWA	East Midland
G331NRC	Nottingham	G709LKW	Blands of Cottesmore	GMS283S	Kime's	H346SWA	East Midland
G332NRC	Nottingham	G727WJU	Leicester CityBus	GMS289S	Hunt's	H347SWA	East Midland
G333NRC	Nottingham	G728WJU	Leicester CityBus	GNN220N	Bestwicks	H348SWA	East Midland
G334NTV	Nottingham	G729WJU	Leicester CityBus	GNN222N	Bestwicks	H397SYG	RoadCar
G335PAL	Nottingham	G730WJU	Leicester CityBus	GNU568N	Trent	H402DEG	East Midland
G339KKW	East Midland	G731WJU	Leicester CityBus	GNU570N	Trent	H482BEE	East Midland
G340KKW	East Midland	G732WJU	Leicester CityBus	GNU571N	Trent	H483BEE	East Midland
G341KKW	East Midland	G733WJU	Leicester CityBus	GNU572N	Trent	H484BEE	East Midland
G342KKW	East Midland	G734WJU	Leicester CityBus	GNU573N	Trent	H485BEE	East Midland
G343KKW	East Midland	G735WJU	Leicester CityBus	GNV656N	Midland Fox	H611EJF	Leicester CityBus
G362SRB	Nottingham	G736WJU	Leicester CityBus	GOG58TN	Virgin Bus	H612EJF	Leicester CityBus
G363SRB	Nottingham	G737WJU	Leicester CityBus	GOL398N	East Midland	H613EJF	Leicester CityBus
G364SRB	Nottingham	G745PNN	Nottingham	GRF264V	Felix	H614EJF	Leicester CityBus
G365FOP	Hornsby	G746PNN	Nottingham	GRF703V	P C Coaches	H615EJF	Leicester CityBus
G365SRB	Nottingham	G747PNN	Nottingham	GSC857T	Isle Coaches	H616EJF	Leicester CityBus
G366FOP	Hornsby	G748PNN	Nottingham	GSO8V	East Midland	H633GHA	Haines
G366SRB	Nottingham	G749PNN	Nottingham	GSO87V	RoadCar	H727LOL	Nottingham
G367SRB	Nottingham	G751SRB	Nottingham	GSU835T	Applebys	H732LOL	Nottingham
G368RTO	Nottingham	G752SRB	Nottingham	GSU844T	Applebys	H737THL	RoadCar
G369RTO	Nottingham	G753SRB	Nottingham	GSU857T	Applebys	H742VHS	Cavalier
G370RTO	Nottingham	G754SRB	Nottingham	GSU858T	Applebys	H751ENR	Leicester CityBus
G371RTO	Nottingham	G755SRB	Nottingham	GSU860T	Applebys	H752ENR	Leicester CityBus
G372RTO	Nottingham	G756SRB	Nottingham	GTM123T	Brylaine	H790RWJ	Reliance
G373RTO	Nottingham	G757SRB	Nottingham	GTO48V	City Rider	H799RWJ	P C Coaches
G374NRC	Nottingham	G758SRB	Nottingham	GTO49V	City Rider	H830RWJ	P C Coaches
G375NRC	Nottingham	G820KWF	East Midland	GTO299V	City Rider	H845UUA	Reliance
G376NRC	Nottingham	G821KWF	East Midland	GTO301V	City Rider	H894AAT	Applebys
G377NRC	Nottingham	G822KWF	East Midland	GTO302V	City Rider	H898LOX	Hornsby
G378NRC	Nottingham	G823KWF	East Midland	GTO304V	City Rider	H998VRR	Nottinghamshire CC
G379NRC	Nottingham	G824KWF	East Midland	GTO305V	City Rider	HAL242V	Travel Wright
G379REG	Wing	G825KWF	East Midland	GTO306V	City Rider	HAL598V	Kettlewell's
G409NAK	Hornsby	G826KWF	East Midland	GTO307V	City Rider	HAX6W	Johnson's
G424YAY	Hylton & Dawson	G827KWF	East Midland	GTO701V	Nottingham	HCS795N	Applebys
G430YAY	Travel Wright	G849VAY	Elsey	GTO702V	Nottingham	HCT990	Wing
G440NET	Butler Brothers	G865VAY	Travel Wright	GTO703V	Nottingham	HD9823	Hylton & Dawson
G440LKW	RoadCar	G870YDU	Mauri Crusader	GTO704V	Nottingham	HDL406N	Hunt's
G495VFU	Applebys	G879TVS	Nottingham	GTO705V	Nottingham	HDX906N	RoadCar
G506SFT	Midland Fox	G881WML	RoadCar	GTO706V	Nottingham	HFL672L	The Delaine
G508SFT	Midland Fox	G882WML	RoadCar	GTO707V	Nottingham	HFU531	Eagre
G509SFT	Midland Fox	G883WML	RoadCar	GTO708V	Nottingham	HHE217N	Bestwicks
G512SFT	Midland Fox	G884WML	RoadCar	GTO709V	Nottingham	HHH272N	Eagre
G513SFT	Midland Fox	G885WML	RoadCar	GTO710V	Nottingham	HHJ380Y	Eagre

HIL3075	Moxon	J182CTO	Nottingham	J914HGD	Travel Wright	K3CAV		Cavalier
HIL3476	Moxon	J183CTO	Nottingham	JAF208W	Brylaine	K3RAD		Dunn-Line
HIL4619	Kettlewell's	J184CTO	Nottingham	JAK211W	East Midland	K4CAV		Cavalier
HIL5677	Paul Winson	J201BVO	Trent	JAL573N	Reliance	K5CAV		Cavalier
HIL6153	Maun Crusader	J213AET	East Midland	JAO477V	East Midland	K6CAV		Cavalier
HIL7198	Unity	J214AET	East Midland	JBR684T	Trent	K101JWJ		East Midland
HIL7771	Kinch	J215AET	East Midland	JBT3S	Johnson Bros	K102JWJ		East Midland
HIL7773	Kinch	J216AET	East Midland	JBT16S	Johnson Bros	K103JWJ		East Midland
HIL8418	RoadCar	J217AET	East Midland	JCT73W	Brylaine	K104JWJ		East Midland
HIL8419	RoadCar	J218AET	East Midland	JCT257W	Kime's	K105JWJ		East Midland
HIL8420	RoadCar	J219AET	East Midland	JDB939V	Brylaine	K106JWJ		East Midland
HOD76	Paul Winson	J241MFP	T R S	JDE972X	Midland Fox	K107JWJ		East Midland
HOR305N	Confidence	J242MFP	T R S	JDO241W	Fowler's Travel	K118KUA		Travel Wright
HOR306N	Confidence	J246MFP	Midland Fox	JFW915T	RoadCar	K120OCT		Elsey
HOR307N	T R S	J247MFP	Midland Fox	JGA183N	Moxon	K131XRE		Midland Fox
HPG316N	Pam's Coaches	J302BVO	Trent	JGU943V	Dee Ward	K148BRF		Midland Fox
HRB932V	Glovers	J303BVO	Trent	JGV317V	Applebys	K158HRF		Midland Fox
HRO985V	Hylton & Dawson	J304BVO	Trent	JHE145W	Midland Fox	K185HTV		Nottingham
HSC104T	Sweyne	J305BVO	Trent	JHE153W	Midland Fox	K186HTV		Nottingham
HSD86V	Applebys	J306BVO	Trent	JHE160W	Midland Fox	K187HTV		Nottingham
HSD87V	Scutt	J307BVO	Trent	JHE167W	Midland Fox	K188HTV		Nottingham
HSK833	Dunn-Line	J308BVO	Trent	JHE177W	Midland Fox	K293GDT		Dunn-Line
HSV194	East Midland	J309BVO	Trent	JHE179W	Midland Fox	K295GDT		Dunn-Line
HSV195	East Midland	J310BVO	Trent	JHE189W	Midland Fox	K301NJL		RoadCar
HSV196	East Midland	J311BVO	Trent	JHE192W	Midland Fox	K302NJL		RoadCar
HTU155N	Johnson Bros	J312BVO	Trent	JHE193W	Midland Fox	K303NJL		RoadCar
HVL611	Applebys	J313BVO	Trent	JHJ139V	Trent	K326FAL		Trent
HVU81V	Brylaine	J314BVO	Trent	JHJ146V	Trent	K327FAL		Trent
HWE826N	Johnson Bros	J315BVO	Trent	JHW103P	Trent	K328FAL		Trent
HWJ620W	East Midland	J316BVO	Trent	JIL2156	Midland Fox	K329FAL		Trent
HWJ621W	East Midland	J317BVO	Trent	JIL2157	Midland Fox	K330FAL		Trent
HWJ922W	RoadCar	J318BVO	Trent	JIL2158	Midland Fox	K331FAL		Trent
HWJ923W	RoadCar	J319BVO	Trent	JIL2159	Midland Fox	K332FAL		Trent
HWJ924W	RoadCar	J320BVO	Trent	JIL2160	Midland Fox	K334FAL		Trent
HWJ925W	RoadCar	J321BVO	Trent	JIL2161	Midland Fox	K335FAL		Trent
IIL6440	RoadCar	J322BVO	Trent	JIL2162	Midland Fox	K336FAL		Trent
IIL7074	Skills	J323BVO	Trent	JIL2163	Midland Fox	K337FAL		Trent
IIL7076	Skills	J324BVO	Trent	JIL2164	Midland Fox	K338FAL		Trent
IIW363	Dunn-Line	J325BVO	Trent	JIL2165	Midland Fox	K339FAL		Trent
J1JBT	Johnson Bros	J328ONE	Haines	JIL4006	Pam's Coaches	K341FAL		Trent
J1PCC	P C Coaches	J349XET	East Midland	JIL7889	Moxon	K342FAL		Trent
J4KEC	Lamcote	J350XET	East Midland	JIL7899	Kettlewell's	K343FAL		Trent
J6BOB	Dunn-Line	J351XET	East Midland	JIL8324	T R S	K344FAL		Trent
J8PJC	Paul James	J352XET	East Midland	JIL8325	T R S	K346FAL		Trent
J9DLT	Dunn-Line	J353XET	East Midland	JIL8326	T R S	K347FAL		Trent
J10PSW	Paul Winson	J394LJL	RoadCar	JIW9464	Woods	K348FAL		Trent
J23HRH	Applebys	J395LJL	RoadCar	JMB329T	Hulley's	K349FAL		Trent
J33MCL	MacPherson	J396LJL	RoadCar	JOV701P	Kettlewell's	K350FAL		Trent
J40PSW	Paul Winson	J401FNS	City Rider	JOV754P	Maun Crusader	K352FAL		Trent
J55MCL	MacPherson	J518LRY	Blands of Cottesmore	JOV777P	Kettlewell's	K353FAL		Trent
J77OLT	Sweyne	J564URW	Felix	JOV780P	Kettlewell's	K354DWJ		East Midland
J82CRR	Skills	J602KGB	Pathfinder	JPM815W	Haines	K355DWJ		East Midland
J91DJV	East Midland	J669LGA	Skills	JRB416V	Travel Wright	K356DWJ		East Midland
J92DJV	East Midland	J688LGA	Skills	JRC682V	Nottingham	K357DWJ		East Midland
J93DJV	East Midland	J693AWB	Hornsby	JRF161V	Brylaine	K358DWJ		East Midland
J94DJV	East Midland	J693LGA	Skills	JRR359V	Kettlewell's	K359DWJ		East Midland
J134HME	RoadCar	J715KBC	Daisy	JSV365	Scutt	K360DWJ		East Midland
J151WEH	Midland Fox	J718MFE	Hornsby	JTD387P	Applebys	K361DWJ		East Midland
J168CTO	Nottingham	J753MFP	Leicester CityBus	JTH54W	Bestwicks	K362DWJ		East Midland
J169CTO	Nottingham	J754MFP	Leicester CityBus	JTH772P	Trent	K363DWJ		East Midland
J170CNU	Nottingham	J755MFP	Leicester CityBus	JTL37T	Wing	K378RFE		RoadCar
J171CNU	Nottingham	J756MFP	Leicester CityBus	JTM105V	P C Coaches	K379RFE		RoadCar
J172CNU	Nottingham	J757MFP	Leicester CityBus	JTU131V	Johnson Bros	K380RFE		RoadCar
J173CNU	Nottingham	J758NNR	Leicester CityBus	JVY676S	Scutt	K390NGG		City Rider
J174CNU	Nottingham	J759DAU	Nottingham	JWF493W	Midland Fox	K481GNN		Nottingham
J175CNU	Nottingham	J759NNR	Leicester CityBus	JWF494W	Midland Fox	K482GNN		Nottingham
J176CNU	Nottingham	J760DAU	Nottingham	JWL993W	Johnson Bros	K519RJX		Elsey
J179CRB	Nottingham	J796CNU	Nottingham	JWL997W	Johnson Bros	K529EHE		Elsey
J180CRB	Nottingham	J813KHD	Moxon	JYG431V	Enterprise & SD	K550RJX		Butler Brothers
J181CRB	Nottingham	J861KFP	Reliance	K2CAV	Cavalier	K617SBC		Leicester CityBus

The East Midland Bus Handbook

K618SBC	Leicester CityBus	KVL442Y	Kime's	L201ONU	Nottingham	L443LWA	East Midland
K619SBC	Leicester CityBus	KVO429P	Trent	L202ONU	Nottingham	L445LWA	East Midland
K620SBC	Leicester CityBus	KVO431P	Trent	L203ONU	Nottingham	L446LWA	East Midland
K621SBC	Leicester CityBus	KVO432P	Trent	L204ONU	Nottingham	L447LWA	East Midland
K622SBC	Leicester CityBus	KVO433P	Trent	L205ONU	Nottingham	L448LWA	East Midland
K633FAU	Trent	KWA24W	Isle Coaches	L206ONU	Nottingham	L449LWA	East Midland
K640FAU	Trent	KWA214W	East Midland	L207ONU	Nottingham	L450LWA	East Midland
K645FAU	Trent	KWA218W	East Midland	L208ONU	Nottingham	L451LWA	East Midland
K651FAU	Trent	KWA221W	East Midland	L209ONU	Nottingham	L452LWA	East Midland
K701NDO	East Midland	KWA223W	East Midland	L210ONU	Nottingham	L453LHL	East Midland
K702NDO	East Midland	KWA224W	East Midland	L211ONU	Nottingham	L483LNN	Nottingham
K703NDO	East Midland	KXI6744	Kettlewell's	L227HRF	Midland Fox	L484LNN	Nottingham
K704NDO	East Midland	KXI7014	Kettlewell's	L228HRF	Midland Fox	L485NTO	Nottingham
K746VJU	Leicester CityBus	L3JBT	Johnson Bros	L230RDO	Applebys	L486NTO	Nottingham
K748VJU	Leicester CityBus	L4HOD	Hodson	L231HRF	Midland Fox	L487NTO	Nottingham
K749VJU	Leicester CityBus	L4PSW	Paul Winson	L233HRF	Midland Fox	L488NTO	Nottingham
K750VJU	Leicester CityBus	L5HOD	Hodson	L256VSU	Pathfinder	L489NTO	Nottingham
K760SBC	Leicester CityBus	L6BOB	Dunn-Line	L257VSU	Pathfinder	L501OAL	Nottingham
K761JTV	Nottingham	L8PCC	P C Coaches	L258VSU	Pathfinder	L502OAL	Nottingham
K761SBC	Leicester CityBus	L29CAY	Travel Wright	L303AUT	Midland Fox	L502YFE	Applebys
K770JRA	Skills	L31ORC	Fowler's Travel	L304AUT	Midland Fox	L503OAL	Nottingham
K813VNF	P C Coaches	L34PNN	City Rider	L304VFE	RoadCar	L504OAL	Nottingham
K860RRH	Applebys	L35PNN	City Rider	L305AUT	Midland Fox	L505OAL	Nottingham
KAL578	RoadCar	L36PNN	City Rider	L305VFE	RoadCar	L506OAL	Nottingham
KAU564V	Confidence	L37PNN	City Rider	L306AUT	Midland Fox	L507OAL	Nottingham
KAX714	Haines	L38PNN	City Rider	L306VFE	RoadCar	L508OAL	Nottingham
KAZ3253	Eagre	L47ORC	Skills	L307AUT	Midland Fox	L509OAL	Nottingham
KAZ3254	Eagre	L48ORC	Skills	L307VFE	RoadCar	L510OAL	Nottingham
KBD22V	Bestwicks	L49OCC	Skills	L308AUT	Midland Fox	L542JJV	Applebys
KBT343S	Reliance	L61LRC	Skills	L308VFE	RoadCar	L547EHD	Reliance
KBV144S	P C Coaches	L63ORC	Skills	L309AUT	Midland Fox	L591CJW	Hornsby
KCG627L	Trent	L65ORB	Skills	L310AUT	Midland Fox	L623XFP	Leicester CityBus
KCH472V	Lamcote	L79VMW	Skills	L311AUT	Midland Fox	L624XFP	Leicester CityBus
KCK201W	RoadCar	L101LRA	Trent	L312AUT	Midland Fox	L625XFP	Leicester CityBus
KCK202W	RoadCar	L102LRA	Trent	L313AUT	Midland Fox	L626XFP	Leicester CityBus
KCK203W	RoadCar	L103LRA	Trent	L314AUT	Midland Fox	L637LDT	East Midland
KCK204W	RoadCar	L104LRA	Trent	L315AUT	Midland Fox	L638LDT	East Midland
KET6	Kettlewell's	L105LRA	Trent	L316AUT	Midland Fox	L639LDT	East Midland
KGY566Y	Daisy	L106LRA	Trent	L317AUT	Midland Fox	L640LDT	East Midland
KHE448P	Sweyne	L107LRA	Trent	L318AUT	Midland Fox	L641LDT	East Midland
KIB6474	RoadCar	L108LHL	East Midland	L319AUT	Midland Fox	L642LDT	East Midland
KIB6527	RoadCar	L108LRA	Trent	L320AUT	Midland Fox	L643AYS	Wide Horizon
KIB6620	RoadCar	L109LHL	East Midland	L321AUT	Midland Fox	L643LDT	East Midland
KIB6708	RoadCar	L109LRA	Trent	L322AUT	Midland Fox	L701MRA	Felix
KIB6828	Woods	L110LRA	Trent	L323AUT	Midland Fox	L702MRA	Felix
KIB6844	Brylaine	L112LRA	Trent	L324AUT	Midland Fox	L705HFU	East Midland
KJD421P	Express Motors	L113LRA	Trent	L325AUT	Midland Fox	L706HFU	East Midland
KKY833P	Johnson Bros	L114LRA	Trent	L339KCK	East Midland	L707HFU	East Midland
KKY835P	Johnson Bros	L115LRA	Trent	L340KCK	East Midland	L708HFU	East Midland
KMW176P	Applebys	L116LRA	Trent	L341KCK	East Midland	L709HFU	East Midland
KMW177P	Applebys	L117LRA	Trent	L342KCK	East Midland	L731LWA	East Midland
KMW178P	Applebys	L118LRA	Trent	L343KCK	East Midland	L732LWA	East Midland
KON326P	Applebys	L119LRA	Trent	L344KCK	East Midland	L733LWA	East Midland
KRO718	Applebys	L120LRA	Trent	L349MRR	Nottingham	L734LWA	East Midland
KSA183P	Confidence	L121LRA	Trent	L350MRR	Nottingham	L735LWA	East Midland
KSK957	Eagre	L122LRA	Trent	L351MRR	Nottingham	L736LWA	East Midland
KSU363	Brylaine	L123LRA	Trent	L352MRR	Nottingham	L737LWA	East Midland
KSU479	Eagre	L124LRA	Trent	L353MRR	Nottingham	L738LWA	East Midland
KTL24V	RoadCar	L125LRA	Trent	L401CJF	Kinch	L739LWA	East Midland
KTL27V	RoadCar	L126LRA	Trent	L402CJF	Kinch	L740LWA	East Midland
KTL27Y	The Delaine	L127LRA	Trent	L403CJF	Kinch	L741LWA	East Midland
KTL43Y	RoadCar	L128LRA	Trent	L404CJF	Kinch	L742LWA	East Midland
KTL44Y	RoadCar	L138XDS	Pathfinder	L435LWA	East Midland	L743LWA	East Midland
KTL45Y	RoadCar	L189MAU	Nottingham	L436LWA	East Midland	L744LWA	East Midland
KTL780	The Delaine	L190MAU	Nottingham	L437LWA	East Midland	L745LWA	East Midland
KTL982	Sleafordian	L191MAU	Nottingham	L438LWA	East Midland	L746LWA	East Midland
KUC179P	Hornsby	L192MAU	Nottingham	L439LWA	East Midland	L748LWA	East Midland
KUC181P	Hornsby	L193OVO	Nottingham	L440LWA	East Midland	L749LWA	East Midland
KUC997P	Hornsby	L194OVO	Nottingham	L441LWA	East Midland	L750LWA	East Midland
KVL261	Sleafordian	L195OVO	Nottingham	L442LWA	East Midland	L751LHL	East Midland

L801MRA	Trent	LRB214W	Nottingham	M135NBE	Applebys	M508GRY	Leicester CityBus
L802MRA	Trent	LRB405W	Camms	M135PRA	Trent	M509GRY	Leicester CityBus
L803MRA	Trent	LRB407W	Camms	M136PRA	Trent	M510GRY	Leicester CityBus
L804MRA	Trent	LRB409W	Camms	M137PRA	Trent	M511TRA	Nottingham
L804YTL	Hornsby	LRB577W	RoadCar	M138PRA	Trent	M512TRA	Nottingham
L805MRA	Trent	LRB578W	RoadCar	M159GRY	Midland Fox	M513TRA	Nottingham
L806MRA	Trent	LRB579W	RoadCar	M160GRY	Midland Fox	M521UTV	Nottingham
L807MRA	Trent	LRB580W	RoadCar	M161GRY	Midland Fox	M522UTV	Nottingham
L807YBC	Kinch	LRB581W	RoadCar	M162GRY	Midland Fox	M594GFE	Applebys
L808MRA	Trent	LRB582W	RoadCar	M163GRY	Midland Fox	M601TTV	Nottingham
L809CJF	Kinch	LRB583W	RoadCar	M164GRY	Midland Fox	M601VHE	East Midland
L810CJF	Kinch	LRB584W	RoadCar	M165GRY	Midland Fox	M602TTV	Nottingham
L811CJF	Kinch	LRR683W	Nottingham	M166GRY	Midland Fox	M602VHE	East Midland
L812CJF	Kinch	LRR684W	Nottingham	M167GRY	Midland Fox	M603TTV	Nottingham
L813DJU	Kinch	LRR685W	Nottingham	M168GRY	Midland Fox	M603VHE	East Midland
L814DJU	Kinch	LRR686W	Nottingham	M169GRY	Midland Fox	M604TTV	Nottingham
L829HEF	Nottingham	LRR687W	Nottingham	M170GRY	Midland Fox	M604VHE	East Midland
L848WDS	Pathfinder	LRR688W	Nottingham	M171GRY	Midland Fox	M605UTV	Nottingham
L865BEA	Pathfinder	LRR689W	Nottingham	M172GRY	Midland Fox	M605VHE	East Midland
L907RDO	Elsey	LRR690W	Nottingham	M173GRY	Midland Fox	M606UTV	Nottingham
L911LRA	Trent	LRR691W	Nottingham	M174GRY	Midland Fox	M606VHE	East Midland
L964VGE	Pathfinder	LTG278X	Brylaine	M175GRY	Midland Fox	M607VHE	East Midland
L965VGE	Pathfinder	LTL388P	RoadCar	M176GRY	Midland Fox	M608WET	East Midland
L967VGE	Pathfinder	LUA251V	Johnson's	M177GRY	Midland Fox	M609WET	East Midland
L971VGE	Pathfinder	LUA278V	Sweyne	M178GRY	Midland Fox	M664KHP	Nottingham
L988AEA	Pathfinder	LUG81P	Fowler's Travel	M196SRR	Nottingham	M665JFP	Pathfinder
LAG188V	East Midland	LUG88P	Fowler's Travel	M197SRR	Nottingham	M667JFP	Pathfinder
LAG189V	East Midland	LUP894T	Trent	M198TNU	Nottingham	M730KJU	Dunn-Line
LAK985W	Travel Wright	LUP895T	Sweyne	M201URC	Trent	M731KJU	Dunn-Line
LAT256	Wide Horizon	LUX536P	Moxon	M202URC	Trent	M732KJU	Dunn-Line
LBH297P	Wing	LVL804V	RoadCar	M212STO	Nottingham	M733KJU	Dunn-Line
LCT980P	Carnell	LVL806V	RoadCar	M213STO	Nottingham	M734KJU	Dunn-Line
LEO734Y	RoadCar	LVL807V	RoadCar	M214STO	Nottingham	M735KJU	Dunn-Line
LEO735Y	RoadCar	LVL809V	RoadCar	M215TNU	Nottingham	M763SVO	Nottingham
LHE601W	Johnson Bros	LVO46W	Kettlewell's	M216TNU	Nottingham	M784RVY	Nottingham
LIB7131	Woods	LWC444V	Paul James	M271URC	Trent	M801PRA	Trent
LIL2512	Bowers	M1OCT	The Delaine	M272URC	Trent	M802PRA	Trent
LIL2612	Bowers	M2JBT	Johnson Bros	M273URC	Trent	M803PRA	Trent
LIL2837	Kettlewell's	M2OCT	The Delaine	M274URC	Trent	M804PRA	Trent
LIL3068	Bowers	M6PCC	P C Coaches	M290OUR	Elsey	M805PRA	Trent
LIL4799	Maun Crusader	M7PCC	P C Coaches	M300ARJ	Paul Winson	M806PRA	Trent
LIL6287	T R S	M8PCC	P C Coaches	M301KRY	Felix	M807PRA	Trent
LIL7568	Bowers	M14ABC	A B C	M332GFW	Daisy	M808PRA	Trent
LIL7910	Bowers	M18ABU	A&S, Leicester	M351BFE	RoadCar	M809PRA	Trent
LIL7912	Bowers	M19ABC	A B C	M352BFE	RoadCar	M810PRA	Trent
LIL9842	Travel Wright	M21UUA	Felix	M353BFE	RoadCar	M811PRA	Trent
LJA608P	RoadCar	M22MCL	MacPherson	M354BFE	RoadCar	M812PRA	Trent
LJA609P	RoadCar	M31TRR	Skills	M354PRA	Trent	M813PRA	Trent
LJA612P	RoadCar	M32TRR	Skills	M355BFE	RoadCar	M814PRA	Trent
LJA622P	RoadCar	M34TRR	Skills	M355PRA	Trent	M815KJU	Kinch
LJA642P	RoadCar	M35TRR	Skills	M356BFE	RoadCar	M815PRA	Trent
LJI5631	Midland Fox	M36TRR	Skills	M357BFE	RoadCar	M821RCP	Reliance
LJI5632	Midland Fox	M37TRR	Skills	M358BFE	RoadCar	M879DDS	Pathfinder
LJI8027	Applebys	M38TRR	Skills	M405HFP	Kinch	M882DDS	Pathfinder
LJI8156	Midland Fox	M42DLN	Pathfinder	M406HFP	Kinch	M919MRW	Nottingham
LJI8157	Midland Fox	M44MCL	MacPherson	M411RRN	East Midland	M953CJN	Sleafordian
LJV273	Applebys	M51PRA	Trent	M412RRN	East Midland	M983CYS	Pathfinder
LJX401W	Brylaine	M52PRA	Trent	M413RRN	East Midland	M985LAG	Applebys
LMS153W	Isle Coaches	M53PRA	Trent	M414RRN	East Midland	M996CYS	Pathfinder
LMS161W	Applebys	M54PRA	Trent	M424GUS	Pathfinder	MAL795P	Enterprise & SD
LMS162W	Enterprise & SD	M64RRA	Skills	M433GFE	Applebys	MAU612P	Dunn-Line
LNU558W	Reliance	M99PCC	P C Coaches	M453LJF	Pathfinder	MAU614P	Dunn-Line
LNU569W	Confidence	M113SLS	Nottingham	M455TCH	Trent	MAU615P	Dunn-Line
LNU577W	Brylaine	M129PRA	Trent	M501GRY	Leicester CityBus	MAU616P	Dunn-Line
LNX319L	Daisy	M130PRA	Trent	M502GRY	Leicester CityBus	MBE613R	East Midland
LOA839X	Midland Fox	M131PRA	Trent	M503GRY	Leicester CityBus	MBZ7142	RoadCar
LRA799P	Eagre	M132PRA	Trent	M504GRY	Leicester CityBus	MCO257H	Grayscroft
LRB207W	Nottingham	M133PRA	Trent	M505GRY	Leicester CityBus	MCS404W	Hulley's
LRB208W	Nottingham	M133TRR	Skills	M506GRY	Leicester CityBus	MFN45R	Enterprise & SD
LRB213W	Nottingham	M134PRA	Trent	M507GRY	Leicester CityBus	MFR17R	Applebys

The East Midland Bus Handbook

MFS579X	Trent Motors	MVO420W	Nottingham	N174PUT	Midland Fox	N358VRC	Trent
MGE8V	Applebys	MVO421W	Nottingham	N175PUT	Midland Fox	N359VRC	Trent
MGR914T	Grayscroft	MVO422W	Nottingham	N176PUT	Midland Fox	N360VRC	Trent
MGR915T	Applebys	MVO423W	Nottingham	N177PUT	Midland Fox	N361VRC	Trent
MGV613V	Wide Horizon	MVO424W	Nottingham	N178PUT	Midland Fox	N362VRC	Trent
MIB648	Emmerson	MVO425W	Nottingham	N179PUT	Midland Fox	N363VRC	Trent
MIB9246	P C Coaches	MWG622X	East Midland	N196DYB	Wide Horizon	N364VRC	Trent
MIL1054	Dunn-Line	MWG623X	East Midland	N203VRC	Trent	N365VRC	Trent
MIL1057	Dunn-Line	MWG624X	East Midland	N204VRC	Trent	N366VRC	Trent
MIL2654	Daisy	MWG940X	RoadCar	N205VRC	Trent	N367VRC	Trent
MIW2418	Wing	N1JBT	Johnson Bros	N206VRC	Trent	N368VRC	Trent
MIW2422	Johnson Bros	N1SMC	Skills	N207VRC	Trent	N369VRC	Trent
MJI7809	Dee Ward	N1TRS	T R S	N208VRC	Trent	N370VRC	Trent
MKP179W	Emmerson	N2JBT	Johnson Bros	N209VRC	Trent	N381EAK	Glovers
MMJ474V	Wing	N3OCT	The Delaine	N210VRC	Trent	N382EAK	Glovers
MMW49X	Haines	N3PSW	Paul Winson	N211TBC	Midland Fox	N401ARA	Nottingham
MNM31V	Paul Winson	N10PCC	P C Coaches	N211VRC	Trent	N401LTL	RoadCar
MNU479P	Applebys	N11PAM	Pam's Coaches	N212TBC	Midland Fox	N402ARA	Nottingham
MNU625P	Confidence	N11PCC	P C Coaches	N212VRC	Trent	N403ARA	Nottingham
MNU631P	Confidence	N12PCC	P C Coaches	N213VRC	Trent	N404ARA	Nottingham
MNU632P	Confidence	N21ARC	Skills	N214VRC	Trent	N429XRC	City Rider
MNU633P	Dunn-Line	N39ARC	Skills	N215VRC	Trent	N430XRC	City Rider
MNU635P	Dunn-Line	N43ARC	Skills	N216VRC	Trent	N431XRC	City Rider
MNU692W	Nottingham	N45ARC	Skills	N217VRC	Trent	N432XRC	City Rider
MNU693W	Nottingham	N66MCL	MacPherson	N217VVO	Nottingham	N433XRC	City Rider
MNU694W	Nottingham	N77MCL	MacPherson	N218VRC	Trent	N472XRC	City Rider
MNU695W	Nottingham	N97ACH	Dunn-Line	N218VVO	Nottingham	N473XRC	City Rider
MNU696W	Nottingham	N101WRC	Nottingham	N219VRC	Trent	N474XRC	City Rider
MOD816P	Camms	N102WRC	Nottingham	N219VVO	Nottingham	N475XRC	City Rider
MPL129W	Midland Fox	N103WRC	Nottingham	N220BAL	Nottingham	N476XRC	City Rider
MRH398J	Applebys	N104WRC	Nottingham	N220VRC	Trent	N477XRC	City Rider
MRJ270W	East Midland	N105WRC	Nottingham	N221BAL	Nottingham	N478XRC	City Rider
MRT7P	RoadCar	N106WRC	Nottingham	N221VRC	Trent	N479XRC	City Rider
MSO15W	Kinch	N107WRC	Nottingham	N223BAL	Nottingham	N480DKH	Nottingham
MSV922	RoadCar	N108WRC	Nottingham	N223VRC	Trent	N480XRC	City Rider
MSV926	RoadCar	N109WRC	Nottingham	N224BAL	Nottingham	N481XRC	City Rider
MSV927	RoadCar	N110WRC	Nottingham	N224VRC	Trent	N523XRR	Nottingham
MTL750V	Applebys	N130AET	East Midland	N225VRC	Trent	N524XRR	Nottingham
MTU116Y	Midland Fox	N131AET	East Midland	N226VRC	Trent	N525XRR	Nottingham
MTU117Y	Midland Fox	N132AET	East Midland	N240NNR	Travel Wright	N539OFE	Applebys
MTU118Y	Midland Fox	N133AET	East Midland	N290DWY	Reliance	N607UTV	Nottingham
MTU119Y	Midland Fox	N134AET	East Midland	N321JTL	RoadCar	N608UTV	Nottingham
MTU121Y	Midland Fox	N135AET	East Midland	N322JTL	RoadCar	N609UTV	Nottingham
MTV309W	City Rider	N135OFW	Applebys	N322WCH	Trent	N610XRC	Nottingham
MTV310W	City Rider	N136AET	East Midland	N322BAL	Nottingham	N611XVO	Nottingham
MTV311W	City Rider	N137AET	East Midland	N323JTL	RoadCar	N612YRA	Nottingham
MTV312W	City Rider	N138AET	East Midland	N324JTL	RoadCar	N613YRA	Nottingham
MTV313W	City Rider	N139AET	East Midland	N325JTL	RoadCar	N614YRA	Nottingham
MTV314W	City Rider	N140AET	East Midland	N326JTL	RoadCar	N615YRA	Nottingham
MTV315W	City Rider	N140ARC	Skills	N327JTL	RoadCar	N661OFE	Hornsby
MTX458	Lamcote	N141AET	East Midland	N328JTL	RoadCar	N691AHL	Fowler's Travel
MUT206W	Leicester CityBus	N142AET	East Midland	N331OFP	Midland Fox	N692AHL	Fowler's Travel
MUT252W	Leicester CityBus	N143AET	East Midland	N344OBC	Midland Fox	N693AHL	Fowler's Travel
MUT256W	Leicester CityBus	N144AET	East Midland	N345OBC	Midland Fox	N743LUS	Pathfinder
MUT257W	Leicester CityBus	N144ARC	Skills	N346OBC	Midland Fox	N744LUS	Pathfinder
MUT259W	Leicester CityBus	N160VVO	City Rider	N347OBC	Midland Fox	N751DAK	Dunn-Line
MUT260W	Leicester CityBus	N161VVO	City Rider	N348OBC	Midland Fox	N752CKU	East Midland
MUT264W	Leicester CityBus	N162VVO	City Rider	N349OBC	Midland Fox	N753CKU	East Midland
MUT777W	Brylaine	N163VVO	City Rider	N350OBC	Midland Fox	N754CKU	East Midland
MVK881X	Brylaine	N164VVO	City Rider	N351OBC	Midland Fox	N755CKU	East Midland
MVL750V	Applebys	N165XVO	City Rider	N352OBC	Midland Fox	N756CKU	East Midland
MVO411W	Nottingham	N166PUT	Midland Fox	N353OBC	Midland Fox	N757CKU	East Midland
MVO412W	Nottingham	N166XVO	City Rider	N354OBC	Midland Fox	N758CKU	East Midland
MVO410W	Nottingham	N107PUT	Midland Fox	N355OBC	Midland Fox	N760CKU	East Midland
MVO414W	Nottingham	N168PUT	Midland Fox	N356OBC	Midland Fox	N760CKU	East Midland
MVO415W	Nottingham	N169PUT	Midland Fox	N356REE	Applebys	N761CKU	East Midland
MVO416W	Nottingham	N170PUT	Midland Fox	N356VRC	Trent	N762EWG	East Midland
MVO417W	Nottingham	N171PUT	Midland Fox	N357OBC	Midland Fox	N763EWG	East Midland
MVO418W	Nottingham	N172PUT	Midland Fox	N357VRC	Trent	N764EWG	East Midland
MVO419W	Nottingham	N173PUT	Midland Fox	N358OBC	Midland Fox	N764RBE	Applebys

N765EWG	East Midland	NGM168G	Johnson Bros	NTL939	Sleafordian	ORA451W	Nottingham
N766EWG	East Midland	NHL301X	East Midland	NTV729M	RoadCar	ORA452W	Nottingham
N767EWG	East Midland	NHL302X	East Midland	NTV730M	Isle Coaches	ORA453W	Nottingham
N767WRC	Nottingham	NHL303X	East Midland	NUB93V	Fowler's Travel	ORA454W	Nottingham
N768EWG	East Midland	NHL304X	East Midland	NVL165	RoadCar	ORA455W	Nottingham
N768WRC	Nottingham	NHL305X	East Midland	NVL692V	Applebys	ORJ366W	Applebys
N769EWG	East Midland	NIB2796	Skills	NWB163X	RoadCar	ORJ442	Applebys
N769WRC	Nottingham	NIB4887	Eagre	NWO455R	RoadCar	ORR904W	Travel Wright
N770EWG	East Midland	NIB6064	Andrews	OCY907R	Hulley's	OSF305G	Johnson Bros
N770WRC	Nottingham	NIB6433	Woods	ODJ587W	Brylaine	OSF307G	Johnson Bros
N771EWG	East Midland	NIB8762	Skills	ODJ593W	Brylaine	OSJ1X	Butler Brothers
N771WRC	Nottingham	NIW2342	T R S	ODJ599W	Brylaine	OTD827R	Blands of Cottesmore
N772EWG	East Midland	NJS45S	MacPherson	ODM499V	Hulley's	OTL3	The Delaine
N773EWG	East Midland	NKU570R	Applebys	OEG283P	Fowler's Travel	OTL633V	Everett
N774EWG	East Midland	NKY146R	East Midland	OEM776S	T R S	OTO540M	Confidence
N775EWG	East Midland	NLG909T	Johnson's	OEM785S	RoadCar	OTO548M	Maun Crusader
N776EWG	East Midland	NLO857V	Emmerson	OEM794S	T R S	OTO551M	Confidence
N779DRH	Nottingham	NNN471W	Nottingham	OFV287T	Applebys	OTO555M	Nottingham
N795PDS	Travel Wright	NNN472W	Nottingham	OGR51T	Camms	OTO557M	Confidence
N816PJU	Kinch	NNN473W	Nottingham	OGU131	Brylaine	OTO562M	Confidence
N817PJU	Kinch	NNN474W	Nottingham	OHE270X	Carnell	OTO569M	Dunn-Line
N818RFP	Kinch	NNN475W	Nottingham	OHE273X	Applebys	OTO570M	Confidence
N819RFP	Kinch	NNN476W	Nottingham	OHL912X	Haines	OTO576M	T R S
N820RFP	Kinch	NNN477W	Nottingham	OHW492R	Trent	OUH738X	Sweyne
N821RFP	Kinch	NNN478W	Nottingham	OIB3509	Brylaine	OWB30X	East Midland
N875AKY	Applebys	NNN479W	Nottingham	OIB9392	Wing	OWB31X	East Midland
N957SAY	Woods	NNN480W	Nottingham	OIW1321	Woods	OWB32X	East Midland
N983XCT	Pathfinder	NNU71W	Glovers	OIW5036	Dunn-Line	OWB33X	East Midland
N984XCT	Pathfinder	NNU124M	Maun Crusader	OJD66R	Express Motors	OWB34X	East Midland
N985XCT	Pathfinder	NNU128M	Camms	OJD89R	Express Motors	OWE854R	Johnson Bros
N991XCT	Pathfinder	NOC396R	P C Coaches	OJD267R	Virgin Bus	OWE857R	Johnson Bros
N992XCT	Pathfinder	NOC406R	Virgin Bus	OJD434R	Brylaine	OWE858R	Johnson Bros
N997BWJ	Dunn-Line	NOC454R	P C Coaches	OJD444R	Brylaine	OWF425R	RoadCar
N998BWJ	Dunn-Line	NOC526R	P C Coaches	OJD455R	Brylaine	OWJ167X	Trent Motors
NAU292W	Travel Wright	NOE555R	Trent	OJL822Y	East Midland	OYJ68R	Marshall
NBF744P	Brylaine	NOE584R	Trent	OJL823Y	East Midland	P1OTL	The Delaine
NBZ1670	Grayscroft	NOE585R	Trent	OJS27T	Brylaine	P2OTL	The Delaine
NDE748Y	Nottingham	NPA218W	Reliance	OJV120S	East Midland	P6KET	Kettlewell's
NDX579	Hunt's	NPA223W	RoadCar	OKY60R	Daisy	P50PSW	Paul Winson
NEE496	Applebys	NPA224W	RoadCar	ONN287R	Midland Fox	P151CTV	Trent
NEV678M	Kettlewell's	NPP328V	Carnell	ONN571P	Trent	P152CTV	Trent
NFB602R	Trent	NRB434P	Trent	ORA446W	Nottingham	P153CTV	Trent
NFP205W	Leicester CityBus	NRB435P	Trent	ORA447W	Nottingham	P227CTV	Trent
NFW35V	RoadCar	NRP580V	East Midland	ORA448W	Nottingham	P228CTV	Trent
NFW110V	Applebys	NRR400N	Nottingham	ORA449W	Nottingham	P229CTV	Trent
NFW501P	P C Coaches	NSU180	Emmerson	ORA450W	Nottingham	P230CTV	Trent

Modern single deck buses have for many years been purchased in small numbers by Nottingham City Transport. The Leyland National was succeeded by the Leyland Lynx and the fleet contains some twenty-eight. One of the 1988 intake is 732, E732BVO.
Colin Lloyd

P231CTV	Trent	PKE810M	Johnson Bros	RDZ4275	Carnell	SDA517S		Applebys
P232CTV	Trent	PNK94R	Avisdors	RFS590V	RoadCar	SDA563S		Applebys
P233CTV	Trent	PNK152R	Bowers	RGS820V	Kinch	SDX26R		RoadCar
P234CTV	Trent	PNL163Y	Carnell	RGS822V	Kinch	SDX28R		RoadCar
P235CTV	Trent	PNW306W	Reliance	RHL174X	East Midland	SFL438R		Fowler's Travel
P236CTV	Trent	PNW308W	Hunt's	RIB2699	Cropley	SGR545R		Trent Motors
P237CTV	Trent	PNW599W	Kinch	RIW8126	Andrews	SGR791V		Travel Wright
P238CTV	Trent	PNW600W	Kinch	RIW8127	Andrews	SHE306Y		East Midland
P239CTV	Trent	PNW605W	RoadCar	RJI1653	Grayscroft	SHE307Y		East Midland
P240CTV	Trent	PRD34	Bowers	RJI1654	Grayscroft	SHE308Y		East Midland
P241CTV	Trent	PRR438R	Trent	RJI1655	Grayscroft	SHE309Y		East Midland
P681SVL	RoadCar	PRR439R	Trent	RJI1656	Camms	SHE310Y		East Midland
P682SVL	RoadCar	PRR441R	Trent	RJI1657	Camms	SHE311Y		East Midland
P683SVL	RoadCar	PRR442R	Trent	RJI1658	Camms	SHE545S		Midland Fox
P684SVL	RoadCar	PRR443R	Trent	RJI2709	T R S	SHE546S		Midland Fox
P685SVL	RoadCar	PRR444R	Trent	RJI4240	Woods	SHE549S		Midland Fox
P686SVL	RoadCar	PRR445R	Trent	RJI4578	Emmerson	SHE552S		Midland Fox
P901CTO	Trent	PRR446R	Trent	RJI5704	Leicester CityBus	SHE553S		Midland Fox
P902CTO	Trent	PRR447R	Trent	RJI5706	Leicester CityBus	SHE555S		Midland Fox
P903CTO	Trent	PRR448R	Trent	RJI8583	Hornsby	SHE559S		Midland Fox
P904CTO	Trent	PRR449R	Trent	RJI8608	Hornsby	SHE560S		Midland Fox
P905CTO	Trent	PRR450R	Trent	RJU129Y	Blands of Cottesmore	SHH85M		Fowler's Travel
P906CTO	Trent	PRR451R	Trent	RKA886T	Camms	SIA4683		Lamcote
P907CTO	Trent	PRR452R	Trent	RKW603R	RoadCar	SIB1358		A B C
P908CTO	Trent	PRR453R	Trent	RKW606R	RoadCar	SIB1998		Woods
P909CTO	Trent	PRR454R	Trent	RKW607R	RoadCar	SIB3709		A B C
P910CTO	Trent	PRR455R	Trent	RKW608R	RoadCar	SIJ385		Pam's Coaches
P911CTO	Trent	PRR456R	Trent	RKW610R	RoadCar	SJI1978		A B C
P912CTO	Trent	PRR457R	Trent	RND212X	Sweyne	SJI3696		Kime's
P913CTO	Trent	PRR458R	Trent	RNU426X	Nottingham	SJI6321		Kime's
P914CTO	Trent	PRR459R	Trent	RNU427X	Nottingham	SJI6322		Kime's
P915CTO	Trent	PRR460R	Trent	RNU428X	Nottingham	SJI6323		Kime's
P916CTO	Trent	PRW137M	Unity	RNU429X	Nottingham	SJI6567		Kime's
PAK690R	Carnell	PS2743	East Midland	RNU430X	Nottingham	SJI6568		Kime's
PAU205R	Applebys	PSU443	East Midland	RNU431X	Nottingham	SJI6569		Kime's
PAY9W	Wing	PSU764	East Midland	RNU432X	Nottingham	SJI6570		Kime's
PCA797R	Avisdors	PSV389	Holloways	RNU433X	Nottingham	SJI6571		Kime's
PCT596M	Carnell	PSV436	Holloways	RNU434X	Nottingham	SKF12T		Camms
PFE39P	RoadCar	PTD641S	East Midland	RNU435X	Nottingham	SKG919S		Trent
PFE540V	RoadCar	PTV583X	Trent	ROI876	Eagre	SKY31Y		East Midland
PFE541V	RoadCar	PTV585X	Trent	ROI5013	T R S	SKY32Y		East Midland
PFE542V	RoadCar	PTV586X	Trent	RRC484R	Applebys	SLJ386X		Elsey
PFE544V	RoadCar	PTV587X	Trent	RRC487R	Trent	SMY631X		Carnell
PFN787M	Bowers	PTV588X	Trent	RSK584W	A B C	SMY632X		Carnell
PFW839V	Brylaine	PTV589X	Trent	RTO461R	Trent	SMY637X		Carnell
PGA833V	Enterprise & SD	PTV591X	Trent	RTO462R	Trent	SND85X	Blands of Cottesmore
PHW986S	Trent	PTV592X	Trent	RTO463R	Trent	SNM74R		Wing
PHW987S	Trent	PTV601X	Paul James	RTO464R	Trent	SNN747R		Travel Wright
PIB2459	MacPherson	PUA917	Andrews	RTO465R	Trent	SNU456W		Nottingham
PIB9214	P C Coaches	PWE531R	Midland Fox	RTO466R	Trent	SNU457W		Nottingham
PIW4456	RoadCar	PWE534R	Midland Fox	RTV436X	Nottingham	SNU458X		Nottingham
PIW4457	RoadCar	PWT279W	Applebys	RTV437X	Nottingham	SNU459X		Nottingham
PIW8618	Andrews	PYE841Y	East Midland	RTV438X	Nottingham	SNU460X		Nottingham
PIW8619	Andrews	PYE842Y	East Midland	RTV439X	Nottingham	SNU461X		Nottingham
PJI3042	Travel Wright	Q364FVT	Hulley's	RTV440X	Nottingham	SNU462X		Nottingham
PJI3043	Travel Wright	RAL795	Marshall	RTV441X	Nottingham	SNU463X		Nottingham
PJI3746	Andrews	RAU597R	East Midland	RTV442X	Nottingham	SNU464X		Nottingham
PJI3748	Dunn-Line	RAU600R	RoadCar	RTV443X	Nottingham	SNU465X		Nottingham
PJI4314	East Midland	RAU624R	Marshall	RTV444X	Nottingham	SPC270R		RoadCar
PJI4316	East Midland	RBA480	Andrews	RTV445X	Nottingham	SRC109X		City Rider
PJI4317	East Midland	RBU180R	East Midland	RVE651S	Bowers	SRC110X		City Rider
PJI5529	Andrews	RCT3	The Delaine	RVL143R	RoadCar	SRC111X		City Rider
PJI5631	A B C	RDT89R	Moxon	RVL445	Applebys	SRC112X		City Rider
PJI7754	Paul James	RDX11R	RoadCar	RWA050N	Johnson Bros	SRC110X		City Rider
PJI7929	Paul James	RDX12R	RoadCar	RWB801R	Moxon	SRC114X		City Rider
PJI7930	Paul James	RDX13R	RoadCar	RWT544R	Johnson Bros	SRC115X		City Rider
PJI7931	Paul James	RDX14R	RoadCar	RWT546R	Johnson Bros	STA361R		Carnell
PJI8334	Maun Crusader	RDX15R	RoadCar	RXI5441	Skills	STK132T		Kinch
PJT268R	Trent	RDX16R	RoadCar	SAE751S	Trent	STK135T		Kinch
PJV36S	Brylaine	RDX17R	RoadCar	SAE755S	Trent	STO529H		A B C

STV122X	City Rider	TFU751T	P C Coaches	TSJ73S	RoadCar	ULS615X	Midland Fox
STV123X	City Rider	THL295Y	Carnell	TTC532T	Trent	ULS618X	Midland Fox
SUA141R	Hornsby	THX120S	Kettlewell's	TTL541R	Moxon	ULS636X	Leicester CityBus
SUR278R	Applebys	THX173S	Hornsby	TUA707R	Unity	ULS637X	Leicester CityBus
SVL177W	RoadCar	THX196S	Kettlewell's	TUB13M	Sweyne	ULS642X	Leicester CityBus
SVL178W	RoadCar	THX212S	RoadCar	TUT888H	T R S	UNA864S	Eagre
SVL179W	RoadCar	THX289S	T R S	TVC402W	Midland Fox	UPB311S	Express Motors
SVL180W	RoadCar	THX305S	Brylaine	TVP852S	Kinch	URA481X	Glovers
SVM378W	Hail & Ride	THX542S	Hornsby	TWF201Y	East Midland	URA605S	East Midland
SVV586W	East Midland	THX643S	T R S	TWF202Y	East Midland	URB467S	Trent
SWE434S	RoadCar	TIB2875	Sweyne	TWJ340Y	Hunt's	URB468S	Trent
SWE436S	RoadCar	TIB4573	P C Coaches	TWJ341Y	Hunt's	URB469S	Trent
SWE439S	RoadCar	TJI1676	Graycroft	TWJ342Y	Hunt's	URB471S	Trent
SWE442S	RoadCar	TJI1677	Graycroft	TWN740N	Trent	URB472S	Trent
SXF319	Maun Crusader	TJI1678	Graycroft	TWO84	RoadCar	URH657	Midland Fox
TAE638S	Trent	TJI1679	Graycroft	TXI2437	T R S	URN154R	Brylaine
TAE643S	Trent	TJI1700	Daisy	TXI8757	A B C	URN155R	Brylaine
TBC40X	Leicester CityBus	TJI4027	Wide Horizon	TYJ394S	Dee Ward	URN158R	Brylaine
TBC41X	Leicester CityBus	TJI4028	Wide Horizon	UBV84L	RoadCar	URN207V	RoadCar
TBC42X	Leicester CityBus	TJI4698	Camms	UBV85L	RoadCar	URN208V	RoadCar
TBC43X	Leicester CityBus	TJI4699	Camms	UBV87L	RoadCar	URN209V	RoadCar
TBC44X	Leicester CityBus	TJI4702	Hulley's	UCK956R	Lamcote	USK207	Cropley
TBC45X	Leicester CityBus	TJI4859	Skills	UDT312Y	East Midland	USO178S	MacPherson
TBC46X	Leicester CityBus	TJI4860	Skills	UDT313Y	East Midland	USO184S	Brylaine
TBC47X	Leicester CityBus	TJI6298	A B C	UDU891W	Bestwicks	USO185S	MacPherson
TBC48X	Leicester CityBus	TJI6713	A B C	UES274S	Dunn-Line	UTC872	T R S
TBC49X	Leicester CityBus	TKW335S	Skinner	UFG53S	RoadCar	UTL798	Applebys
TBC50X	Leicester CityBus	TMR66Y	Wide Horizon	UFP233S	Leicester CityBus	UTV213S	Hail & Ride
TBC51X	Leicester CityBus	TNN696X	Travel Wright	UFP236X	Fowler's Travel	UTX727S	Camms
TBC52X	Leicester CityBus	TRN467V	RoadCar	UFW39V	RoadCar	UVE288	Applebys
TBC53X	Leicester CityBus	TRN468V	RoadCar	UFW40W	RoadCar	UVL653W	Applebys
TBC54X	Leicester CityBus	TRN469V	RoadCar	UFW41W	RoadCar	UVL89W	Applebys
TBC55X	Leicester CityBus	TRN471V	RoadCar	UFX628X	Unity	UVO125S	Confidence
TBC56X	Leicester CityBus	TRN472V	RoadCar	UFX849S	Trent	UWA150S	East Midland
TBM263R	MacPherson	TRN473V	RoadCar	UFX852S	Trent	UWA151S	East Midland
TCH116X	City Rider	TRN479V	RoadCar	UHG146V	RoadCar	UWA154S	East Midland
TCH117X	City Rider	TRN484V	RoadCar	UHG752R	RoadCar	UWA155S	East Midland
TCH118X	City Rider	TRN485V	RoadCar	UHG756R	RoadCar	UWA157S	East Midland
TCH119X	City Rider	TRN803V	RoadCar	UHJ495V	Paul Winson	UWA159S	East Midland
TCH120X	City Rider	TRR814R	Eagre	UHW101T	Trent	UWY65X	RoadCar
TCH121X	City Rider	TRS332	T R S	UIA7089	A B C	UWY70X	RoadCar
TDC853X	RoadCar	TRS574	T R S	UJI2439	RoadCar	UWY73X	RoadCar
TDT864S	Johnson Bros	TRS835	T R S	UJL270	Sleafordian	UWY76X	RoadCar
TET745S	Isle Coaches	TRT96M	T R S	UJV489	Applebys	UWY85X	Eagre
TFJ61X	Camms	TSJ46S	RoadCar	ULS321T	RoadCar	UXI6833	Unity
TFU61T	East Midland	TSJ58S	RoadCar	ULS335T	RoadCar	VAT176S	Applebys

Two of a large batch of Leyland Tigers with Duple Laser bodywork that were new to Ribble have found their way into the Leicester Citybus fleet. Seen in Southsea is B165WRN shortly after gaining the GRT-style livery and Citycoach lettering. *Philip Lamb*

143

VAY57X	Leicester CityBus	WDA948T	Applebys	XAU702Y	Trent	YDM354W	Brylaine
VAY58X	Leicester CityBus	WEE584	Applebys	XAU703Y	Trent	YFC19V	Enterprise & SD
VAY59X	Leicester CityBus	WFP360X	Pam's Coaches	XAU704Y	Trent	YFR649Y	Dunn-Line
VBH40W	Emmerson	WFS149W	RoadCar	XAU705Y	Trent	YIA6276	Lamcote
VBH50W	Emmerson	WFU466V	East Midland	XBF54S	Camms	YIA9006	Reliance
VCH473S	Trent	WFU467V	East Midland	XCH706Y	Trent	YJK932V	RoadCar
VCH474S	Trent	WFU470V	Scutt	XDU178	Leicester CityBus	YJK934V	RoadCar
VCH475S	Trent	WFU561V	Emmerson	XFC486	Emmerson	YJK935V	RoadCar
VCH476S	Trent	WIA7680	Brylaine	XFK173	Emmerson	YJL655T	Brylaine
VCH477S	Trent	WJF8X	Dunn-Line	XFP1Y	Kettlewell's	YJV178	Applebys
VCH478S	Trent	WJS200X	Cropley	XFP2Y	Kettlewell's	YNA887	Applebys
VCH479S	Trent	WJY760	Applebys	XFP502S	Hunt's	YNN396Y	Glovers
VCT418	Sleafordian	WKE65S	Hylton & Dawson	XFU126V	East Midland	YNR778	Paul Winson
VCU400T	Enterprise & SD	WKY676K	Bowers	XFU129V	East Midland	YNY586T	Brylaine
VCX340X	RoadCar	WLT655	Confidence	XFW951S	Hunt's	YPD104Y	The Delaine
VEU228T	Trent	WNW160S	Hornsby	XFW983S	Hornsby	YPD105Y	The Delaine
VEU229T	Trent	WOC740T	Applebys	XGS736S	East Midland	YPD107Y	The Delaine
VEU230T	Trent	WOI3001	RoadCar	XJF60Y	Leicester CityBus	YPD108Y	The Delaine
VEU232T	Trent	WOI3002	RoadCar	XJF61Y	Leicester CityBus	YPD112Y	Hulley's
VFA70X	Paul James	WOI8022	Lamcote	XJF62Y	Leicester CityBus	YPD114Y	Daisy
VFW721	Applebys	WPR150S	Trent	XJF63Y	Leicester CityBus	YPD121Y	Carnell
VFX985S	Trent	WRA688Y	Kettlewell's	XJF64Y	Leicester CityBus	YPD129Y	East Midland
VJG810T	Grayscroft	WRC419	Lamcote	XJF65Y	Leicester CityBus	YPD133Y	East Midland
VJU261X	Skinner	WRC826S	Felix	XJF66Y	Leicester CityBus	YPD136Y	Fowler's Travel
VKE565S	Trent	WSV317	Applebys	XJF67Y	Leicester CityBus	YPL80T	Camms
VKE566S	East Midland	WSV418	Elsey	XJF68Y	Leicester CityBus	YRB652Y	Brylaine
VKU72S	East Midland	WUG532X	Hail & Ride	XJF69Y	Leicester CityBus	YRH808S	Applebys
VKU73S	East Midland	WUK155	Hornsby	XJF888S	Skinner	YRR3	Marshall
VKU77S	East Midland	WUM127S	P C Coaches	XJG815V	Grayscroft	YRR501T	Trent
VKU79S	East Midland	WUY713	Cropley	XJV146	Applebys	YRR502T	Trent
VNH155W	Emmerson	WVL515	RoadCar	XNK199X	Brylaine	YRR503T	Trent
VNH160W	Applebys	WXH612	Kettlewell's	XPA110	Midland Fox	YRY188T	Leicester CityBus
VNH162W	Applebys	WYV51T	Kinch	XPK52T	Camms	YRY198T	Leicester CityBus
VPP957S	Johnson Bros	WYV53T	Kinch	XPM41	RoadCar	YRY200T	Leicester CityBus
VRC479S	Marshall	WYV54T	Kinch	XPM42	RoadCar	YSF73S	RoadCar
VRC480S	Marshall	WYV62T	Kinch	XPP281X	Everett	YSF74S	RoadCar
VRC605Y	Trent	XAK453T	RoadCar	XRR298S	City Rider	YSF80S	RoadCar
VRC606Y	Trent	XAK904T	RoadCar	XRR616M	Confidence	YSF81S	RoadCar
VRC608Y	Trent	XAL481S	Trent	XRW510S	Avisdors	YSF82S	RoadCar
VRC609Y	Trent	XAL482S	Trent	XSG71R	RoadCar	YSF89S	RoadCar
VRC610Y	Trent	XAL483S	Trent	XSG72R	RoadCar	YSU906	Holloways
VRC611Y	Trent	XAL484S	Trent	XSJ647T	MacPherson	YSX929W	RoadCar
VRC612Y	Trent	XAL485S	Trent	XSJ649T	MacPherson	YSX930W	RoadCar
VTL358	Hodson	XAL486S	Trent	XSJ650T	MacPherson	YTO861Y	Travel Wright
VUA151R	RoadCar	XAL487S	Trent	XSU978	Haines	YTO996T	Reliance
VUA152R	RoadCar	XAL488S	Trent	XSV839	Cropley	YUH115T	Applebys
VUA473X	Enterprise & SD	XAL489S	Trent	XTL466X	RoadCar	YVW902S	Express Motors
VUD32X	Applebys	XAL490S	Trent	XTL467X	RoadCar	YWG465T	RoadCar
VUR118W	Brylaine	XAL491S	Trent	XTL468X	RoadCar	YWG466T	RoadCar
VWA34Y	East Midland	XAL492S	Trent	XTL469X	RoadCar	YWG470T	RoadCar
VWA35Y	East Midland	XAL493S	Trent	XWG653T	Holloways	YWH978	Bowers
VWA36Y	East Midland	XAL494S	Trent	XWG655T	Holloways	YXI5503	Skills
VWG360Y	Wide Horizon	XAL495S	Trent	XYK766T	Daisy	YXI5860	Skills
VWM83L	Confidence	XAL496S	Trent	XYN670	Wide Horizon	YXI7380	Skills
VWM89L	Confidence	XAL497S	Trent	YAU126Y	City Rider	YXI7381	Skills
WAC828	Applebys	XAL498S	Trent	YAU127Y	City Rider	YXI7906	Skills
WAD642S	Avisdors	XAL499S	Trent	YAU128Y	City Rider	YXI8421	Skills
WBR5V	Camms	XAL500S	Trent	YCF826	Midland Fox	YXI9243	Skills
WCK137V	Hulley's	XAT586	Applebys	YCS92T	Midland Fox	YXI9256	Skills
WCK141V	Maun Crusader	XAU700Y	Trent	YCT463	Sleafordian	YXI9258	Skills
WCK143V	Hulley's	XAU701Y	Trent				

ISBN 1 897990 16 2
Published by *British Bus Publishing*
The Vyne, 16 St Margarets Drive, Wellington,
Telford, Shropshire, TF1 3PH
Fax and order-line: 01952 255669

Printed by Graphics & Print
Unit A13, Stafford Park 15
Telford, Shropshire, TF3 3BB